SAY NO!

SAY NO!

by

Ruth Adams

The paper in this book has been made from waste paper that normally winds up at the city dump. This reclaimed paper is an example of how today's wastes can be converted into a worthwhile resource, thereby helping to solve the solid waste disposal crisis and preserving the quality of our environment.

RODALE PRESS, INC.

EMMAUS, PENNA. 18049

Standard Book Number 0–87857–002–0
Library of Congress Card Number 74–152855

PRINTED IN U.S.A.
B–147
FIRST PRINTING________________JUNE 1971

Contents

Introduction

"We have plenty of debaters, blamers, provocateurs. We don't have plenty of problem-solvers. A relevant call to action would address itself to that complacent lump of Americans who fatten on the yield of this society but never bestir themselves to solve its problems, to powerful men who rest complacently with outworn institutions, and to Americans still uncommitted to the values we profess to cherish as a people."

John W. Gardner quoted in an article in the Spring, 1970, *Temple University Alumni Review*

Definition: "Ecology is the science which warns people who won't listen about ways they won't follow of saving an environment they don't appreciate."

L. G. Heller in a letter to the *New York Times,* April 2, 1970

INTRODUCTION

"It is the first step of wisdom to recognize that the major advances in civilization are processes which all but wreck the society in which they occur."

Alfred North Whitehead

"When you really understand the situation, it is worse than you think."

Dr. Paul Ehrlich, author of
The Population Bomb

Has the planning commission just announced they are going to bring in lots of new industry to help "broaden the tax base"? Have the bulldozers arrived to fill in the salt marsh, dredge the river, slash down the oak trees, level the hill, dig the foundation for the new shopping center?

Will the new superhighway demolish the children's park and the last historic house in town? Have the councilmen decided to get along somehow with the ancient town incinerator, in spite of the tons of fly-ash it spews into the air every waking hour?

Are the few pleasant roads and lanes left in your community so bristling with the litter of plastic bottles, beer cans, aluminum plates, hair curlers, paper cups, old tires and hub caps that you can't take the dog for a walk for fear his feet will be torn, to say nothing of the insult to his sensitive nose?

Are the venerable trees coming down around your ears, because their leaves are too much trouble to pick up and burn every fall, or because they interfere with the new parking meters or because somebody thinks they bring too many squirrels? Has the AEC proposed a nuclear power plant in your community, which will heat up the river while they cool the reactor?

Is a mining company moving in to devastate your land with strip mines, drain off all the water from your water table and leave streams and rivers flowing livid with acid waste? Has your lovely river become a cesspool of garbage, trash and unmentionable pollution, offensive to the eye and the nose, deadly to the swimmer? Does the dump fire burn eternally, creating stench and smoke? Has your congressman voted against the bill which would save part of the national forest for your grandchildren to enjoy?

Say No!

Dig in your heels, set your jaw, button your coat against the frigid wind whining around the edge of your picket sign. Say no. Say to the commissioners that you don't want new industry and that there's not a chance that new industry will decrease taxes. Lie down in front of the bulldozers, if you have to, and tell the drivers they dare not fill in the salt marsh.

Knock on the doors of your neighbors. Get them to say no, too. Say no to the bulldozers. Say no to the superhighways. Say no to the plastic bottles and the aluminum cans. Say no to the shopping centers. Say no to the new industry which will pollute the air and befoul the water, while the bill for cleaning up the environment comes to you. Say no to the housing development. Say no to the oil tanker shoving through the Arctic ice and the oil pipeline threatening destruction to the most fragile ecosystem on earth. Say no to the new plastic furniture, the new detergent, the new speed-hungry cars. Say no to the power company's wail that they must have a nuclear reactor over the hill from you.

Take no for an answer. This book is about people who said no. In all parts of the world, in city slums and mountain villages, alone or strengthened by hundreds of fellow activists, in words, actions, votes, letters, broadcasts, silent demonstrations, songs, posters, plays, books, speeches, these people have said no. They are the new pioneers, bent not on "conquering the land" but on saving it from the conquerors.

Join the club. Take no for an answer. Make no mistake about it. If you don't take no for an answer now, there will be no future in which you have any choice. The crises we are facing in the areas covered in this book are real crises. The earth which we are despoiling is a fragile battleground, already badly frayed around the edges. The most important thing to keep always in mind is that much of the damage we do the earth is irreversible. When the concrete of the superhighway and the shopping center covers the last bit of good farmland in your township, there's no way to bring the farmland back—not for thousands of years in the future.

Once the lake has succumbed to the eutrophication process, nobody knows how to restore its clean, sparkling waters. Once the endangered animal species is extinct, there is no conceivable way to bring it back to life. Once the green things that manufacture our oxygen are poisoned or bulldozed out of existence, there is no other substance we can breathe.

The purpose of this book is to put you in touch with

the ways in which people all over the land are saying no. Some of them are winning their battles, some are losing. In most cases, the lines are still drawn. Nobody has finally won.

The purpose of this book is to be helpful to you in your efforts to take no for an answer. The chapters are arranged according to battlefields. In the index you will find the weapons. If your problem is saving a tree, read the chapter on how other tree-lovers have saved trees. If your little conservation group is fighting on all fronts, but nobody there quite knows how to write an effective letter, or whom to write to, turn to the index under letters, and see how other groups have carried out this assignment.

People will ask you, "Do you want to stop progress?" And you will have to answer "yes," because, in essence, you are trying to stop what we have up to now defined as "progress." You are asking for a new definition of "progress" and to do this you must say no to the old kind.

CHAPTER 1

Our Air Is an Unlicensed Dump

". . . Forty years ago, a first-hand survey conducted by an engineer of a leading oil company . . . showed that diesel trucks smoked for any of four reasons: inadequate maintenance, engine overload, poor fuel or poor lubricant. Today, diesel trucks spew objectionable smoke for exactly the same reasons."

Power
August, 1970

"We don't really know how we're polluting the environment. We don't know how the biosystem functions. We don't understand the implications of so-called 'technological progress'. We don't even know how many people would be an ideal population for a country or the planet as a whole. So one of the biggest challenges of the 1970's is to find out what the heck we're talking about when we wring our hands over 'the environmental problem' ".

Robert C. Cowen
Technology Review
Feb. 1970

"Never in history has society been confronted with a power so full of potential danger and at the same time so full of promise for the future of man and for the peace of the world. . . . The menace to our people of vehicles of this type hurtling through our streets and along our roads and poisoning the atmosphere would call for prompt legislative action, even if the military and economic implications were not so overwhelming."

Speech on the automobile by a Congressman
Congressional Record, 1875
(Why didn't we listen then?)

One half of all the air pollution in the entire world comes from automobiles, carbon monoxide alone amounting in just the United States to some *230,000 tons every day.*

By the beginning of 1969 there were almost 100 million cars on the roads in the USA. By 1975 we will probably have 20 million more. They use up 20% of our steel, 51% of our lead, 60% of our rubber. Our present 41,000 mile interstate highways system has, at present, used up more land in right-of-way than the entire state of Rhode Island.

There are 3,600,000 square miles of land in the USA and we have built 3,600,000 miles of highway across it, paving over an area as big as the state of West Virginia.

Everyone knows that one of the most worrisome headaches of our cities is the burgeoning traffic that pours in every morning and pours out every evening, meanwhile gobbling up most of the city's land during the day in parking lots, creating insolvable crises of keeping streets clean of dirt or snow. Finding a parking place has become the great national joke. And many expressways are deemed nothing but skinny "parking lots" by the helicopter pilots who hover overhead reporting on the bumper-to-bumper situation below.

Are cities moving forward bravely to meet this crisis with daring new plans? In our locality, the bulldozers flattened the entire center of an old and charming small town to create a large parking lot which now stands next to empty, since all the stores which might have attracted shoppers were destroyed to make the shopping center! In a neighboring city, already almost immobilized by traffic jams, many millions of dollars will be spent in the next 20 years to turn the main avenue where the shops are into a "mall", roofed over to protect customers from the weather. This project, for which many millions will come from the state, has the blessing of the city fathers and planners. To accomplish it, about half the downtown part of the city will be razed, the rest completely renovated — to accomplish a roofed over mall, you understand, where people can loiter under the trees (trees?) and enjoy themselves.

This plan is bound to bring thousands and thousands more cars into the already narrow, stuffed streets and bridges that funnel traffic into the city. Presumably, to handle the cars, most of the rest of downtown will be destroyed to provide parking places. The city prides itself on its beauty, its cleanliness, its historic background. One by one, the stately trees have gone down to make room for cars and parking meters. Cleanliness becomes a joke when there's no way to clean around the cars. There is, at this moment, only one restored historic house left. All the rest have been devastated to make room for cars. One cannot help but wonder why anyone looking for beauty, for cleanliness, for history, would come here, since, by now, the city has assumed just about the same aspect as any other city — beleaguered by traffic to the point where nothing else seems to matter. But the roof over the main street, planted with sapling trees (which presumably will have to be cut down as soon as they grow large enough to be interesting or gracious) seems to bemuse the entire citizenry, since it has apparently never occurred to anyone how they will manage 10 years from now to get to this fabulous shopping mall over streets which, even now, cannot handle the traffic.

A highway "explosion" not too different from the population explosion and perhaps a result of it was prophesied by a University of Chicago professor who told a meeting of the American Institute of Physics that the number of miles of highway in any country will grow in the same exponential way as population growth, and that this will ultimately yield a situation *where America is essentially all paved over* — as in downtown Los Angeles.

Each new mile of highway generates new traffic that will quickly fill it to capacity. According to many state laws all highway revenue dollars must be spent on highway construction, he said. He suggested that students in science and mathematics (able to analyze and predict the results of a given set of conditions) should jump in and help by pointing out what we are headed for and, if possible, preventing it.

In a "Threatened America" article in *Life* magazine, Paul O'Neil states that the reason for most of the highway explosion is the Highway Trust Fund — a pork barrel "of such magnitude that no congressman, senator, governor or state highway official can possibly ignore it." The money comes from a tax on the sale of spare parts and gasoline. It goes back into highways. A congressman or governor risks political suicide if he does not bring home his state's share of this bounty.

He tells us further that former President Johnson tried to head off inflation by freezing about one billion of the Trust's 4 billion dollars. But six months later, pressure had grown so great that he was forced to restore the money. Pennsylvania's former Governor Shafer called his efforts a "complete farce".

Governor Shafer's name is signed to a full-page ad which appeared in the *New York Times,* January 11, 1970. It points out that Pennsylvania leads all major states in completion of our Federal Interstate Highway System "and we have added it to what was already the nation's greatest highway network. . . . Pennsylvania has the best transportation system in the world." There's a map showing the state crisscrossed with highways.

Yet according to an article in the *Wall Street Journal* for February 4, 1970, Pennsylvania was planning to spend another 6 hundred million dollars in 1970 building new highways, instead of the four and a half hundred million spent in 1969 or the 2 hundred million in 1964. It's anybody's guess why we needed to spend this when we had just boasted that our Interstate Highway system was the best in the country.

In an interview with a group of students, reported on page 200 of *Ecotactics,* Representative Paul McCloskey answered this question which was put to him: "Congress has to take the money away from those projects that are facilitating land destruction, such as the Federal Highway Trust Fund. Nothing is going to prevent the destruction of all the open space in the country, if the highway program continues at the enormous rate it's going. I think we're just kidding ourselves, otherwise. Do you?"

And McCloskey answered, "I agree with you. But the great enemy of open space is not the Federal government. It's the local governments. There's no local government in this country that is suited to turn down a new payroll or a new property tax. Our country's built on a property tax supporting local government. Every impoverished county that has lovely open space, every city that wants to expand is going to permit development."

It seems to me that this is no answer to the question that was asked. Obviously, if the money for new highways is not given to the "impoverished county" by the state or federal government, no new highways will be built there — right? And "lovely open space" will be saved. So it's not the impoverished local government's fault at all, but the fault of the state and federal governments which give them all this lovely free money with which to betray and despoil the "lovely open space."

So one government blames another. Most everybody blames Detroit. Detroit blames that pernicious consumer who "demands" all these cars! Everybody — or almost everybody — agrees that the only final answer is a public transportation system that works, but nobody does much of anything to bring this any closer to realization.

Yes, somebody does. On page 89 of *Audubon* magazine for March, 1970, appears an ad of the National Association of Railroad Passengers. It says, "The maps don't show it, but an area exceeding that of the states of Connecticut, Delaware, Massachusetts, New Hampshire, Rhode Island and Vermont has now been taken over for motor traffic. How many trees have fallen, how many scenic areas have been scarred and leveled by the roadbuilders' bulldozers is anyone's guess. And the demand for more and bigger and wider and longer highways and expressways goes on."

"Meanwhile only a small fraction of the nation's safest, most efficient and economical means of transportation — the railroads — is being put to use. Passenger trains make no new demands on our diminishing land area. Compared to other modes, railroads create a negligible amount of pollution." There was a box for your name, address and the kind of membership you wanted to pay for. I sent a check to them at 41 Ivy Street, Washington, D. C. 20003. You can, too.

And what is the reason railroad passenger service has declined into almost nothingness in the US? A letter to the *New York Times,* April 19,1970, explains: "The United States is the only country in the world in which the railroads are not nationalized (except 50–50 in Canada) and it is also the only industrial nation in the world in which railroad travel has almost ceased to exist. Obviously, this is no coincidence.

"For years it has been official Government policy in this country to spend endless billions of dollars on highways, airports (which are tax-free) an air-control system and aviation research and development. On the other hand, the total Federal contribution to intercity rail travel to date is about eleven million dollars . . . or about enough to build a mile or so of expressway. The nationalized systems of other countries are given equal treatment with other forms of transportation which is why trains are still running there."

So now we have Railpax, a quasi-governmental corporation which will take over what is left of our passenger service and try to recreate a satisfactory, even a profitable, system of rail passenger service. Although their first announcement that they would cut back our present 285 passenger trains to 160 to 180 trains was hardly encouraging to most of us, Paul J. C. Friedlander, writing in the *New York Times,* March 7, 1971, states that "Railpax believes that it can in three years reorientate the thinking of American travelers back to the railroads, improve the equipment from some of the Civil War coaches still in use today to modern, clean, efficient and comfortable cars, and at the end of three years run its trains at a profit." Let's keep our fingers crossed and hope he's right.

Air pollution comes from many other sources than cars. Every time you breathe you pollute the air with carbon dioxide. If you smoke, the pollution is magnified with all the elements present in tobacco smoke. When you burn your trash outside you put into the air an astonishing amount of what is called "particulate matter" and gases, much of it carcinogenic (causing cancer). If we all lived in isolated spots this would bother no one. The air above us has the capacity to carry the pollution away harmlessly.

But we are crowded together in cities and suburbs. And the total pollution arising from a city's airborne waste can and has produced death for many of its citizens. We all know the stories of Donora, London and the Meuse Valley when temperature inversions kept the rising smoke and fumes close to the ground, so that people simply couldn't breathe. Those who died were mostly children, sick people and old people — heart and respiratory patients, mostly. There is no way of knowing when the weather will be just right to produce another inversion, or where. Most large cities now have alert systems which give warning when the pollution rises beyond the safe point. Alerts go out by radio and newspapers: close down the factories, stop driving cars, don't go outside, tell the children not to play actively but to rest — it takes less air! Supposedly we are equipped to handle the acute emergencies, although no one will ever be able to tell whether we have managed to save lives this way. But what about the eternal air pollution that goes on and on, day after day, all over the planet — from factories, from jet aircraft, from burning dumps, from incinerators?

Our favorite stories these days are the ironic ones involving high-flown promises and strict laws almost immediately transgressed by the very people who made the promises, passed the laws or are empowered to enforce them. The day after President Nixon made his impassioned anti-pollution address to the nation, the *New York Times* revealed again, for perhaps the 50th time, that federal government installations are probably the largest polluters of both air and water in the nation — his people, the nation's employees, over whom the President has almost absolute power.

In our locality a highway is being widened. Piled along the side of the road are the trees and shrubs that were grubbed out to make the right-of-way. Piled beside them is a mountain of old tires. Passersby apparently spotted the tires and decided to add to the pile some of their own, so they cleaned out their garages and tossed the old tires on the heap. One sunny day hideous black smoke fumed from the pile of tree stumps, blackening the air for half a mile. The contractors building the highway had set fire to the heap, to get rid of it in the quickest possible time.

Now Pennsylvania has a very fine, very strict air pollution law — one of the best in the country. The week before the "burning", as it has come to be known locally, the Governor had made a lofty statement announcing that all state agencies were to cease all forms of environmental pollution. Fine! Why then were they polluting? The township supervisor, in a hassle with the contractors, was told that our area is outside "the air pollution basin" covered by the law and a lot more such equivocation. The head of our local conservation group went to the next meeting of the supervisors armed with the township ordinances against air pollution. I telephoned everyone in the area supposedly concerned with enforcing the state air pollution laws. No one would assume any responsibility for this matter. It was somehow out of their jurisdiction.

The newspapers, a few weeks later, hailed the appointment by the governor of a new air pollution expert assigned to the "Lehigh air pollution basin" — an area which apparently would *not* include our township. I wrote to the governor and to the state secretary of highways telling the story and asking just why the average citizen, working against pollution, should be continually thwarted by the very state organizations assigned *not only to enforcing the law, but also to encouraging private citizens to report violators!*

I got a speedy answer from the governor and from the highway department. I got a copy of the state air pollution law governing open burning and an assurance that it would not happen again. Furthermore, I was assured that a new regulation had made it possible, somehow, for the new air pollution expert *to include our township in his jurisdiction.* So the next time there is an air pollution infraction here I will go armed with the letter from the State Health Department, and demand that the new expert stop the pollution.

In case you are wondering about the fate of the old tires, they are still there. We were told that it is customary to start such highway trash fires with oil and old tires, so that they will burn briskly. And we were told that we should be grateful the contractor didn't use the oil and the tires!

Where the whole process bogs down even more discouragingly, is when a giant industry is involved. Bethlehem Steel dominates the area where I live. Most people who live around me work at "The Steel." It has been accepted by all of us for years that Bethlehem Steel is the worst polluter in the area. All you have to do is drive past the seemingly endless smoking chimneys to see the amount of stuff poured into the air, and the differing hues of the Lehigh River water after it has passed the steel plant.

As part of their Earth Day celebration, the Lehigh University EcoAction Group arranged a meeting one evening to listen to the man who is chairman of the Pennsylvania Air Pollution Control Commission and also Environmental Quality Control Division of Bethlehem Steel. Immensely knowledgeable, fast on his feet, impossible to fault, bait or challenge, he told us that making steel is dirty business and that all the pollution involved in making steel will never be completely eliminated. It can't be. He gave us facts on the amount of pollution created by a given amount of steel-making.

The Bethlehem plant uses 250,000,000 gallons of water a day. Even at the end of their 67 million dollars anti-pollution program, there will still be water and air pollution. By 1972, he said, they hope to be able to comply with the state's codes.

The implications of his facts were so overpowering, so well documented and they came at you so fast, that his audience, consisting mostly of young, earnest engineering students, was all but overwhelmed. There was nothing you could say. How could you challenge his figures? This is top man in the business and in the state! He tells you it is costing his company 67 million dollars to give our community a certain amount of pollution abatement. Can you tell him this is not enough? Can you threaten to close down this mighty industry if pollution standards are not met? The idea is laughable. The industry is doing all it can, he says.

But in Pittsburgh, a steelworker forced by incapacitating emphysema to retire, joined what the *Wall Street Journal* calls "a curious collection" of protesters, the "Breathers' Lobby". They were women's clubs, health societies, union organizations, garden clubs and teenage militants, who attended a Pittsburgh hearing on air pollution — 500 of them. Industry representatives, startled at the turnout, moved the meeting hall to a bigger room. The Lobby continued its pressure, with hearings and letters to the state officials. They — along with a Philadelphia group, the Delaware Valley Clean Air Committee — forced through recommendations for an air pollution law so strict that industry spokesmen predict that it will fail, that industry cannot comply, with their present technology.

The proposed regulations now go to the Federal government which will accept or reject them. Throughout the hassle, the clean air people claimed that the state's air pollution laws were written to protect industry. They pointed out that the top men in some of the industries that pollute the most are also in charge of the state's anti-pollution commission. They charged that scientists and professors who work on the commission also have close ties with industry. They turned out hundreds of people to every meeting and every hearing. They provided free bus transportation. The man in charge of air pollution enforcement in the state said, finally, that their recommendation of the strictest pollution law in the country had come about chiefly because of "the many, many comments at the public hearings plus the many, many comments and letters we got in the mail." In the light of this, who can claim that mass meetings, letters to industry, letters to the editors don't work? They do work. They have worked.

In Italy a chemical plant grossly polluting a nearby river got an anonymous letter threatening to blow up the plant if the pollution did not stop. In Venice, a parade of barges and boats protested pollution which is destroying the art treasures, as well as the canal waters. Thousands watched the demonstration. In Milan, an ardent air pollution campaign has resulted in a much cleaner city. The cost of switching to cleaner fuel was estimated to be 29 million dollars.

London, we are told, has cleaned up its air pollution so successfully that winter sunshine has increased by 50%. The last bad smog was in 1962. The Clean Air Act was aimed primarily against the open coal fires in private households which provide heating for most London houses. The act enables a local authority anywhere, not only in London, to declare its area a "smokeless zone". This means that some fuel other than coal must be burned: gas, oil, anthracite or electric heat are permissible. People have been complaining about the pollution of London air from coal smoke since the year 1273. Nothing worked until the Clean Air Act came along. Smoke from domestic chimneys has dropped to 13% of what it was in 1952. The smoke output of industry is down to 18 percent.

In Texas several plants have closed down, unable to meet the pollution standards. A chemical company, two lumber companies, two rock plants have closed. Citizens of El Paso and Juarez, Mexico have instituted a one billion dollar law suit against American Smelting and Refining Company, alleging that the health of residents in both cities is endangered.

In Los Angeles in 1960, physicians advised more than 10,000 patients to leave the area because of health hazards caused by air pollution. At least 2500 of them left. In August, 1968, 60 members of the UCLA medical faculty issued a statement to the Los Angeles *Times* saying that "air pollution has now become a major health hazard to most of this community during much of the year." They advised anyone to leave who does not have compelling reasons to stay there. In Los Angeles, the problem is compounded by the action of sunlight on the various elements of pollution changing them into other substances of unknown toxicity. Newspapers and radio stations provide smog forecasts along with the daily weather reports.

The Los Angeles area, plagued chiefly with air pollution from cars, has taken massive measures to guard against other kinds. Coal is outlawed. Oil cannot have a high sulfur content. 57 open burning dumps have been eliminated, along with about a dozen large municipal incinerators, most commercial building incinerators and about 1½ million domestic incinerators. On September 6, 1968, however, *Science* reported "there has been essentially no improvement in the quality of Los Angeles air in this decade . . . The smog hasn't gotten any worse — it's more or less stabilized."

Private aircraft pilots got into the air pollution act at Missoula, Montana when they formed an airborne picket line over a large paper and pulp mill, circling overhead in planes emblazoned with anti-air pollution signs. Fifteen planes participated, one of them trailing a streamer which called for "Life, Liberty and Livability". The pilots claim that smog from the paper mill is the main cause of lack of visibility at the Missoula airport.

"Nagging the power structure" is the phrase used by Mrs. Linda Fosburg of the New York City Citizens for Clean Air, a group which boasts 10,000 dues paying members. She means activities like pasting stickers on the doors of firms who pollute the air, picketing their buildings, calling rent strikes or boycotting businesses which do nothing about their air pollution problems.

On December 7, 1966 two experts in the field of urban air pollution wrote to the *New York Times* suggesting a number of solutions for the New York traffic problems. During rush hours, counting-machines could measure numbers of cars and/or pollution levels at critical points near tunnels, bridges and highway approaches. When the count showed that no more cars should be permitted, a barrier would simply close off the road and instructions would be given for alternate routes. So you'll be late for work that morning. It's not your fault.

Then they suggested electric cars for moving around within city limits. In London, England there are 50,000 electric delivery vehicles which greatly reduce pollution. The use of electric cars for the city could be encouraged by lowering license costs, equipping parking meters with electric outlets. Cars running on electricity would greatly reduce pollution. Bus and truck terminals should be located at the city limits. Within the city, trucks and buses should be replaced by electric ones, as railroads must switch from diesel fuel to electric power before they come into the city. So far as we know, nothing has been done to implement any of these excellent suggestions made by H. Dickson McKenna, Executive Director of American Institute of Architects and Rhodes W. Fairbridge, Columbia University, an expert on smog.

Here are some brief thoughts on air pollution that you can use on posters at your next meeting:

By the early 1980's air pollution with a temperature inversion will kill thousands in some American city.

By 1985 air pollution will have reduced the amount of sunlight reaching the earth by one-half. No one has any idea what this will mean to agricultural production or just the health of all the green, living things on earth.

In the 1980's some major ecological system — soil or water — will break down somewhere in the United States. New diseases that we cannot resist will reach plague proportions.

15% of everyone presently living in Los Angeles now shows noticeable measurable pulmonary distress from air pollution — 700,000 people. There were 58,000 cases of lung cancer in 1968 with 50,000 deaths. The 1900 figure was only 1,000. Much of this is admittedly due to air pollution.

Bronchitis and emphysema cause at least 25,000 deaths per year in the United States. Probably the figure is nearer to 75,000. Chronic bronchitis affects one man out of every five between 40 and 50 in our country.

86 percent of all our air pollution comes from transportation, 25 percent from power generation, 20 percent from industry, 8 percent from heating homes and other buildings, 4 percent from trash burning, the total reaching 286,000,000,000 pounds or *143 million tons per year*— in the air over our country.

Automobiles produce 90 percent of all carbon monoxide in the air.

In New York City turbo jet planes dump 1139 tons of carbon monoxide and 409 tons of particulate matter on the city every year.

Lung disease is the fastest growing disease in the country. The effect of carbon monoxide is to cut off the oxygen supply to the blood, thereby impairing the brain and nerves. The carbon monoxide level on many expressways during rush hours is often above the danger level for impairing judgment.

Lead is another air and soil contaminant which is causing great concern in areas where traffic is dense. Dirty air costs each individual American 65 dollars a year in cleaning bills, doctor bills and so on. It seems rather obvious that we should be willing to pay that much more in taxes to keep it cleaned up if we can be assured that our money will indeed be used for this.

The conservationist need not wait until all gasolines are lead-free. Amoco now sells lead-free gasoline in some parts of the country. Switch over. And let the companies not selling lead-free gasoline know what you are doing and why. Cancel your charge cards. Buy only lead-free gas.* Another way to help curb pollution from cars is to keep the motor of your car in perfect shape, mechanically speaking. This involves locating an honest, concerned mechanic and then treating him fairly and considerately, so that he will continue to give you good service. Make appointments with him and keep them. Don't make unreasonable demands on him. Don't treat him like a subordinate. He's a businessman and a craftsman. If you want good service, pay him well in both money and consideration.

Granted that the automobile is probably our single greatest problem not only so far as air pollution is concerned, but also in regard to the destruction of our cities and countrysides with expressways, and the despoiling of our natural resources just to make the cars, why not go on a war basis with cars?

For those of you who are too young to remember World War II, let me describe to you what happened then in regard to the automobile. There were no new automobiles. None. So we just used our old ones. They rattled, they swerved, they chattered; grass grew in the back seat, the trunks rusted out, the tires blew. Never mind all that. We were at war. We were proud of their condition of ill-use. It was a matter of status whose car was oldest, in worst shape.

Gasoline was rationed. That's what I said. Rationed.

* Although lead in gasoline is undoubtedly harming us, it now appears that additives which substitute for lead may contribute as bad or possibly worse pollution than lead. The controversy has bogged down into acrimonious debate between those companies which have lead-free gas and those which don't. No one seems to have a final answer.

Once a month you got your ration book of stamps. You gave one stamp for each gallon of gasoline. Every time you wanted to go somewhere it was a matter of deciding whether the trip was worth the ration stamps. If you worked in a war industry you got a few more stamps — not many. It was forbidden, it was illegal to come to work with only one person in the car. Every department arranged car pools and if you were the one to drive that week you picked up the list of folks you were to drive and you made the rounds. And you didn't drive in the gate and show your security badge unless you had six people in the car. Or you had a regular pool of folks for weeks and months. If they had cars (and lots of people didn't!) they chipped in their ration stamps for you.

If you wanted to visit your friends in the country, you took a trolley to the nearest spot and walked the rest of the way — walked, carrying lunch or a coat or bunch of flowers or whatever else had to be carried. Walked, you did, along the country road for five miles or six, or however far it was. Then you walked back and took the trolley into town again.

And do you know what? We got along perfectly all right. We didn't suffer from air pollution or from lack of cars. We were infinitely healthier than we are today. We kept our figures. One reason for that was that butter, sugar, lard and coffee were all rationed, too. But the walking was responsible for a large part of our good health. The situation today in regard to air pollution appears to be infinitely more threatening than any danger we feared in the 1940's. Why not go on a war basis? Why not ration gasoline? Why not ration new cars?

Another alternative is strict legislation governing the

advertising of cars. It appears that cars kill, injure and maim more people than cigarettes do. So a campaign against car advertising should be as effective as the anti-smoking campaign. Let's suppose that, after every TV commercial for a car, it is mandatory for the next commercial to give all the horrendous facts about what the car is doing to our lives. All of them, including the yearly death toll from accidents. Doesn't it seem that the burning desire for a new sex symbol might cool down a bit? What about the electric car? Won't it solve all our problems? Read the dreary story in Chapter 5.

During Earth Week, many demonstrations centered around cars. Students showed their understanding of our present slavery to this object by ferocious attacks on old cars, chopping, axing, burning and burying them. These are all negative manifestations. More positive were the symbolic acts in which substitutes were featured. Bicycle fleets carried people to work and students to class. In California a 400 mile Survival Walk from Sacramento to Los Angeles engaged hundreds of people who camped at night, and went entirely by foot, proselytizing along the way for a new life style. Get out and walk instead of riding.

There are, of course, excellent reasons for walking, apart from the nuisance of the automobile — good health, for instance. We were meant to move about, not sit immobile most of the time. While our hearts and circulatory systems fail simply from lack of exercise, we are also damaging our nervous systems with the frustrations that come from most driving. Human beings, like other animals, are equipped with an alarm system, involving glands, nerves, circulation, heart, brain. When something happens that is frightening or threatening, we are equipped to fight or run, because, down through all the millions of years, those were the only alternatives to being killed.

Today these same reactions continue. But the threat this time is a truck which swerves in front of us. No chance to fight or run. What happens to all the complex mechanism that is preparing us for either of these two choices? It goes on functioning. Blood sugar and blood pressure rise. Our coagulation mechanism begins to thicken blood. Nerves are alerted. Digestion stops. Do we run or fight? No, we sit frustrated, profane, and the mechanism continues to do its subtle damage while we wait for the traffic to clear, the truck to move. No one knows what this syndrome is doing to overall health. It *is* known that blood pressure and heart rates in commuter traffic on expressways are far more shockingly disordered than those of astronauts careening through space or going through the stress of take-off and re-entry.

Walking or bicycling use up the energy, work off the tension, take off the pounds, correct the heart rate, the circulatory disorders, the poor digestion, the insomnia. Walk. Bicycle. Walk to work if you can possibly manage. Walk part way to work. Walk to the supermarket. Walk to church. Walk to the shopping center.

Do you have two cars, or three? Apply the Law of Tolerable Inconvenience. You can get along with only one. Of course you can. It may mean you have to get up earlier, go to bed later. It may mean you have to cancel an appointment with the hairdresser or the dentist or miss the White Sale. But you can do it. By getting along on one car rather than two you can reduce, by half, the air pollution your family is contributing to the total.

Make up a car pool when you go anywhere. Getting to work is the most obvious time. Arrange right now that anybody from your neighborhood going your way to work can have a ride. Or you will drive this week; he will drive next week.

CHAPTER 2

Water's Too Precious to Foul

"Surface water can contaminate ground water and ground water can contaminate ground water and ground water can contaminate surface water. Everything that man himself injects into the biosphere — chemical, biological or physical — can ultimately find its way into the earth's water. And these contaminants must be removed, by nature or by man, before that water is again potable."

Charles C. Johnson, Jr.
Administrator, Consumer Protection
and Environmental Health Service

"Paris casts twenty-five million francs yearly into the water. What is done with this golden manure? It is swept into the abyss . . . Every hiccough of our sewers costs us a thousand francs."

Victor Hugo in *Les Misérables,*
1862

"Regardless of the fact that $5.4 billion has been expended since 1957 for waste treatment facilities, little or no cleanup has been achieved for the nation's waterways, according to a recent report of the General Accounting Office. Although the federal government contributed $1.2 billion, cleanup efforts simply are overwhelmed by increasing industrial waste discharges and poor planning in the choice of Federal Water Pollution Control Administration's 9400 projects."

Environmental Science and Technology
December, 1969

"Unfortunately the majority of the people and even a majority of the Congress still do not understand the gravity of our water-pollution problems. Cleaning up the rivers is viewed by many as part of the 'beautification' program, like getting the automobile junk piles out of sight. Improving the scenery does not purge the water. In my opinion the League of Women Voters is doing the best job countrywide in educating people to the importance of the water problem. It has placed water pollution high on its list of continuing responsibilities."

Donald Carr, "The Death of the Sweet Waters"
Atlantic Monthly, May, 1966

"A simple way of diminishing some of the pollution of rivers is to insist that the effluent from any factory which uses river water for any purpose shall be returned to that river upstream of the factory's water intake. Users of river water are thus encouraged to make an effort to clean up their effluent before dumping it."

T. F. Shaxson in a letter to the Editor, *New Scientist*
October 22, 1970

Nothing could illustrate our dilemma with technology any more clearly than what has been happening around the detergent problem. Until a very few years ago everybody used soap, a harmless, nice, germ-killing cleanser which came in bars, chips or beads. You poured it into the washing machine, it frothed up and you started the machinery. If you had hard water, there was trouble with the greasy scum that accumulated around the top of the tubs and under the hems and collars of things. So you put in washing soda, and you soaked the clothes overnight. And somehow you got them clean.

I grew up in Pittsburgh long before there was any such thing as air pollution abatement. Winter mornings you opened the front door of the house to a thick, smelly curtain of greasy soot that sank, clammy and filthy, into your nostrils and lungs, over your face and hands, and, of course, clothing. There was no question of wearing any piece of clothing longer than an hour or so before it was grimy. You came home from "town" on the trolley car, your face streaked with soot. This was the accepted condition of life. We never even thought of complaining.

The water was so hard that any amount of Ivory soap still left a thick, greasy scum around the top of the washer. You just scrubbed it off with hot water and Old Dutch Cleanser which in those days consisted, I am sure, of some sand and finely ground ashes. Of course there never was much hot water and when you took the clean laundry off the line (of course there were no driers then) it, too, was usually streaked with soot. But we managed. Nobody complained. We washed all the curtains and bedspreads every month and, even so, they looked dirty most of the time. But we managed. And because everybody lived in the same condition nobody thought there was anything unusual about it.

When the phosphate content of modern detergents first made headlines in 1969, we read in our newspapers and magazines that after the laundry water and dishwater is flushed out into sewers, the sewage goes into lakes, rivers, streams where the detergents' phosphates create an excellent growing medium for small water plants called algae. Because of the phosphates in sewage from many cities and towns, lakes and rivers show deterioration from immense growths of algae which take oxygen from the water, so that fish and other living things disappear rapidly. Water becomes thick, scummy, polluted. As the algae die and sink to the bottom, they create more fertilizer for more algae, and the condition worsens.

Lake Erie is spoken of as "dead" by many scientists because of phosphate and nitrate pollution. The nitrates come largely from commercial fertilizers which are spread lavishly over agricultural land and leach away into nearby waterways. If we continue to pour this kind of pollution into our waterways, we are facing a grave pollution crisis because the waters simply cannot cleanse themselves from this kind of pollution. Lake Michigan is the next to go, we are told gloomily.

Other forms of pollution — millions of industrial chemicals, for example, are of course involved. And the mechanics of getting even a small part of these removed in time to save ourselves appear to be insurmountably difficult. But detergents! Surely just doing the laundry and the dishes with something else shouldn't be too difficult a change to make, now, should it?

But technology and everything that accompanies it in modern life has made this seemingly simple step so unbelievably difficult that it appears that detergents may have us licked. The industry, you see, has sunk millions of dollars of advertising into this 5 billion dollar a year business and they won't give them up without a struggle. They have persuaded not only practically all Americans, but many millions of people in other countries as well that they are not socially acceptable unless their laundry is whiter than white. They have set up standards of "whiteness" preferred by folks in different localities and then put in chemical "whiteners" to produce the desired shade of white. This is a purely chemical "brightener" you understand. It has nothing to do with making the clothes any cleaner. As a matter of fact, so much of the chemical content of detergents remains *on* any clothing you wash in detergents, that, if you want to change over to soap, you have to "strip" the detergent leavings out of the clothes with washing soda before making the change, or everything will turn streaky yellow!

This is what the formula for a typical detergent looks like. The active ingredient is something like alkylbenzene sulfonate or fatty alcohol sulfate, the "foam booster" (you have to have foam!) is something like lauryl alcohol or cocomonoethamolamide. Then there's the sodium tripoly phosphate which is the compound that causes all the trouble with algae. This is there to keep soapy curds from forming in hard water. Then there's sodium carboxy methyl cellulose which keeps the dirt from re-depositing itself on the clothes after it's washed off. And sodium silicate, an anti-corrosion agent. A bleach like sodium perborate plus a stabilizer like magnesium silicate which keeps the bleach working longer. Plus, of course, filler which might be sodium sulfate. And, possibly, enzymes.

Enzymes are a natural product put in to remove stains that are protein-based, like blood or grass. Nobody knows very much, actually, about the effects enzymes may have on us or on our waterways. If this kind of pollution behaves as most other kinds have in the past, we won't know what effects enzymes may produce until we have managed to spread them over most of the world, then noticed some peculiar things happening as a result. That is, if anybody manages to connect the effects with the cause. Sweden has banned enzymes in detergents because of dermatitis among women who used them. Our detergent makers declare flatly that no such thing is possible.

After the FTC pestered the detergent industry for months about the possible skin injuries enzymes might cause in housewives, the industry announced they were phasing out enzymes. This upset scientists from the American Academy of Allergy who had been poised to carry out a three-year, $750,000 study on possible harm, partly financed by industry. As this is being written, nobody knows what the final results will be.

Meanwhile, a number of communities banned the sale of phosphate-rich detergents. In Akron, Ohio, an ordinance which would have curbed the detergents and outlawed them by 1972 was stopped by a court injunction on behalf of the detergent industry. The City Council then moved to circumvent the injunction. And the Food and Drug Administration seized, as a hazardous substance which must be so labelled, one of the most widely advertised "safe" detergents — Ecolo-G. The dangerous ingredient is sodium metasilicate. The FDA spokesman said plaintively that some of the chemicals used as substitutes for phosphates "may all have harmful direct physical dangers."

And, finally, there's the arsenic. A University of Kansas researcher, Dr. E. E. Angino, also on the Kansas Geological Survey, did some tests and found up to 70 parts of arsenic per million in several household detergents. This, he said, in an article in *Science,* April 17, 1970, is potentially dangerous for water pollution and for those of us who use the products. He also found arsenic levels of 2 to 8 per parts per billion in the Kansas River. These are close to the 10 p.p.b. recommended as the tolerance level by the Public Health Service. In other words, PHS tells us we're taking a chance if we get 10 p.p.b. of arsenic in drinking water. The Kansas River already contains 8 p.p.b. What about the river you get your drinking water from? Has anybody tested it for arsenic lately?

Dr. Angino said, "We are dealing with a possible pollutant to our environment that is considerably more insidious and potentially far more dangerous than any reported to date." Arsenic can be absorbed through the unbroken skin. It is a cumulative poison which may not produce any symptoms for up to six years or more, at which time the damage has been done. Spokesmen for the detergent industry say the arsenic is a pollutant of the phosphates. It's been there for all the years we've been using detergents, they say, which somehow doesn't make you feel much happier about the whole thing. They say, too, that it's chemically "bound" to the phosphates, so that it can't be absorbed by human beings. No one knows for sure.

These are very serious claims. We could be poisoning all our waterways irretrievably and condemning our children and grandchildren to unimaginable horrors by careless continued use of detergents containing arsenic. If detergents were a life-giving substance we simply could not get along without, maybe there would be some sense to going through what must be done to get rid of the phosphates and the arsenic and substitute something else or put in elaborate, hideously expensive additions to sewage plants to take them out. *But the only reason any of us use detergents at all is to avoid a little bit of soap curd and get our sheets whiter than our neighbors!* Can any intelligent person — let alone any conservation-minded person — believe for a moment that it's worth it?

The detergent industry threatens us with total breakdown in health and sanitation if we abandon detergents. They don't once mention the fact that soap is a fairly effective germ killer while some detergents have been found to encourage the growth of germs. Industry spokesmen do mention in their handsome, cheerily-worded promotion pieces — that by now many washing machines have been manufactured so that you just can't use soap in them and of course soap won't work at all in a dishwasher. So we are the complete prisoners of our washers and dishwashers and they have apparently condemned us and our waterways to lingering death. For some high and noble cause? No. Just so that we can get our sheets whiter than our neighbors! This is the sole reason for using detergents and it is hammered home every half hour of every day with commercials whose idiocy would be nauseating except that we have long since given up being nauseated by commercials and now just accept them in numb, silent compliance and — most of us — believe them!

In the frenzied discussion about detergents that went on around Earth Day I could not find any individual — young or old — who was not in a veritable panic, unable to plot any course, foresee any bearable future! What could they use, they asked. "Soap", I said. "But where do you get soap?" "At the store." "What does it look like? How can I tell whether it's soap or detergent and why don't the detergent makers say on the box how much phosphate is in their product?" "How can I get my clothes clean with soap?" "How dirty are your clothes?" "Oh, we never wear anything more than a few hours or so." "Why do you need detergents, then? The detergent industry itself says that these are 'heavy duty' cleansers. Is your husband a coal miner?" "Of course not. But what if he gets a grass stain on his shorts? How will I get it out?" "Soak it out." "But I have no place to soak the laundry." "Let him wear the shorts with a stain. It's not going to kill him. The arsenic in the detergent may."

I have sat, literally, for hours, discussing quite seriously with individuals who identified themselves as desperately concerned about what's happening to our environment, and they actually thought it was worthwhile to spend a great deal of time weighing the relative merits of destroying all the waterways in the world or having sheets less white than their neighbors'! This is the state to which technology and the advertising industry have brought us.

The detergent industry is rushing around claiming, first, that local sewage plants should take phosphates out — not them. Equipment to do this would be so expensive that few localities could afford it. And most small towns have no sewage plants. They just dump the whole business, raw, into the nearest water. The industry ignores these facts. They are also trying to find substitutes for phosphates. The latest is something called NTA which stands for nitriolo-triacetate. Some scientists feel it may present much more of a potential hazard than the phosphates. We won't know, apparently, until the industry has invested millions of dollars and spread the stuff all over the planet. Then we'll find out that we've made another hideous mistake.

Late in 1970 the Department of Health, Education and Welfare announced that their studies had found that NTA is teratogenic to Laboratory animals — that is, it causes deformed offspring. The largest user of NTA agreed to phase it out. But, according to chemical industry publications, the detergent industry is trying to prove that the NTA tests were inconclusive, so that they can continue to use it. No one has apparently paid much attention to the fact that NTA is an excellent "chelator" which means that it has the ability to take up from the bottom of waterways highly toxic heavy metals like lead, cadmium and mercury and make them available to living things in the waterways.

Chemical Week for March 3, 1971 announced that a new ingredient, disodium oxydiacetate, is front-runner in the race for a phosphate substitute. One of its glorious attributes is its ability to act as a "chelator" — one of the things that made NTA so dangerous!

What's wrong with using soap? I wrote a nice letter to the President of Proctor and Gamble which makes Ivory soap, which I have used exclusively since I was a child. I mentioned all the furor over detergents and asked why P and G is not advertising soap — the good, unpolluting, wholesome, harmless substance that is still available. I received a charming letter from a lady in "Consumer services" who told me a great deal about detergents, which I had not inquired about — and enclosed a "Dictionary of Cleanliness Products" which tells you everything the industry wants you to know about detergents — nothing more, nothing less.

Officially the industry says we can't go back to using soap because of the great scarcity of animal fats of which it is made. Their promotional piece, "The Facts About Today's Detergents", implies without actually saying it, that anybody who uses soap is condemning millions of people in underdeveloped countries to starvation because soap contains animal and vegetable fats which should be going to maintain good health in these folks. They neglect to mention that an important part of water pollution in many areas is the incredible quantity of animal fat tossed into waterways from slaughterhouses which not only goes completely to waste but contaminates miles of rivers and lakes.

I think some of the best things about the detergent crisis were said by a Wisconsin lady, Carol A. Duller, who wrote to *Chemical Week,* protesting their tongue-in-cheek editorial on the subject. She said, in part, "detergents don't do the hot job of cleaning you seem to think they do! . . . . Wash your hands thoroughly and dry them on a freshly laundered towel. See the dirt on the clean towel? Well, that's not from drying your clean hands . . . . you have now wiped off whatever it is that made the towel look so clean and bright. . . . If you really want to get clothes clean these days, it costs a fortune for presoaks, detergents, bleaches, bluing and, of course, the detergents make the clothes so stiff you need a fabric softener . . . . the presoaks and softeners are loaded to their box tops with phosphates, too. . . . If Lake Michigan dies as Lake Erie has, there will be an awful lot of very thirsty people in Michigan, Indiana, Illinois and Wisconsin. And they won't be able to wash their clothes in ANY product."

What should you do about laundry? Use soap. If you have hard water, use washing soda along with it. If you feel you have to "taper off", begin using less and less detergent (and use only the kind with as little phosphate as possible) and gradually switch over to soap entirely. If your family is all that fussy, use bleach to get out stains. Or just leave the stains and wear them proudly to indicate that here's an individual who cares more about the welfare of the planet than some trivial stain. Of course you should be washing dishes only by hand in a good old dishpan, using soap — in chips, beads, flakes or however you prefer it.

Finally, there's an apocrophal-sounding story which we are assured is true. At Marquette University they were testing a new detergent. (Oh, yes, universities are occupied all the time these days with important things like testing products for big industries.) They used dirty cloths, washing them in either (1) plain hot water, with no soap, no detergent added, (2) the new detergent they were testing, or (3) an old detergent loaded with phosphate. They then established several criteria of cleanliness and tested the cloths after the washing period was over. Care to guess what the results were? *Plain hot water with nothing added came out as the best all-around cleanser.*

I have told this story to scores of women with the

most elaborate and expensive laundering equipment at home and all the hot water they could ever need. They listen — all of them — uncomprehending and unbelieving — and then ask "But if I switch over from the high phosphate detergent to the lower, what . . . ." and so on.

Say no to detergents. Don't buy them. Write to the manufacturer and tell him why. And when you get in reply a splendid promotion piece in full color telling you the glorious story of detergents and how we can't get along without them, throw it away without looking at it. It's a pack of lies.

The Jewel Food Stores in Chicago, incidentally, have posted signs above the detergent counters in their 220 supermarkets listing the phosphate content of all detergents they sell. Your local supermarket might be interested in doing the same, with a little friendly pressure from you.

Is there something other than detergents polluting our waterways that we should worry about? You bet there is.

The *New York Times Magazine* on July 17, 1966 printed an article by Peter T. White on the dreadful condition of the Hudson River, which is a typical American river, pollution-wise. Thirty six million gallons of raw sewage a day goes into the Hudson from New York City. The untreated or partially treated waste from all the other municipalities in New Jersey combines with that discharged from upriver to create what the Public Health Service estimates is equivalent to the waste of 10 million people.

Governor Rockefeller calls the Hudson from Troy to Albany one great septic tank. John W. Gardner, former

Secretary of Health, Education and Welfare, called it, in 1966 — "a torrent of filth." Robert Kennedy called it "little better than an open sewer." Senator Clifford Case of New Jersey said, "The time for words has long since passed."

Mr. White's article expressed hope that, at last, something was going to be done for the Hudson. Former President Johnson had asked for funds. The state was determined to clean up the river. Signs still appearing on the shores in 1966 stated that "disposal of any oil, sludge, sewage, bilge oil, garbage or refuse of any kind" anywhere in the tidal waters of New York harbor or its tributaries is forbidden by the New York Harbor Act of 1888, the Federal Refuse Act of 1899 and the Federal Oil Pollution Act of 1924. Penalty — $2500 fine and/or prison for one year.

The pure waters program of the state called for a billion dollar bond issue. The law, supported by many conservation and political groups, was passed by an overwhelming 4 to 1 vote — a billion dollars just for cleaning up pollution in the Hudson! Did it work? Is it working? Industries promised that they would get busy right away planning abatement measures. Cities promised they would make plans for sewage treatment plants. The head of FWPCA predicted that the river would be cleaned up in seven to ten years. Engineers and municipal authorities were pessimistic, muttering that the amounts of money being talked about were a drop in the bucket.

What about New York City itself? By 1971, said Mr. White in 1966, all the West Side sewage will be pumped into sewage treatment plants. Six more will have been built and New York City will have spent more than one billion dollars on water pollution. Most of Manhattan's sewage will be treated in a new plant built right into the river. Sounds cheerful enough.

But on May 3, 1970 Wade Greene wrote an article for the same magazine entitled "What Happened to the Attempts to Clean Up the Majestic, the Polluted Hudson?" None of the predictions appear to have materialized. Less than a third of the major polluters have built treatment plants in the past four years. All the municipalities are years behind in their schedules and plans. The Health Department of the state decided that regional plans might get the job done better and less expensively. This means getting local officials together from different communities and getting them to agree on plans, prices and participation.

The bickering and maneuvering is endless. When officials finally manage to produce a workable plan, it may be vetoed by referendum. Shall polluting industries be included in village sewage plans or must they go it alone? A paper mill near one of the small communities pollutes an estimated six times more than the village. Plans for combining the pollution in one treatment plant fall through. The highway department then announces that the planned sewage line will conflict with their plans for a highway and more difficulties arise. And so on and so on. State authorities believe there is faster progress this way than by litigation. If they tried to stick by the letter of the law and enforce penalties, they say cases might drag through the courts for years while nothing was done in the way of cleaning things up.

In 1970 the chairman of the water resources committee of New York's state Conservation Council, who is one of the nation's major and early crusaders against water pollution, said, "We have suffered more deterioration in the last four years in the waters of the state of New York than in a like period of time in the history of the world."

Author Greene points out that even if or when pollution efforts succeed in shutting off the flow of some of the filth from the cities and industries upriver from New York City, there are some seven feet of organic sludge lying along the bottom of the Hudson River around and south of Albany. Nobody knows what form of pollution will emerge when decomposition of this thick ooze begins or how long it will take to disperse.

An article by John Barnett in the *Wall Street Journal* for December 18, 1969 tells much the same story, quoting the executive director of Scenic Hudson Preservation Conference as saying, "The thing that's important and frightening is that we're working on a series of best engineering guesses with no real marine research behind them." His organization has spent more than $500,000 in the past years fighting a Consolidated Edison pumped storage hydro-electric power plant at Storm King Mountain. Mr. Rod Vandivert is also incensed about the four nuclear power plants being planned in the area where one is already operating. Thermal pollution may upset the delicate balance of life in the river resulting in much greater and speedier destruction of the health of the waters. Algae proliferate more readily in heated water. And, of course, many kinds of water creatures cannot survive increases in temperature. The billion dollar bond issue appears, at present, to be totally inadequate to deal with the problem of constructing sewage facilities.

In May, 1970 Governor Rockefeller said perhaps his promise of a Hudson River clean enough to swim in by 1970 would come true by 1975. In his speech he said that we must get used to doing without many products we are accustomed to, if their long-term "damages outweigh any short-term value." Asked if he meant products like DDT, the governor said that, well, no, he didn't mean DDT, for this is the only spray we can use "in certain epidemic situations." Nor did he mention any other products which might have to be dispensed with before we can clean up water pollution. It was a very general statement, which could offend no one.

An associate commissioner of the Federal Water Quality Administration told businessmen at the same meeting that he foresees a sewage treatment plant *in every home* within the next 30 or 40 years. Apparently he feels that making every man his own sewage works manager is the only possible solution. The trouble is, of course, what it always is with pollution. You can't just make the stuff disappear. It has to go somewhere. And no matter how skillfully you design a home sewage apparatus, there is bound to be something left over that must be disposed of elsewhere. What do you do with the sludge? Put it out for the garbage man to take? Where is he going to take it?

On June 21, 1970, Merril Eisenbud of the Hudson River Environmental Society, asked that part of the five billion dollars now planned for its power plants and sewage treatment plants in the next five years be devoted to a complete scientific study of the life balance of the river. That's how far along we are in even beginning to understand what possibly irreparable things we have already done to our waterways. You frequently hear cheerful prognosticators say that all we have to do is foresee the effects of any new technology before we loose it on the world, then we'll be able to avoid possibly hazardous consequences.

How do you manage to do this? Here's the Hudson, at the heart of the intellectual, industrial and scientific center of the world. But nobody has any idea of what it contains — there must be millions of compounds that have been dumped in over the years. How could anybody — even with unlimited funds — make any sense out of what might happen with some new technology that was going to dump still more compounds into the Hudson?

"Long Island Sound is in danger of becoming another Lake Erie," said Representative Ogden Reid, in October, 1969. "The water is twice as dirty as it was 10 years ago and the pollution is spreading out from the shoreline." *(New York Times,* October 25,1969). Most of the pollution comes from the discharges of 179 municipal sewage facilities that empty into the Sound, and from commercial navigation, recreational boating and dredging operations. Less than half the municipal sewage facilities now provide secondary treatment for sewage. In addition, the Sound is to be the site of five nuclear fueled power plants in the 1970's. These are bound to raise the temperature of the water almost immediately.

Pete Seeger, well known folk singer, took a dramatic step on behalf of the Hudson, which flows past his home. He and a group of friends bought and refurbished an old-time sloop, the *Clearwater,* and sailed up and down the Hudson for a year giving concerts of songs about pollution and showing slides from the State Pure Water Authority. They drew as many as 400 spectators an hour on pleasant Saturdays, more on Sundays. Many of the people who came had never realized the extent of the Hudson's pollution until they saw it first-hand and close.

The *Clearwater* sailed down to the Potomac and Washington for Earth Day. Pete said, "We've sailed for a year now up and down the river showing people what the river used to be, how it's polluted now and what it can be. But now we're going to Washington because the problems of the American rivers can't be solved by people who live on them. Only the federal government has the power to enact and enforce the laws that are needed."

There is not enough oxygen for fish to survive in the Potomac River for 12 miles from Georgetown to Mount Vernon. The bacteria count is 100 times too high to permit swimming. The imperfectly treated sewage of the entire Washington area is dumped directly into the river at the rate of 240 million gallons daily. The Department of Interior, questioned by representatives of the League of Women Voters, opined that the government would surely have the Potomac "cleaned up" by 1973 or, at the latest, 1975.

In January, 1970 seven New York concerns and 13 from New Jersey were haled into court to answer federal charges of water pollution. These were companies not exactly penniless or unaware of the vast problems of water pollution. They included: Consolidated Edison, White Rock, Commander Oil Corporation, duPont, Texaco, Central Railroad of New Jersey, General Aniline and Film and so on. The charges were brought under an 1868 law prohibiting the "deposit of refuse in New York Harbor and adjacent waters."

Science reported on August 8, 1969 that "All of the 50 states have now submitted (clean water) standards to the Secretary of Interior, but only 21 states have had their standards fully approved and about half of those are now considered inadequate and subject to further tightening. . . . The first deadlines for polluters to meet in designing and ordering pollution-control equipment occurred last year. Also still unresolved is the question of how compliance with abatement schedules is to be enforced, *or even whether the federal government itself has the authority to enforce them in situations where the states fail to do so.*" (My italics)

Nobody knows what to do about Iowa, for instance, which has flatly refused to go along with federal programs for cleaning up waterways, in this case, the Mississippi and Missouri. Iowa sent in the required formulations or standards for clean water which are so far removed from what federal officials believe are necessary that they held four days of hearings with the Iowa officials trying to come to some agreement.

Iowa refuses to adopt secondary treatment of sewage as a uniform requirement for sewage discharge into the two rivers. Citing "state's rights", the Iowa Water Pollution Control Commission chairman said, "When the federal people show us that secondary treatment is necessary to maintain the rivers' quality, we'll do it, but not until then." The federal spokesmen produced days of evidence that the rivers are "filthy with chemicals, germs and packing house wastes", according to Gladwin Hill writing in the *New York Times* for April 21, 1969.

The Iowa people claimed they and they alone could decide how much of the pollution came from Iowa, how much from neighboring states. They also said they would not abide by a federal policy requiring that any generally unpolluted waterway should not be "degraded" in the course of cleaning up the badly polluted cases. Iowa seems to feel that in some cases it might be advantageous to the state to pollute a stream!

In January, 1968, a biologist employed by Gulf Coast Research Laboratory in Mississippi told federal researchers who came to study the pollution of the estuaries of the River, "These are our estuaries. They do not belong to the federal government. If we want your help we shall request it. Otherwise, kindly keep out." He went on to say that, in his opinion, estuaries *should* be used as open sewers. Conservation is not a "feasible way of life" in the 20th century, he said. Industrialization is paramount. He is a realist and he realizes that pollution is here to stay, he said.

He went on to say that, "The official public position of the Federal Government and, particularly, of the Department of the Interior, has been that the general public wants and will support water pollution control, regardless of cost. How this position is maintained in the face of repeated instances of defeat of bond issues for sewage treatment facilities is not clear. Apparently some thoughts are publicly unthinkable — for example, that pollution is not necessarily bad, or that the majority of citizens simply do not care whether or not the water is polluted." And "because of rapid increase in knowledge in recent years, management of estuaries is approaching the stage where the problems tend to be more economic than biological. We have grave doubts that the Federal Government is any more sensitive or adept politically than local governments in estuarine management. Thus, we are states righters, following an old tradition. . . . The Gulf States are getting along well with local control."

A headline in *Business Week,* March 7, 1969 states "Chesapeake Bay Fights for its Life." The Bay is the largest of this country's 500 estuaries. Estuaries are the mouths of rivers, where they meet the sea. As such they are breeding grounds and homes for millions of organisms, fish, shellfish, wading birds, and all the elaborate cycle of life that needs the shallow water, the edges of the river and the sea in which to survive and procreate. Estuaries are among the most ecologically elaborate and, hence, the most easily damaged of all natural areas, in terms of pollution.

Scientists are already predicting a Lake Erie fate for the Bay if present trends are not reversed speedily. Four million gallons of untreated sewage dumped into the Bay poison fish and create conditions favorable for eutrophication. There are already so many coal-fired and nuclear power plants around the Bay that those which are being planned will bring the total to 17. This means thermal pollution of water, for it is used to cool the plants, then returned to the Bay. Six thousand merchant ships a year discharge their human waste into the Bay. The Army Corps of Engineers are dredging to deepen the Baltimore harbor and the Chesapeake and Delaware Canal. The Army conducts chemical warfare tests nearby; the Navy sets off underwater explosions. Pesticides and fertilizers run off from surrounding farmland.

Where is the hope? The Army Corps of Engineers has gotten into the act and one shudders to hear it. When this crew offers to help somehow one thinks of the fox offering to help feed the chickens. There is a Chesapeake

Bay Foundation headed by Jess Malcolm who speaks at group meetings about the pollution in the bay and who is chiefly concerned with preventing the building of the proposed atomic power plants. It's the radioactive wastes that, understandably, worry Mr. Malcolm. But he presses on, trying to awaken the public's awareness of the seriousness of the situation in regard to every kind of pollution.*

What one would like to think is an unusual threat to potable water occurred recently in our part of Pennsylvania where 3 million gallons of highly toxic chemical waste had been stored in a crumbling lagoon at the site of a chemical plant which had long since moved away. The director of Bucks County natural resources, asking the governor for an emergency fund of $200,000, pointed out that, if the lagoon gave way, the copper sulfates and sulfuric acid it contained would cause massive and serious pollution which would shut down water systems in a number of neighboring towns and force Philadelphia to seek another source of drinking water.

At the time he made his request 30 gallons a minute of the toxic wastes were flowing into a local creek which empties eventually into the Delaware River. The lawsuit pending against former owners cannot proceed since most of them cannot be found. The local authorities decided that three procedures could be undertaken to safeguard the water supply. The chemicals could be loaded into tank cars and barges, taken out into the

* The *Washington Post* announced the resignation of Mr. Malcolm in January 1971 because of lack of funds. His Save-The-Bay campaign had been literally snowed under with requests for information and help. Although his organization had 900 members, they were trying to get along on donations of $10,000 a year. Mr. Malcolm had been preparing TV documentaries, had served on discussion panels, lectured, edited a monthly bulletin, organized conferences and seminars, testified at hearings and issued reports on pollution.

ocean and "slowly released into the sea" — (the universal sink!) Or processing operations could reclaim much of the waste on the spot. Or a silica jell could be used to solidify the waste and keep it from dispersing into waterways.

This appears to be no kind of a guideline for the future. Just what can we do with all the millions of gallons of toxic liquid waste which are stored in many spots all over our country? How long will it be until storage tanks fail? Where is the pollution likely to spread and how soon? How can it be mopped up quickly enough or dispersed gradually enough to do no harm? Who knows?

These are the questions you should ask in any local situation where water pollution is the issue. There are no answers. No one, scientist or engineer, can come forward and declare flatly that this or that measure will forever mop up or disperse or render harmless the mess that has been made. We must still find the answers! There are years of hard work ahead until the answers are found. We must make a start at once!

In 1965 a survey by the House of Representatives found that 68 federal installations, mostly defense department bases, were dumping millions of gallons of sewage into streams and rivers daily. The committee recommended that these bases be surveyed to find out what they are doing to improve the situation. Money intended for use to clean up the pollution was being used for other things, like football fields.

The New Republic reported in 1964 that the Water Pollution Control Program of 1956 had a provision for taking polluters to court if the pollution is not stopped. In the 8 years since the measure was passed, *only one case went to court.* And "In the 8 years that the present water pollution control act has been in existence, the federal government has started fewer than two dozen enforcement actions and most waterways are filthier now than they were in 1956 when the program began."

On February 24, 1960 a *New York Times* editorial announced happily that "The heart of President Johnson's message on conservation is his program on water resources. At last, the nation appears to be moving toward an effective confrontation with the urgent problem of polluted water." In 1971, eleven years and oceans of filth later, most editorials on water pollution sound glum, even totally hopeless. There is nobody to blame, it seems. The whole mechanics of enforcing any law on water pollution appear to be just unmanageable.

"Where is the money to come from?" we all tend to inquire. And editorials and speakers point out time and again that building sewage plants takes enormous amounts of money, especially when they involve secondary or tertiary treatment. The federal government promises to pay the states a given portion of the amount necessary. Congress duly appropriates the money and sets it aside for this purpose. But it is up to the executive branch of the government to spend it. And, said the *New York Times* for January 11, 1970, "Officials in the Executive branch department make no secret of the President's intention not to use the $586 million that Congress has appropriated above his request."

In Europe the situation is no better. Forty million fish died in the Rhine River in June, 1969. The Mediterranean and Adriatic Seas are repulsive with sewage, industrial waste and oil slicks. Ammunition and mustard gas dumped into the Baltic is a perennial threat to the safety of everyone living on the shores. Nuclear wastes in massive amounts have been dumped into the ocean on both sides of the Atlantic. Most English rivers are heavily polluted. Denmark is surrounded by "No Swimming" signs on magnificent beaches and there is a stench of sewage as you near Copenhagen. In colorful Austria sewage from camping sites and tourist hotels threatens the lakes and rivers which the tourists come to enjoy.

In the Netherlands, there was a widespread kill of sandwich terns in 1964 and 1965, when birds died in convulsions 100 miles away from any possible source of pollution. The mystery was solved years later. A chemical plant had dumped the chemical *isodrin* into the water which had come to rest in the mud at the bottom of Rotterdam's inland waterways. The chemical was evidently carried "some kilometers" offshore with the mud when the waterways were dredged. Currents in the water then apparently washed it northward *and while on its way it underwent a chemical change into endrin* the highly toxic pesticide. How? It was thought to have been caused by bacteria in the mud and "enzymes in shellfish"! So much for the extent of our knowledge of what can happen once a seemingly harmless substance is dumped into the complex environment of the ocean. The story by Eric Pace was in the *New York Times,* February 22, 1970.

Representative Henry S. Reuss of Wisconsin, who has done so much to keep detergent harm in the light of public and legislative scrutiny, has a plan for overcoming water pollution. He is suing 149 industries in his home state for water pollution. They include slaughter houses, canneries, chemical plants, paper mills, auto companies, glue factories, cheese factories. He is bringing them into court under the provisions of the Rivers and Harbors Act of 1899 which forbade the dumping into navigable waters of refuse of any kind, without a permit from the Army Corps of Engineers.

The 1899 Act provides for a fine of not less than $500 and not more than $2500 *a day* for each day's violation and a prison term of not less than 30 days and not more than one year. In the past 71 years the law has been, you might say, totally ignored, as we have proceeded on our careless, destructive way filling every available body of water with as much and as varied pollution as can be imagined. Now federal courts are using the Act to bring suits against companies in several states, including one power company which is causing thermal pollution in Florida. (Is thermal pollution actually water pollution, in terms of the ancient law? No one knows. The courts will have to decide.)

An interesting provision of the 1899 Act states that one half the fine shall be paid to the individual who "gives information to the United States attorney which shall lead to conviction." That, obviously, was a big incentive in days when a real polluter might be a fellow who snuck out in the middle of the night and dumped a dead animal into the stream from which the townspeople drew their drinking water. Today the facts about most heavy polluters are all well known in their localities. No one has to sneak out and actually behold the offender doing his dumping. Steel mills and paper mills openly admit, through their public relations officials, that they are polluting the water. And as for any United States attorney, he surely does not need anyone to tell him that certain industries are polluting the nation's waterways. He needs only to read the newspaper or almost any magazine of national circulation.

What is missing, of course, is the complainant, the fellow who brings the suit, who alleges the damage, who claims that he has been harmed. And this is where you, the ordinary citizen, come into the picture, says Representative Reuss. He has a handy "kit" for guidance in these affairs which you can obtain by writing to him at the House Office Building in Washington, D. C.

Representative Michael Harrington of Massachusetts, who has asked the U. S. Attorney to begin suits against 151 Massachusetts industries, has also recommended that private citizens follow his lead and that of Representative Reuss. Harrington has available at his office an outline describing how you go about it. You can write for it. Address him at 1205 Longworth Building, Washington, D. C., 20515.*

The procedure is rather complicated and may prove to be costly, depending on whether you win or lose the case. If you lose, you would probably have to pay all court costs, plus the cost of your lawyer. It's not a game to be played on a summer afternoon just to collect a few dollars. But certainly if your local conservation group is working hard to stop pollution of a local river and if you have run out of expedients this might be the time to try Representative Ruess's plan to get the 1899 Act enforced. It is becoming increasingly apparent that, if antipollution laws are to be enforced, citizens will have to take the initiative.

When Congressman Reuss asked the Attorney Gen-

* An excellent booklet, *Here's How to Fight Back Against Water Pollution,* covers the 1899 Refuse Act. Write to Connecticut Action Now, 152 Temple Street, Room 310, New Haven, Conn. 06510

eral's office why they were not prosecuting polluters under the 1899 Act, he was told officially that the department would not prosecute industries "where satisfactory results are being achieved under state or federal programs with which participating industrial producers are in full compliance."

Reuss told the press that "The law doesn't exempt polluters who spend money to clean up their mess . . . . it is folly to allow the polluter, regardless of the sums of money he may be spending now for pollution abatement, to disregard the prohibition against such discharges under the Refuse Act."

So, the law has been on the books of our federal government for 70 years. No one has made any attempt to enforce it. Some of the worst polluters are agents of the federal government, one of whose departments (the executive) has the job of enforcing the law. When a Congressman asks why the law is not being enforced, he is told by the government that they do not intend to enforce the law, except under certain conditions. It is not clear just what a private citizen can do in circumstances like this, but it appears rather obvious that federal officials clamoring loudly for "law and order" might well begin to look around at some such actions as these to see how they measure up. It isn't really the job of private citizens to enforce federal laws, you know. Yet the lackadaisical point of view of federal enforcement officers is underlined by the apparent helplessness of the government to do anything without a massive protest — almost an uprising — on the part of the majority of citizens who have been, or expect to be, injured by the pollution. And officials appear to know this, as it becomes, every day, increasingly apparent that all of us are the injured parties — even, or perhaps mostly, all the generations yet to come.

Assistant Interior Secretary Carl L. Klein, in charge of Water Quality and Research, is quoted in *Science* as advising "Don't let up on government. Hammer it. Worry it. Keep after it." In other words, force the government to enforce the laws.

The findings of a nationwide sampling of community drinking water supply systems "underline the need for upgrading our treatment and distribution systems and illustrate the danger of complacency with regard to drinking water safety", according to Charles C. Johnson, Jr., Administrator of Consumer Protection and Environmental Health Service. Mr. Johnson went on to catalog the findings in the entire state of Vermont, and eight metropolitan districts of varying size. Nine per percent of the samples show contamination in the distribution systems. Judging from 6 per cent of the samples which contained colon bacteria, eight million people served by municipal water systems consume water which exceeds the bacteriological criteria contained in federal Drinking Water Standards. In Vermont, the contamination rate was found to be 31 percent for both the total number of samples and the total number of systems.

Of 79 analyses for pesticide completed to date, pesticides were detected in 76. In rural areas about 40 per cent of all water supplies were found to be contaminated with objectionable material, 40 per cent of which is colon bacteria. In many places the people in charge of the water works were "moonlighting", or working full-time at other jobs. Safety measures for chlorine handling were "often nonexistent in the smaller water treatment plants and often limited and ineffective in the larger ones." Mr. Johnson asked, "Are we going to wait until public health statistics reveal a drinking water crisis? Or are we going to begin now to upgrade our water treatment and distribution systems to cope with the problems of our own time and place?"

Commenting on these findings in *American City,* June, 1970, past president of the American Waterworks Association, Henry J. Graeser, admitted that "the results are not flattering to the water-supply industry." In many cases they could very easily have met the standards by following the minimum requirements for bacteriological analysis and enforcing plumbing codes. Towns with populations under 5,000 were the most serious offenders. And 85 per cent of all Americans still live in such towns. "The situation is simply this — " said Mr. Graeser, "we have received adequate warning."

What's the situation in your own town or city? When did you last inquire? When was the last report made? Have you ever visited the waterworks and asked about the procedures used? How many operators are on hand there? Are they full-time? Do they actually use the safety measures provided for in your state code and federal codes for assuring the safety of drinking water? Why not check it out? It's a good project for your club.

In Easton, Maine a local boycott against a water polluting industry was instituted by the State Biologists' Association. The boycott climaxed a ten-year hassle to get a potato company to stop polluting the Prestile stream. According to a former engineer on Maine's water pollution control board, the Vahlsing Potato Company, dumping wastes into the stream were producing as much pollution as a city of 270,000 people would produce. Said he, "Locating an industry or a city with this magnitude of waste on a stream which is hardly more than a brook could not be based on good judgment or foresight."

For ten years, Maine had supposedly been trying to get the potato company to do something else with its wastes. At the time the boycott was instituted, the company faced legal action by the state for "illegal pollution". When the plant was built, the stream was reclassified to take care of the pollution — but temporarily classified, it was noted by Senator Muskie in a speech in 1965. Just until the factory was built and put into production, the state would put up with a given amount of pollution, but not a minute longer! The company promised. The state lent them money to proceed with the building.

Fish died in the Prestile. A Fish and Game Department spokesman said, "It's a dead stream. It couldn't be any deader. You could grow trout better on the main street of Augusta than you could up there." Said a former mayor of Centerville, N. B., "We threw some trout into the stream this week and they lived less than a minute. Dead salmon fry line the banks of the Prestile like sardines in a can."

The pollution continued. In 1966 a petition with 420 signatures was sent to the Maine Water Improvement Commission, the governor and the attorney general. Nothing happened. In 1969 the State Biologists' Association, under the leadership of Dr. Robert M. V. Chute of Bates College, voted to institute a boycott of all Vahlsing products. And the Vahlsing Potato Company applied for a state loan to build still another factory!

The biologists' association points out in the literature which they circulated widely to other conservation groups, asking for their cooperation, that the potato company obviously had enough money to stop polluting their stream, since they had enough money to start a new plant. Dr. Chute told me in a letter that the boycott had not been highly successful, mostly because the company sells their products in other states and under other labels. However, he said, "As a stimulus to further action — as a warning to the industries and politicians of the state that we have shifted from talk to action — it has been well worth the effort. It was much more effective than several expensive full-page ads would have been to attract support for our cause. . . . Next time we boycott we'll pick an easily identified product for which substitutes are available. These seem to be necessary conditions for a product boycott to work. On the local level boycott against individual businesses is a real possibility."

On March 15, 1970, the first anniversary of the boycott, Dr. Chute placed a wreath on the "Monument to Vahlsing Pollution" on the New Brunswick-Maine border. The wreath said, "Pollution is Dirty Business."

Our almost total lack of protection from those agencies of government assigned to protect us shows up clearly in the story of mercury which was being written in horrifying headlines as this book was being written. No government agency had apparently ever thought of testing water for mercury. A young Canadian student tested some water and found alarming levels of mercury. Public health officials came to attention, saluted, and began to test water for mercury.

Headlines screamed. State after state announced that fish was too contaminated to eat, in one lake and river after another. By November, 1970, 33 states had found dangerous amounts of mercury in fish caught in their waters. Our casual, careless assumption that the oceans are so vast no amount of pollution can damage them was roughly shaken when the livers of seals caught off the Pribilof Islands in Alaska were found so badly contaminated with mercury that a food supplement made of them was taken off the market. Ten times the safe level of mercury was found in the hair of residents of Pribilof Islands who eat seal meat and livers. Then high levels of mercury began to show up in tuna and swordfish.

Many industries use mercury in their operations and, apparently, dump the wastes into any nearby waterway without giving a thought to the consequences, although the toxic nature of mercury has been known for years. In 1966 an international symposium on "Mercury in the Environment" should have been warning enough.

About 80 percent of all commercial crop seed in this country is coated with mercury to protect it from fungus. The mercury disappears into the soil after the seed sprouts. Almost no one gave a thought to any possible harm this might do until cattle and pheasants were found to contain dangerously high levels of mercury. And a New Mexican family was poisoned when they ate pork from a pig which had been fed mercury treated seeds.

How poisonous is mercury? How much should we allow in food to prevent damage to health? How do we get it out of our food and water supply? No one has any answers to these questions. It may take years to discover the answers, if indeed, there are any satisfactory final answers. Meanwhile we can cross our fingers and hope that our families won't be permanently damaged by today's or tomorrow's burden of mercury in what we are eating and drinking.

Mercury is only one of hundreds, perhaps thousands, of industrial chemicals of unknown toxicity we are turning loose on the environment in unknown quantities. In *FDA Papers* for September, 1970, Dr. Henry Fischbach, FDA Director of the Office of Pesticides and Product Safety, Bureau of Foods and Pesticides, outlines what must be done immediately to forestall future damage to waterways, air and soil. And, eventually, to people.

The finding of mercury in tuna and swordfish illustrates well how the food chain operates. The poisons are taken up in small amounts by small organisms which are then eaten by larger ones, then by small fish which are eaten by larger fish and so on. At each step, the poison is concentrated. Tuna and swordfish are large fish. The poison is most heavily concentrated in them. And, like man, they are near the top of the food chain.

Dr. Fischbach mentions a chemical PCB, widely used, whose potential for harm is very much like that of DDT. Chemicals used in rubber processing and rubber worn from tires on roads is washed into waterways. In 1967 our rubber processing plants used 264 million pounds of such chemicals! Says Dr. Fischbach, "Except for PCB's, about which only limited information is available, essentially nothing is known about possible residues of these many nonpesticidal industrial chemicals in man's food supply and in man himself . . . there is a dearth of information on the toxicology of these chemicals. In most cases, little is known about the toxic effects of low levels ingested over long periods."

In *Chemical and Engineering News,* October 12, 1970, Richard A. Carpenter, Chief of Environmental Policy Division, Legislative Reference Service, Library of Congress, takes up the problem of "New Chemicals: Risks Versus Benefits". He points out that, even if we knew the potential damage of one or another of these chemical pollutants, there is no way of knowing what the "synergistic" effect may be — that is, what happens when you ingest or breathe two, three, a dozen or several hundred at the same time! Toxicologists know well that one poison can potentiate (or render much more toxic) another poison.

Dr. Carpenter says that all these dangerous new chemicals have the following qualities: they are alien to the environment, they are persistent like DDT; they are highly toxic to living things; they are mobile and diffuse; they represent a great departure from a natural situation in regard to quantity, concentration and formulation.

Two attractive booklets are available from the Department of Interior, *What You Can Do About Water Pollution* (15 cents) and *Showdown* (65 cents). You can get them from the Superintendent of Documents in Washington, D. C., 20402. Perhaps the most significant paragraph they contain is this: "One central fact is beginning to emerge from all this — *there is no way to avoid the costs of pollution.* Either we must put up with the more and more costly consequences of pollution, or we must accept the costs of pollution prevention and control. This is the stark either-or of the situation. There is no other choice."

According to *Showdown,* which was published in 1968, the Secretary of Interior is empowered "to institute an enforcement action" when (1) the water quality standards adopted for inter-state and coastal waters are violated; (2) the health and welfare of persons in a state other than the one in which the pollution originates are endangered; (3) the pollution causes damage to the health and welfare of persons within the state in which it originates and the Governor of the state requests such action; (4) pollution has damaged shellfish so that substantial economic injury has resulted from the inability to market shellfish products in inter-state commerce; and (5) international pollution is involved.

Since, by its own admission, the Interior Department apparently needs all of us to hammer at it, worry it, keep after it, let's hammer at it, worry it, keep after it.

CHAPTER 3

Solid Waste Can Be a Resource

"We calculate that each ton of recycled waste paper saves 17 trees and that the current recycling activity conserves close to 200 million trees annually. This is equal to the annual yield of five million acres of woodland."

Edwin A. Locke, Jr., President
American Paper Institute *New York Times*
March 22, 1970

"Everyone wants us to pick up their garbage, but no one wants us to put it down."

Louis Welch, Houston, Texas Mayor

Ask anybody you know what they do with their garbage. If they live in a city or town they'll tell you they set it out for the Man to collect. Ask them what he does with it. They'll tell you they don't know. Unless their community has had a recent hassle over a new incinerator, a fire at the dump or a ruling that their landfill won't pass state inspection, chances are they have no idea what happens to the garbage after the Man picks it up.

Ask them next what they do with their trash, that is, bottles, cans, old furniture, broken toys, worn-out tires. They give that to the Man, too, either in a separate collection on a special day, or else mixed in with the orange peels and the coffee grounds. What does the Man do with it? "I really don't know," they'll tell you. "He disposes of it whatever way he's supposed to and we pay him for it."

Until the past few years, most people knew something about air pollution (temperature inversions and all that) and water pollution (you can't drink out of just any old spring when you're in the country) but no one knew or cared very much about garbage and trash. Fifty years ago when most of us still lived on farms or in small towns, garbage was fed to the pigs or spread on the vegetable garden to disintegrate into soil. What did we do then with the trash?

There just wasn't much trash, to begin with. When you married, you bought furniture for the house or you inherited it from your folks and it lasted you for life. You handed it down to your children as very valuable and expensive stuff. You grew most of your own food or bought it from the Man who came around in a truck or a buggy, so you had almost no cans or bottles to dispose of. In fact, bottles were rather precious artifacts handed down from one generation to the next and the few cans we accumulated were used for all kinds of practical things: to make bird houses or dollhouses, to plant cuttings or store seeds, and so forth.

You used waste paper to start the fire every morning. There wasn't much paper, anyway. Letters from friends and relatives, the address book, the mail house catalog, the butcher paper the meat came in and the daily paper were just about all most people had to dispose of. Bulky things you just couldn't use any longer like the leaking ice chest or wash boiler you allowed to collect in the cellar and took to the town dump once a year.

The town dump was a fairly unattractive place with rats and rotting hulks of things, but nobody minded. It was on the edge of town where nobody lived, usually in an abandoned quarry or hole and although it sometimes caught fire, it didn't really cause much inconvenience.

How does it happen that, all of a sudden, in the middle of the 20th century, we have a solid waste explosion of such dimensions that it promises to bury us all long before we ever start that promised colony on the moon? Here are some of the reasons for the explosion.

Most of us no longer raise our own food. We buy food and many other items in vast establishments where the aisles stretch for blocks and the shelves are loaded with many varieties of every item. Each item is enclosed in layers of wrappings which you fight your way through when you get home, breaking fingernails and kitchen shears in the process. By the time the groceries are stowed away, you have a heap of wrappings higher than the kitchen sink.

Whatever food you don't buy at the supermarket, you may get from a vending machine or an ice cream or candy stand. This, too, is encased in quantities of packaging material. Your soft drinks, which used to come in returnable bottles, now come in the non-returnable kind, or in cans. Gadgetry made of aluminum foil proliferates on all sides. There's almost nothing today you can't buy wrapped in aluminum. The TV dinner, the disposable cake pan, the florists' bouquet — the aluminum part is dumped into the trash can. Aluminum doesn't disintegrate in the soil, doesn't burn, lasts practically forever.

Whatever isn't made of aluminum may be made of plastic. And here we'd better give you some statistics, because, unless you've studied this problem recently, chances are you won't believe what we are about to tell you. Plastic things are what environmental specialists call "non-biodegradable". That is, they last for a very long time. No one knows exactly, because we've had the avalanche of plastic things only within the past 10 years or so and no plastic ever shows signs of wear in that length of time. It will scratch, of course, and maybe some part will snap off to render it useless. But the hard, glittering, impermeable surface of that plastic Thing remains almost indestructible.

The *New York Times,* in its end-of-the-year financial section, 1969, told the following story, "When Monsanto's plastic house of the future in Disneyland was torn down after a one-year display, neither steel balls, torches, chain saws nor jackhammers were able to help the wreckers. What finally solved their problem, after two weeks of effort, were choker cables that tore the modules into pieces small enough so they could be carted away." The *Times* does not say where they were taken or what happened to them. Plastic does not burn unless it is subjected to great heat, then it more or less melts into a rubbery mass instead of burning. It doesn't seem likely that an incinerator large enough to burn pieces of an entire house has yet been built, so presumably that Disneyland house is still piled up somewhere, impermeable to heat, moisture, cold, rain and freezing.

This gives you some idea of the long-lived quality of this new substance which is remaking our world. The plastics industry, in an attractive booklet entitled, *Plastics: a 15-Year Outlook,* welcomes you to the world of 1980 "where cities nestle under plastic domes . . . where high speed plastics-based trains zip along at unbelievable speeds and where plastic appliances pop out of walls on command, clean your house, launder your clothes, make your bed, cook your meals — within the next 15 years."

By the middle of the 1980's world-wide production of plastics will be up to *273 million tons.* By the year 2000 this will be six times greater — 1,790 million tons. "What is more, these materials will collectively dominate nearly three-quarters of the total materials market at that time" — close to 4 billion pounds of plastics will be produced annually in the USA as we enter the 1980's.

This is cause for rejoicing for the plastics industry. As this book is being written, several soft drink companies are announcing plastic non-returnable bottles that will be on the market soon. We are speaking, you will remember, of a substance that, virtually, we can't dispose of. The big chemical companies which make plastics have no way of disposing of scraps and discarded material at their plants. They just bury them.

When I requested information about plastics from the Society of the Plastics Industry, 250 Park Avenue, New York, 10017, I asked specifically if they are making some provision for disposal of their products after we've used them. Here is the answer, from a staff administrator:

> "There is nothing as yet in print in this office, on pollution control as several major projects are still being field-tested. At present it is safe to say that the major disposal routes for plastic products will be chemical incineration, compacting for land fill and possible construction uses, and possibly far in the future, atomic disintegration for recycling of the basic material by laser fusion."

Four billion tons of plastic items a year, some of them so evanescent that you use them only once, and the industry itself sees no way of disposal except to burn them in city incinerators (which you and I pay for) which will infinitely increase the hazards of air pollution from these incinerators, or burying them in landfills (which you and I pay for), many of which are filling up at such a rate they will last only a few more years. Then we must find some new way of disposing of trash.

The plastics industry has been making plastics since the early days of celluloid, more than 100 years ago. They have apparently given hardly a thought to disposal problems even though, as the plastic industry boasts, "new plastic materials have been introduced at such a fantastic rate that even the specialist finds keeping track requires some fancy footwork." The man in charge of your local incinerator is certainly not a specialist in plastics. Yet every new kind of material introduced in plastics creates new problems for him.

Polyvinyl chloride, used in making plastic pipe, flooring, packaging material, insulation and phonograph records, produces, when it is burned, hydrochloric acid resulting in new and possibly very dangerous air pollution. Nobody knew this or, if they did, just didn't care. It seems to be the point of view of the plastics industry that they make the products; disposing of them is somebody else's headache. They couldn't care less. Well, you and I have to care, for it's our expensive city incinerator whose grates will be eaten away by the hydrochloric acid and our lungs that will be irritated by the fumes. What final harm these fumes will do to trees, animals, human beings, buildings and homes, no one knows and probably no one will know for years to come, at which time we will discover we have an enormous pollution crisis to solve just because a new ingredient was introduced into certain plastic products years before.

If we don't burn the stuff, we can always bury it. Can we? Where will we have room, around our crowded and rapidly expanding cities and small towns, to bury 4 billion pounds of plastic, this material that never disintegrates, never disappears, just stays there? New York City, San Francisco, Los Angeles, Philadelphia, to name but a few, are already almost out of space for landfill. Certainly all the rest of us will be, too, before the plastics industry sticks us with 4 billion pounds a year of indestructible things.

An ad in *New Scientist* for July 17, 1969 calls the

1970's "the decade of planned obsolescence". Almost everything you buy should last only so long as you like the look of it, says this ad. Plastic furniture is what they are talking about. They promise you they are making this stuff precisely because it will become obsolescent in a short time. You just throw it away and buy something new. If he sells you something that could last forever, there has to be some incentive for you to get rid of it, or how can he sell you something else? So there will be built-in flaws or a built-in boredom element.

The plastics industry promises us automobiles with bodies made entirely of plastic, as soon as they can manage it. There are now millions of abandoned cars left on highways with no identification. In New York City it may cost up to ten dollars a car to tow away the almost 60,000 abandoned vehicles, every year, to a junk yard. There they sit while the junk men tear them apart to provide parts for other old cars which will soon be abandoned. We produce more than nine million cars annually, of which about 21 per cent are abandoned and become a public charge. Steel mills, which used to recycle metal into steel have changed their ways of doing things, so that they don't take much scrap metal any more. The scrap piles up in the auto graveyards, the landfills and the dumps.

But metal eventually succumbs to weather and rusts away. Metal can be burned and its elements recovered. Metal cars can be sunk into the ocean, as one engineer proposed recently, to make living space for fishes. Eventually the metal will enrich the sea water. But when the plastics industry finally achieves an all-plastic car there will be no final disposal means at hand. The junked car which we cannot crush, hack to pieces, burn or recycle in any way will clutter the highway or the park. The men who haul it away can do nothing with it but bury it. It will then clutter the soil for who knows how many years? Plastic things we now send to the landfill create problems. They don't compact well. But the plastic industry, avidly developing new products and new materials, has no plans for giving us any help on this.

Here are some further statistics on solid waste, as garbage and trash are called "in the trade". Every year Americans discard 3½ billion tons of it: 48 billion cans, 26 billion bottles, 30 million tons of paper, 4 million tons of plastic, 100 million rubber tires and so on. With the exception of paper, no one has done much about planning any way of putting this gigantic waste basket of stuff to any use. The glass in the bottles, the rubber in the tires, the metal in the cans is, in addition to a monumental and possibly insolvable problem of disposal, a hideous waste. We are running out of metals. We are logging our forests faster than they can be replaced. And our Madison Avenue experts are charged with getting us to throw away everything we buy just as fast as we can. "Get a new one" chant the ads. "Throw away your refrigerator and buy a color-coded one". "Throw away your car if the ash tray is dirty." "Wear a paper dress. Use paper napkins and disposable dishes."

So we have arrived at a crisis. The consumer gives the trash to the Man who takes it to: 1. the dump. 12,000, 73% of all American communities still dispose of all waste in open, burning dumps which spew pollution into the air, pollute water and soil, bring flies, rats and other pests, as well.

2. the sanitary landfill. There are few in the country,

some well-managed, where tractors and bulldozers compact the waste into the soil, cover it with several inches of soil, then compact the soil over the waste. Ideally there are no rats, flies, odors, fires or pollution. But all too often the landfill is not ideal. Just a bit less than the optimum soil cover, winter weather which freezes the ground, a poorly selected location — and you have water, air and soil pollution, as well as odors, blowing papers, rats.

3. the incinerator. Expensive, likely to become inadequate as communities grow, and probably managed unsatisfactorily. Said Senator Edmund Muskie at hearings on the Resource Recovery Act of 1969, "94 percent of all land disposal operations and 75 percent of the municipal incinerators are unsatisfactory from the standpoint of public health, efficiency of operation, or protection of natural resources."

In some communities in the U. S. A. and in many more in other parts of the world, the part of solid waste that decomposes in the soil is made into compost. This includes all garbage, grass clippings, tree clippings, sawdust, bark, paper, clothing, wastes from food processing industries, dead animals and so on. In a rather simple and inexpensive operation, which involves grinding this stuff fine and exposing it to just the right temperature, air and soil bacteria, a fine, fragrant topsoil is made in a few days or weeks depending on the process used.

The only acceptable final answer to the solid waste problem, all experts agree, is to recycle everything, and the sooner we start this task the better. Organic waste — that is, things that have recently been alive and hence will easily decompose — must be separated from tires, cans, bottles, furniture, plastic, aluminum and so on. These items must be returned to the manufacturers and recycled into usable products again. Perhaps you can't make new rubber tires out of old ones. Possibly they can be made into road material, as one researcher suggests. Bottles can be melted down and made into any glass objects.

There are several reasons why this kind of recycling is not being done at present. First, methods of recycling have not been perfected in most industries. Second, the place where the recycling takes place is far from the spot where the cans, bottles and old tires were discarded. Who will pay for transporting all this junk? How much will it cost? Then there is the problem of competition among industries as well as among individual members of the same industry. The glass people declare their pollution is not nearly so bad as that of the can or plastic people, because glass, crushed small enough, will eventually break down into tiny sand-like particles which actually help to condition soil. So why recycle? The aluminum people contend that their cans are superior to tin cans. It's not their fault that the aluminum is so resistant to rust and decay. People prefer aluminum things, they say, so they have to make them!

The organic stuff, the garbage listed above, should, of course, be returned to the soil in the best possible condition for remaking land that has been mistreated or eroded. It can be composted into fine, fragrant, crumbly topsoil which can be spread all over the garden year after year to recondition the soil. In places where municipal composting plants are thriving, the final product is sometimes bagged like peat moss and sold. Or it is used by the city to improve parks, golf courses, school grounds, flower boxes, tree plantings and so on.

Here are some facts on the way we are wantonly wasting our single most valuable asset — the agricultural land on which we depend for all our food. We lose one billion tons of topsoil every year. It washes away into rivers and lakes because of unwise, shortsighted agricultural methods, because of unneeded dams, highways and constructions. We are losing other extremely valuable agricultural land to housing developments and shopping centers. Millions of acres of fine farmland are simply being paved over every year, to build highways, factories or homes.

One biologist, Professor Wayne Davis of the University of Kentucky, tells us that we now have 2.6 acres of agricultural land per person — that is, the food for each of us Americans must be raised on this amount of land today. At the rate we are going, this will be cut to 2.2 acres by 1975, the critical point for the maintenance of what we consider a decent diet. By the year 2000 we will have left only about 1.2 agricultural acres of land per person. And we are the breadbasket of the world. We are the nation on whom all the hungry world is depending to prevent future famines!

In the light of these figures, it seems criminal folly to burn or bury the mountains of organic waste which could, in a few weeks, be made into rich topsoil, by a method that is economical, easy, pleasant and does not require a great deal of urban space. In the Netherlands about 20 per cent of all garbage is composted and returned to the soil. European cities where problems are more acute than here, are finding that composting is the only solution that does not result in further air or water pollution, that requires little space and little initial expense.

What can you do to help stem the solid waste explosion which threatens to bury us, disfigure our landscape, pollute our air and water and probably bankrupt us, for estimates of what it will take to come up with some workable solutions are astronomical.

Apply the law of tolerable inconvenience. See chapter 14. Decide now what you can do without every day, and still find life tolerable and interesting. Your coffee probably comes in cans with additional plastic lids, so you can open the can, pop on the lid and keep the coffee fresh. Then you must dispose of both the can and the lid, every time you buy coffee. The can will eventually disintegrate in the dump or landfill, if it's some metal other than aluminum. The plastic lid is forever.

There's some place nearby where they still sell coffee in paper bags. You grind it yourself at a grinder. Hunt up this place and buy coffee there from now on. Put it in an airtight container at home and refrigerate it to retain freshness. Fold the paper bag and put it in the pile for the scrap paper drive. Then write to the people whose coffee you have abandoned because of its can and plastic lid.

Be polite but firm. Tell them you like their coffee and will find it hard to become accustomed to another brand. But you feel that the problem of disposing of both the can and the plastic lid is more important than how the coffee tastes. Tell them you believe in recycling solid waste and you are doing this, in your own small way, in everyday matters. You will not buy anything made of plastic, if you can help it. You will not buy anything made of aluminum. You won't buy anything made of any other substance which cannot eventually be returned to the manufacturer and recycled, or decomposed in the landfill or compost bin.

You will accomplish little by just discontinuing the coffee and not writing to the manufacturer. He won't have any way of knowing what you're doing or why. If sales in your community fall off, his market research men may think they should start a contest or give away a premium or something equally silly. Let him know just why you will not buy his product. Get others to do the same. Tell your friends and neighbors.

How will you know where to write? Every product in a container must have the manufacturer's name and address on it. If the label says, "General Foods, White Plains, New York, 10602" you can be fairly sure that a letter addressed this way will reach them. If the label says "So-and-So Company, New York" chances are a letter will not reach them. Call your local public library and ask for the address. They will be glad to help you. Your public library, especially the reference librarian, can be a source of much important and helpful information on many aspects of life, not the least of which is information about how to reach people you want to write letters to.

What can you do about paper products? Recycle them yourself. Save the envelopes the junk mail comes in. Use it to mail something. Save paper bags. Use them again and again until they're worn out, then fold them and add to the scrap paper drive. Buy paper sandwich and storage bags, rather than plastic ones. They can be recycled. They decompose in landfills or compost piles. Leave the coat hangers at the cleaners and ask them to use them over again. Do the same with the plastic bag they pack things in.

When your community arrives at the solid waste crisis which it will certainly face someday soon, your local paper will bristle with information about incinerators.

Specialists will look over the terrain to decide whether you can find space for a landfill. In all probability, nobody will mention composting. You should then proceed, with information in hand, to a meeting of the governing board to ask why composting is not being considered. Probably you will be met with blank stares and shaking heads. You will be told that composting doesn't work, that every municipal compost plant has failed, that it's not economical, that the compost can't be sold.

Take heart. Come back to the next meeting with more facts. Or, better still, before the next meeting mail the facts to the home of each councilman or selectmen or whoever is doing the deciding. For more facts, write to Rodale Press, Emmaus, Pa. 18049. We can send you copies of our publication, *Compost Science, Journal of Solid Wastes and Soil,* and the book by its editor, *Garbage as You Like It. Compost Science* is mostly for engineers and specialists. The book is for laymen. You can understand it. Your councilman can, too.

You can also write to the Bureau of Solid Waste Management, Department of Health, Education and Welfare, 222 East Central Parkway, Cincinnati, Ohio, 45202, asking for information on municipal composting. They look very favorably on it there. But they also have on hand much material on incineration and landfill. Tell them you want material only on composting.

Then get busy and organize a letter-writing campaign to the editor of your local paper. Newspaper editors thrive on controversy. They want to get everybody in the community to talking publicly in their pages on community issues. It sells papers. Write your letters with care. Make them short and to the point. Firm, never angry. Full of conviction and information. Never wordy.

There has to be some reason why otherwise sensible men would behave so stubbornly and blindly in refusing to consider municipal composting. There is. Some communities have gone into composting with the idea that they would make enough money selling compost to pay for the whole operation. They piled up the rich, crumbly black stuff and waited for the world to come flocking to carry it away at five dollars or so a hundred pounds. They didn't come. City officials turned to compost-minded citizens and said, "See, we told you it wouldn't work. We're not making any money. We'll have to close the plant." And they have closed plants, just for this reason.

They are willing to pay, let's say, 15 million dollars for an incinerator that is bound to foul the air one way or another, bound to wear out eventually, bound to attract rats and flies and cause noisome odors. After the trash has been incinerated, they have a pile of unburnable stuff that must be carted off somewhere and buried. The operation is expensive. Nobody ever suggests that it should pay for itself. Who makes money out of a landfill? After 25 years or so it may be possible to put a park or a golfcourse where the landfill has been. It may take that long for the soil to settle. But this is the only dividend you get from a landfill.

Once you have made a beautiful, rich, loamy, fragrant product out of your most objectionable waste, garbage, somehow city politicians feel that you must make a profit selling this product or they just won't put their okay on it. People who started out with the sound idea that compost would be something good to have around, whether it was profitable or not, have succeeded with their composting operations.

Auckland, New Zealand has been composting its city garbage since 1960, selling it through an attractive promotional leaflet which explains what compost is and how it should be used. Retail customers can buy at the plant, they can phone and have their compost delivered to them in a city truck. Altoona, Pennsylvania has been composting its garbage since 1951, through a contractor who manages the plant and sells the compost — 2000 tons a year — by the ton or by the 40-pound bag. In Houston, Texas, the Metropolitan Waste Company runs the plant and sells the compost. There are as many ways to work out the details as there are communities. The point is, composting works, if you want it to work.

The eventual solution must be the same for that other dreadfully unpleasant-sounding substance which emerges from our sewage plants. You wouldn't believe what people are doing with sewage sludge — in their efforts to dispose of it cheaply. Or maybe you never thought about what happens to the stuff you flush down into the sewer. In communities throughout our polluted country, municipal sewage is simply flushed out into the nearest waterway — just as it is, full of the most sickening pollution there is, as well as the phosphates and nitrates which abound in this kind of waste.

If there were only a few people per stream or lake or river, the water would have the ability to cleanse itself within a few miles, so great is nature's cleansing power, when we do not overburden her. But there are far too many people, far too much sewage and far too little room left in the waterways. If your community pours its untreated sewage into the river, the folks downstream must drink it, just as you must drink the sewage poured in by the towns upstream from you.

So, in some communities, sewage is given either primary or secondary treatment before anything is released to a waterway. This involves many complicated steps of settling and aerating the stuff. What finally emerges is fairly clean water which is sent back into the waterway, and sewage sludge — the solid part of the sewage which accumulates and must be disposed of. You can truck this to the landfill where it disappears gradually among all the other litter or you can use it constructively to help rebuild soil, to make gardens, to replenish eroded areas, or for almost any other purpose for which compost could be used.

In Allentown, Pennsylvania, a large attractive sign directs people to the Waste Water Treatment Plant where soil conditioner (sewage sludge) is piled up free for anyone who wants it. There is also available plenty of information on its safety, which kinds of plants it should and should not be used on, and anything else the customer wants to know.

"An End to Solid Waste" crows a headline in our local paper for March 15, 1970. The fellows who work in nuclear fusion have decided that the way to do it is to use a "fusion torch" that would disintegrate the waste into its elemental parts. That is, a junked car would disappear under the onslaught of the torch. In its place would be a little heap of iron, copper, silicon, aluminum, chromium, lead and whatever other metals and elements were used in making the car.

True, says the article, there are some technical problems still to be solved. Nobody has discovered yet how to produce the thermonuclear power, derived from the fusion of charged components of heavy hydrogen. As soon as they do (100 years from now, perhaps) we will have this excessively hot gas which would decompose the waste into electrified particles of its own constituent elements.

The thermonuclear power they're talking about at present exists only in the stars and in hydrogen bombs. Nobody has, apparently, given any thought to the possible side-effects or indeed any of the practical aspects of using this kind of power for a crowded community in an American locality. It appears obvious that any such installation would be astronomically expensive. The dangers inherent in its use boggle the mind, for this would be not just a little old nuclear reactor sitting there by the river down by the sewage works, but a full-fledged hydrogen bomb, you understand, with everything that this means in terms of possible hazards.

Who would be in charge? Well, the people from the solid waste department, the sanitary engineers and their assistants. Since we have not been able to guarantee the absolute lack of hazard in any atomic or nuclear installation to date, there seems to be no reason why we should expect such assurances from this device, especially when it is new and untried.

One would suppose that anything heated to the temperature involved here would involve some mighty effective cooling devices to keep it from fusing itself out of existence. This, we assume, would be the function of the river, as it now is the function of the river or the lake wherever atomic installations are built. You cool the plant by heating the river. But the job of keeping the river cool is not the province of the specialists who are busy designing the nuclear fusion stuff! That's a job for another expert and, so far as we know, he hasn't been born yet. When you get into problems of thermal pollution, we have the word of one of our state's experts in pollution that there is just no solution for this problem in the foreseeable future.

But never mind. "Fusion Torch May End Waste" makes a good headline. It keeps everybody from getting depressed about the garbage and trash situation. It brings in a lot more money in federal grants to the AEC which continues to proclaim pretty regularly that atomic power will solve most of our problems, eventually.

Shortly after Earth Day, 1970, the concept of recycling solid waste suddenly began to take hold on a neighborhood basis all over the nation. We heard of many different kinds of groups collecting glass, paper, "tin cans" and aluminum, transporting it to various spots where a glass factory, a paper plant or a secondary materials dealer would accept it and pay a small bounty in return.

Somehow this seemed to bring great relief to everyone. At last, here was something constructive, something active, anyone could engage in to help make a dent in this vast mountain of garbage and trash. There are problems, of course. The spots at which you can turn in glass and aluminum are often too far away. The amount of money you make seems inconsequential for the amount of work involved. You have problems of storing materials and arranging for collection points and manpower. Some people lose interest; others never get really enough concerned to help.

But successful projects are continuing at a very satisfactory pace. In nearby Bucks County, the Audubon

Society has a recycling operation continuing once a month in various spots around the county. They are overwhelmed with the response. They are all but buried in glass, paper, aluminum. They have done an outstanding job of publicizing their project. They have Scouts, civic organizations, and women's clubs and many other groups helping out.

They are not making money at a rate which would satisfy the stockholders of a mighty industry. But who expects this from a group of nature lovers, who aren't organized to make money, but are chiefly concerned with getting people involved in preserving our environment. Even if they made no money at all, the recycling operation is driving home, as nothing else could, the seriousness of the problem and the necessity for everyone to get involved in solving it, on a community basis.

You can start a recycling operation in your own community. To obtain a sheaf of valuable, helpful ideas on recycling, write to the Bucks County Audubon Society in care of Lefferts Hutton, Box 289, Aquetong Road, New Hope, Pennsylvania, 18938. And write to *Environment Action Bulletin,* Rodale Press, Emmaus, Pennsylvania, 18049 for their very fine material on neighborhood recycling.

CHAPTER 4

Litter: Children Lead the Crusade

"The promises of ownership and management that they will voluntarily reduce their profit by instituting proper controls can be considered as another kind of advertising — and we should not consider it to be other than advertising until convinced by action, not words. . . . We cannot afford to believe such promises by either industry or government officials."

Statement of Intent of State Biologists' Association instituting a boycott against a Maine potato company polluting a stream.

"I don't think most of the politicians who are jumping on the environmental bandwagon have the slightest idea what they're getting into. . . . I don't think they realize that students see this as a long and serious fight for a profound change in what this country is all about . . . They're talking about emission-control devices for automobiles; we are talking about bans on automobiles. They are bursting with pride over plans for municipal waste-treatment plants; we are challenging the ethics of a society that, with only 7 percent of the world's population, accounts for more than half of the world's annual consumption of raw materials."

Denis Hayes, Coordinator
Environmental Action, Earth Day, 1970

"Let me remind you of an important thing to understand about any institution or social system, whether it is a nation or a city, a corporation or a federal agency; it doesn't move unless you give it a solid push. Not a mild push — a solid jolt. If the push is not administered by vigorous and purposeful leaders, it will be administered by an aroused citizenry or by a crisis."

John W. Gardner, former Secretary
of Health, Education and Welfare

Keep America Beautiful completed a litter survey in 1969 which showed that each month American motorists drop an average of 1304 pieces of litter on every mile of the nation's highways, superhighways, small roads and lanes. This comes to nearly 16,000 pieces of litter per mile, per year. Paper items make up 59 percent of the litter, generally. Cans and bottles are a big percentage of the rest.

But as anyone knows who has ever walked along a highway or a quiet country road, the items you turn up are varied. Whitney North Seymour, Jr., then a New York State Senator, wrote an article in *The Conservationist* for February–March, 1968 in which he told of walking one-tenth of a mile on New York State Highway 9W and finding about the same amount and kind of litter found by the Glass Container Manufacturers' Institute on a one-mile stretch of highway in five different states. Here it is:

1,652 pieces of paper, ranging from full-sized magazines to cigarette packs and crumpled paper cups
396 cans, principally beer containers
254 bottles, most of which would be non-returnable

12 bits of clothing
86 miscellaneous items including dead animals and loose change

Michigan highway officials estimated that it costs about 32 cents, or about $2500 per mile, to pick up each piece of litter. New York State has 85,000 miles of road. At $2500 a mile, the total cost of picking up litter in New York State would come to $212,500,000 a year. In 1959 almost 10 million gross of non-returnable beer bottles were sold in this country, and about 1½ million gross of non-returnable soft drink bottles. A gross is 144. By 1970 these figures had reached the staggering total of over 8 billion beer bottles and 4 billion soft drink bottles — all of them destined to end along a highway, in a town dump, landfill or incinerator. The appalling cost to us taxpayers of the non-returnable bottle is apparent, if you think only in terms of picking the bottles up from the roadsides at 32 cents a bottle. It comes to almost 400 *billion* dollars just to pick up disposable soft drink and beer bottles.

Of course, most of them are not picked up. The rest end in the garbage can where they complicate immeasurably the work of the incinerator or landfill people. We, the taxpayers, pick up the tab for that, too, of course. Why should this be? Mr. Seymour tells us that supermarket managers simply don't want to foot the bill for the labor costs involved in checking in returnable bottles. So they apply pressure on the suppliers to obtain nonreturnable bottles. "The effect is to shift the cost of handling empty bottles to the taxpayer . . . This is an expensive way to underwrite private industry . . . Those who are making profits out of bottles (and cans and other containers, too) should bear some part of the expense of disposal," says Mr. Seymour.

He goes on to suggest a state law requiring a deposit from every manufacturer who sells such a product in the state. He would have to pay a fixed amount on each bottle or can shipped by him in the state. His deposit would be returned for every empty can or bottle returned to him. The way he gets it back is of no concern to the state. The deposit on unreturned containers would go to help pay the cost of handling them in the solid waste program.

But Mr. Seymour goes farther than this in proposing a state Technology and Reclamation Council which would combine the knowhow of private industry with government responsibility to deal with refuse of all kinds by recycling as much of it as can be saved and disposing harmlessly of the rest. He suggests laws that certain kinds of containers *must* be biodegradable — that is, easily disintegrated into the soil in a landfill. To take care of the problem of junked cars, the state might imposed a personal property tax to encourage their removal.

A second proposal is a conservation patrol. Why not, asks Mr. Seymour, put to work some of the many unemployed and untrained young people we are now supporting with unemployment payments? Give them jobs picking up litter and otherwise being useful in conservation terms. How do you pay them? With the disposal fees paid by the sellers of disposable containers. Handled wrongly, it seems to us such a conservation patrol might degenerate into an undignified "make-work" project that would never succeed. But if it were promoted as a civic-minded worthwhile kind of activity, contributing immensely to the health and welfare of the community, who knows? We might have so many applicants that there would not be enough jobs!

A New York City Councilman introduced a bill in January, 1970 that would require a deposit on every glass, metal or plastic drink container sold in the city, to keep the containers from littering the streets and overburdening the sanitation department. "The people who put these articles on the market should be responsible for getting rid of them", he said. Anyone who has ever threaded his way through the flying paper, plastic and rattling cans on a windy day in downtown Manhattan should be forever grateful.

But somehow there's more to the litter story than passing laws and transferring the cost from the taxpayer to the people who make the things that create most litter. Somehow, we have to begin to awaken in people a sense of responsibility about not creating litter. It has apparently never occurred to most people that someone has to pick up the litter they discard, or soon the entire landscape will be impossible to walk or drive through. We'll be buried alive in our litter!

And the more the burden of eliminating litter is kept somehow behind the scenes with laws and disposal fees, the less responsibility each of us will have to remind himself not to throw away that candy wrapper, not to discard that beer can, not to drop the plastic spoon at the ice cream stand. We'll shrug it off with "Let the government take care of it" as we have been trained to do with hundreds of other issues down through the years.

But the government, especially the small local government, is already staggering under the load of finally disposing of all solid waste. See Chapter 3 for this gruesome story. Each of us is individually responsible for the thing he discards without a thought of who's going to pick it up. It seems obvious that a nation grown so mature and so conscious of its own responsibility in this aspect of life that litter would cease to exist, might also be ready to assume those much more complex responsibilities the future is going to demand of us prisoners in a technological society.

Why not make every effort we can to lick the ever so trivial litter problem ourselves, without relying on "the government" to do it for us? You can fight litter by simply setting an example. Next time you go outdoors, take along a bag of some kind and an old pair of gloves and pick up everything in sight that doesn't belong there. You'll draw a lot of curious glances and you can explain to anyone who asks that litter just plain offends you and you've decided it has to go. Then you can ask, "Want to help?" Maybe you'll get some takers.

There's an 82-year old lady in a little town in Connecticut who takes her bicycle out every pleasant day and rides the two miles of highway near her home, getting off to pick up any litter she finds. One day in the schoolyard across the street from her home she picked up over 400 gum wrappers, paper wads and soft drink cups and bottles. If the children saw her, it shouldn't take long to impress them with what she was doing.

Anti-litter drives are popular all over the country. You could make such projects permanent affairs in your community, not just something the Scouts get interested in every spring. At the University of Illinois, a group of students, concerned with litter, visited a nearby creek and picked up everything they could find and haul to the shore — six tons of it. Then they called in the city government and used the heap to persuade the city to begin a clean-up program.

The *New York Times* told of a Manhattan clean-up project that began in a slum where a vacant lot collected trash and garbage. The people of the neighborhood got together and cleaned it up. It looked so attractive, clean, that they decided they'd go a little further and make a park of it. The city gave them some money, a local merchant contributed some more. They bought trees, shrubs, flowering perennials and bulbs. Somebody went to the library and learned enough about gardening to supervise the plantings. The kids joined in, enthusiastically. The men made park benches. The old folks discovered they had a fine place now to sun themselves on pleasant days. The kids could romp and play without fear of cars. There was some money left over to pay for outings, perhaps to start a little library, some arts and crafts. And it all started with an anti-litter campaign. The civic pride that kept the enthusiasm going was worth the whole affair.

In Missouri a group of young canoe enthusiasts meets every year to clean up the 26-mile stretch of a cherished canoeing river. From five states they come to collect a grand total of almost 300 burlap bags of trash, mostly cans and bottles.

In upstate New York 15 college students walked a stretch of country road, picking up everything that didn't belong there. They filled an entire dump truck by noon. They called it a protest march. "We'll be weird in a different way", said the youngsters. They told the local paper. The story was picked up by the *New York Times.*

A fine pamphlet *Youth Power,* available from National Youth Conference on Natural Beauty and Conservation, tells triumphant stories of young peoples' campaigns against litter. (You can get a free copy from: National Youth Conference, 830 Third Avenue, New York City, N. Y. 10022). In a small Louisiana town 18 year old Loretta Shadow organized CRUD, Campaign to Remove Unsightly Debris. She called in the press, she got a police escort, a sanitation truck and a mobile radio station to broadcast the proceedings. She and the group of young folks who worked with her covered one mile of highway picking up everything they found.

But this was not all. Loretta itemized the rubbish, counted it. The results were sent to every 4-H club in the state with an appeal for them to do likewise. Young peoples' groups flocked to the banner. Girl and Boy Scouts, Future Farmers, Red Cross Youth, YM and YWCA staged a campaign along a 16 mile highway stretch. They collected and listed 11,711 pieces of paper, 6,327 beer cans, 3,043 cigarette butts, 1,691 liquor bottles, 1,960 soft drink cans and bottles, and assorted other trash. It costs Louisiana 34 cents to pick up any single piece of litter. Loretta's campaign saved the state $8,412.28. Reports of her campaign were requested by the Gulf States Research, the National Soft Drink Association, the U. S. Department of Agriculture, the U. S. Department of Health, Education and Welfare, and the governor of the state. One eighteen-year-old girl undoubtedly made a sizeable dent in the national problem of litter.

There's some encouragement to be found in the attitude of some members of industry on the subject of litter and solid wastes in general. In January, 1970, William F. May, Chairman of the Board and President of American Can Company, told a group of the New York Board of Trade that a national body must be created to set policy and make regulations for the orderly use of the country's environment. He suggested an agency like the Federal Reserve System. Otherwise, he said, there would be a hodgepodge of regulations that would be unfair to some industries. Three years ago the same Mr. May counseled relevant participating corporations at the National Packaging Conference to solve these environmental problems within the family, before the federal government must be called in to make regulations.

He went through all the arguments we would expect the head of a great industry to present. One company can't spend millions to produce a non-polluting product unless other competing ones will do likewise. Not only pollution but scandalous waste of irreplaceable resources must be stopped, he said. "We are profligate in our use of limited resources. We use once and throw away minerals and metals that are not inexhaustible. We must recycle them if we are to preserve something for future generations." He ought to know. American Can produces much of the paper and metal litter that presently graces our landscape. He said his company has spent two million dollars a year trying to find a container that would disappear after it was used, rather than creating a disposal problem. It's difficult to make a can strong enough to hold things, that will just fall apart after you remove the contents.

Sounds reasonable. But it does not explain the whole picture. There seems to be no earthly reason why we should now be buying things in cans that could just as easily be packed in paper bags. Popcorn comes to mind. Tea. Coffee. And Mr. May did not make any attempt to explain away the multitudinous paper products his firm makes which serve no useful purpose whatsoever except to pretty up a party table. These could certainly be disposed of easily with perhaps an advertising campaign to show the public that doing without them is in the best interests of Mother Earth and all of us who inhabit it. "Tolerable inconvenience", he might call it.

The paper industry has a curious tendency to think of themselves as saving mankind because they produce some disposable items that are used in hospitals and laboratories which can be thrown away after one use. One paper company, in a full page ad in the *Wall Street Journal* boasted of its fully disposable products. You use them once and throw them away — hundreds of things! Disposables! What could be better for us all! This is the "disposable decade", crowed the ad. Buy our products, use them once and toss them away carelessly and casually.

A friend of mine, just back from a township meeting where she heard the grim facts on the sanitary land fill and what it was going to cost to bring it up to the state health standards, read through the ad and wrote the paper company president that she would never again buy any of his products, since his attitude, as expressed in the ad, appeared totally irresponsible on two counts. First the enormity of the solid waste problem all over the country and, second, the appalling rate at which our forests are disappearing under the lumbermen's axes —

much of it for the sake of profits for the paper industry.

My friend went further. She reminded the captain of the paper industry that during the last war we got along perfectly well with almost no paper products at all. We shopped with a big market basket and carried home the food unwrapped. We used scrap paper for letters, notes and countless other uses. We saved paper bags and used them until they were worn out. We used cloth napkins, tablecloths and handkerchiefs and used them until they were threadbare. We can do it again, for the present emergency is a greater emergency than war, she said.

She received a two-page reply on the heavy engraved paper of the president of the company. It was not a form letter. Every comment she made was answered in carefully chosen words. And the letter was, as you would expect, a masterpiece of equivocation. Paper things present hardly any problem of disposal compared to things like junked cars or plastics, said the letter. Besides our disposables are essential for health! (Paper dresses?) If you launder diapers, napkins and handkerchiefs, you just create another problem of pollution because of the phosphates in your detergents.

And as for the forests, well, as anybody knows, the best way to keep a forest healthy is to keep cutting it down. The trees like to be cut down, you understand, because then the little trees can grow better and you can cut them down. Besides this paper company "farms" their trees in such a way that they grow a lot faster than they naturally would — and of course, we all prefer that, don't we now? And the paper company is public-spirited. Any of us can use their forestland for hunting and camping and hiking — except where they are lumbering.

A few days later another ad appeared boasting this time of the marvels of forest management the company engages in. They own 3,200,000 acres of forests and where it used to take 35 years to grow a tree, they now believe they can get a tree to grow in less than 20 years. They raise trees the way farmers raise corn (famous last words!) They fertilize, they breed, they harvest in cycles that "produce crops of trees that grow faster and bigger" and that produce superior cellulose fibers.

They've improved greatly on nature, you see. Nature knows almost nothing about how to produce a tree compared to this paper company. They are also "evaluating the mineral potential of the woodlands." Well, that probably means strip mines, doesn't it? Just what we need! And, perhaps the most significant sentence in the ad — "the worldwide demand for paper is expected to double in the next 15 years."

Well, there go the rest of the forests, down the hillsides. Do you care? Do you believe, with me, that preserving forests is more important for the health of the planet than disposable dresses, party favors, diapers, sheets, napkins, lab coats, and dishes?

In 1969 Wade's supermarket took a full page ad in the April 10 *Christiansburg-Blacksburg, Virginia, News Messenger.* Mr. L. E. Wade, owner of the store, had a few words to say about non-returnable soft drink bottles which I think are wise enough that you should read them here. Mr. Wade has taken into account all the aspects of trouble with non-returnable bottles, what it will cost him and what, in the long run, it will cost his customers. This is what he says:

"Who Will Pay for Throw-Away Softdrink Bottles?

"Presently if you buy a carton of nationally-advertised

soft drinks you pay from 8 to 14 cents more per carton than if you purchased them in returnable bottles. In addition you will sooner or later have to buy extra garbage trucks to haul them off, or to have them picked off the highways, or perhaps to buy a new tire for your car. I have mixed emotions about them. As a retailer selling them for 61 cents per carton, I make 7 cents. I make 8 cents when I sell a carton of returnable bottles for 51 cents, and the extra 1 cent does not cover the extra costs of handling the bottles. So as a retailer, I prefer to sell the throw-away bottles. As a citizen, I wonder if they are not one more thing that will in the long run cost more than the convenience is worth. Can you imagine Clayton Lake full of throw-away bottles? Even cans eventually rust."

Environmental Action, Washington, D. C., where Earth Day, 1970 began, took a full page ad in the *New York Times* on May 3 to announce that Earth Day failed. "Nearly 20 million people participated," the ad said, but nobody accomplished anything to alleviate pollution. "And the vast majority of Americans drove to work in their own fumes, ate their daily chemicals and pesticides, discarded millions of tons of junk and wondered why the earth was in such bad shape. It seems like everybody wants somebody else to do something about pollution." The ad went on to say that Environmental Action plans to continue with the Earth Day program on a slightly different basis and asks for funds.

I want to disagree with the ad. True, 20 million people participated in Earth Day. There were speeches, parades and demonstrations of every conceivable kind, but nobody actually *did* anything about cleaning things up except the children. Children can't make speeches, don't parade very well unless someone organizes them and can't usually turn out a very large group to a demonstration. So all over the country, in large groups and small, the children turned out, millions strong, and *worked* to clean up America. Some of the activity got into the papers and we read it and said, "how nice that the children helped", without ourselves realizing that the children didn't just "help". The children did everything that was done, while we adults made the speeches.

And in many parts of the country, the children are still working, every day, every week, all year long, cleaning up the mess we adults are totally responsible for. They get no credit, no rewards — a pat on the head and a "That's nice, dear — be sure not to get your clothes dirty, or cut your hands".

In classrooms — elementary and high school classrooms — all over the nation, a big part of Earth Day celebration was just going out into the school ground, onto the highways, into the swamps and vacant lots and cleaning up. In every case, the children were astonished at the amount of litter they brought in. In many cases, the litter-collecting programs have continued and will continue.

As I was going home at five o'clock from Earth Day celebration at Lehigh University near where I live, I met two little girls, perhaps nine years old, scurrying along the highway up the steep hillside, shopping bags in hand, picking up broken bottles and beer cans, paper containers, plastic bags and all the other disgusting welter of junk that had accumulated there. We adults had driven past it for years, hardly aware that it was there. When I stopped, the children told me they just weren't satisfied with coming home from Earth Day at school and doing nothing more. They had, on their own, started out to pick up litter.

I got out of the car to help. They told me in scandalized tones of a few children at their school who didn't seem to care that the landscape was littered with trash. As we worked our way up the hill in the hot sunlight, a group of boys came along planning a ball game. We enlisted their help. The girls told them a local drive-in stand had promised free burgers and a soda to any child who brought in five pounds of picked-up trash on Earth Day. All of us worked harder at this announcement. The children had made their own posters in crayon on construction paper — "Stop Pollution" and "Don't litter." As the cars passed us, they waved the posters and shouted "Stop pollution" at the motorists.

As enthusiasm increased, the trash piles grew higher, the frenzied cries at motorists grew more urgent. Most cars stopped to listen and their drivers told us "good work — keep it up." The hillside was at last clean. Standing by the side of the road, we organized ourselves into an anti-pollution club and elected a president. The kids went home to interest the mother of one of them in taking them and the litter to the drive-in stand to collect the reward. They called me that evening, heartbroken, to announce that the drive-in people said they had never made such a promise. The kids had been betrayed. However, they agreed that the anti-litter campaign must continue.

I got a story about the undertaking in the local paper's *Teen Times* section and did a story on it for our SAVE newsletter. SAVE then arranged to put a sign on the hillside saying

"50 pounds of litter were picked up on this hillside by young people from Schnellmans on Earth Day, 1970. Please help us keep it clean.
S.A.V.E."

There are two reasons, I think, for these inspiring and encouraging success stories involving children and litter campaigns. First is the wonderful, natural enthusiasm of children in any campaign. They don't discourage easily. They look for rewards that are so easy to give them — a badge, a story in the paper, a sign, a citation to put on the wall. And they work with such direct ferocity that nothing stands in their way.

Second, litter is absolutely the only aspect of pollution that lends itself to immediate, direct action. The governor of Pennsylvania, on the day after Earth Day, expressed his wish that the people of his great state would continue their fine Earth Day activities all year around — would just go on and on picking up trash. Apparently he thought this was all that was involved — picking up trash. It had never gotten through to him, or perhaps he chose to forget — that Earth Day celebrants all over the state had attacked his highway building program, assailed his feeble efforts at controlling air and water pollution, his neglect of immense problems of strip mining, slums, both rural and urban, poor management of land, no public transit system worth the name, and all the other things wrong in the environment of our state. Earth Day was for picking up litter, he thought, because that's the one thing anybody can step outside and do immediately and effectively, without any bureaucratic doubletalk or diplomatic stalling.

So be it. Let's clean up the litter! If we can manage to interest only the young folks in it, let's do that. The young folks are way ahead of us in so many ways already that, if we turn them loose on litter, they just may show us how to make an effective start on some of the other problems whose complexity is manifold.

CHAPTER 5

You Want to Go Back to Kerosene Lamps?

"The solutions do not lie in exhortations for the objectors to disappear; they will not disappear but will increase in numbers, in sophistication and in stature, for the problems are large already and growing fast. The solutions lie in addressing the problems: how much power for New York, Boston or Reston? How many people? How can we contain or use the 'waste' heat? How can we make reactors acceptable neighbors and not destroy all beauty spots in the interests of unlimited electricity? . . . The power companies would do well to use their enormous political power not in resort to demagoguery but in attempting to convince the public and political leaders of the need for enduring answers to the real problems of power development."

G. M. Woodwell
Senior Ecologist, Brookhaven National Laboratory —
in a letter to the *New York Times*
January 2, 1970

"It isn't a matter of capitalism versus socialism. It's a question of materialism versus survival. People must come to understand that there is an equation — that every time we turn on an electric toothbrush or carving knife in Philadelphia, it destroys a little bit of our environment. . . . If everyone would just stop using a single small electric appliance, for example, it would not make a significant dent in the buildup of pollution in our environment, but it would prepare people to take the next, slightly larger step in the battle. Once people have some little success behind them, they are ready to tackle greater problems with much more assurance."

Ian McHarg, Chairman
University of Pennsylvania
Department of Landscape
Architecture and Ecological Planning

"The direct cost of air pollution to the consumer from all sources has been roughly estimated by the Public Health Service as about $60 per person per year. (Electric) power production from fossil fuels (coal and oil) accounts for about one-third of this. This means that for a family of four, about $80 per year must be added to the cost of power production — an appreciable amount compared to the annual electric bill".

Environmental Cost of Electric Power
Dean E. Abrahamson

"I do what I am told. At Con Edison's insistence, I leave an electric light on at night and am loaded with unnecessary appliances. I follow New York Telephone's directives by having extensions in every room. Now I am told to cut down on electrical usage to ease a critical power shortage. My beautiful Princess phones have been silent for two weeks, with no repair in sight. ('We have you on our list. It's just a question of too many phones.') Isn't it about time that Con Edison and New York Telephone spend some money on satisfactory service instead of elaborate and self-defeating promotion?"

H. Jeremy Wintersteen in a letter to the *New York Times,* August 9, 1969

As everybody knows, there was a gigantic blackout in the New York metropolitan area in the fall of 1965, when, for one entire night, nobody over a wide area had any electricity. In August, 1969, Consolidated Edison lost 20 per cent of its power, "creating a crisis that could last for weeks" according to a *Times* headline. For days beforehand power supplies had been low, necessitating pleas over the radio and TV for consumers to turn off their air conditioners. Lights were turned off in public buildings. TV pictures wobbled.

In May, 1970, a power cutback dimmed lights in five states around New Jersey. It was a precautionary move because of unseasonably hot weather and a spring check-up of generators. The New York Public Utilities Commissioner predicted "brown-outs" for the city during the summer when air conditioners are on. An urban ecologist said in November, 1969 that a brownout might be beneficial in Southern California "because it would discourage additional people from moving here." He went on to say that "as far as living a healthy, satisfying life, it will soon be impossible. The environment has declined steadily for three decades."

Federal power officials have already announced that there will be more interruptions of power and "brown-outs" in 1970 and 1971. The federal officials have no power or authority to compel any power company to increase its generating plant capacity, according to the FPC Chairman. This is up to the individual companies. Legislation is not the answer to the problem, he said. "It is going to be worked out by thousands or hundreds of thousands of sound decisions with everybody pulling together to meet a common problem."

Let's take a look at a pamphlet published by *Electri-*

cal World, 330 West 42nd Street, New York. *"The Power Crisis, A Handful of People Are Pulling the Plug on America."*

"In the last ten years," says this pamphlet, "the American family's use of electricity has nearly doubled. . . . The reasons for these constantly increasing demands for electric power are not hard to find. The average family has purchased a host of new electric devices including refrigerators, food freezers, ranges, water heaters, toasters, blenders, razors, toothbrushes, fans, dehumidifiers, waste disposers, dishwashers, air conditioners, dryers, ironers, washing machines, vacuum cleaners, radios, television sets, home heating equipment and stereo sets."

Industry, too, has been using more electric power, says the pamphlet. "As industry finds more ways to use power to improve production the output and wages of the individual employee rise." And finally, the clincher. The use of electricity is an index of our standard of living. We use 83 times more electricity than India uses. That means, presumably, we have an 83 times higher standard of living or should we say 83 times better life than the Indians have.

"And the use of electric power will increase," continues the pamphlet. "40 percent of all American homes now have air conditioners. In ten years this figure will rise to 80 percent. The number of homes using electric power for heating will triple in the next 10 years." And "it is not inconceivable that we will be driving exhaust-free electric automobiles whose batteries are charged nightly by plugging into a household power circuit."

However, power reserves have dropped from 27.1 percent in 1958 to 17.2 percent in 1969. "Brownouts" may become common. "The basic needs of society and commerce will have to come before the luxuries of consumers," says the trade publication of the power industry. 250 new power plants are needed now, just to keep up with the present demand. What's the difficulty? "Skilled labor is becoming scarce and a shorter work week lies just ahead. Materials are in short supply. Financing is becoming more and more difficult and expensive. Building sites are increasingly impossible to find."

Now about these building sites. Nobody wants a power plant in their backyard. "Because of the opposition of a handful of people, the country as a whole is falling behind in its efforts to build the plants and lines that are needed." The pamphlet goes on to describe the three kinds of power plants we can choose from: hydroelectric, fossil fuel (coal or oil) or atomic power. Then it goes on to say: "What can the concerned citizen do about the power crisis? Become as informed as you can on the power needs and the utility proposals in your immediate community. . . . If your area is not involved in controversy, you can prepare for the time when it might be. Look for articles pro and con in the general press. . . . If your local utility is making proposals to build facilities and there is local or regional opposition, become involved. And get your neighbors and friends involved. Attend hearings. Listen carefully to the reasons why some oppose power plants and transmission lines that you need. Understand the issues." And finally, write to *Electrical World* for help.

This pamphlet has obviously been written by highly skilled public relations experts. Although not openly stated, the suggestion is cleverly and subtly made that those who oppose the power plant on the mountainside or the riverbank have some sinister purpose in mind. "Listen carefully to the reasons why some oppose power plants and transmission lines that you need," says the pamphlet. (Maybe they're radicals of some kind? Maybe somebody is paying them to fight the power company?)

It seems obvious that when a scenic area is destroyed by building a plant of any kind everyone in the community suffers. It also seems obvious that those who fight the proposal are working for the good of the entire community against forces that hold most of the cards, in terms of prestige, power and money. How do you weigh the advantages of an unspoiled riverbank, an unbulldozed mountain against the delights of an electric toothbrush? It seems incredible but this is the kind of decision that must be made.

Now the power companies say, in essence, just as the aluminum companies and the paper companies say, "You consumers *demand* these products. We must supply them. Then when our efforts pollute the environment, you claim it's our fault. It's your fault for demanding the products!" Now which of us "demanded" an electric toothbrush? Which of us ever dreamed that such a thing was possible? Which of us "demanded" an electric carving knife or an electric oven or an electric outdoor grill or an electric broiler or any of the other gadgets which the power companies and the people who make electric gadgets advertise so shrilly, so continuously and so ubiquitously that it is impossible to get away from the sound or the sight of them?

Let's turn now to the March, 1970 issue of *Environ-*

ment magazine in which the St. Louis Committee for Environmental Information talks about electric power from a somewhat different point of view. The article is based on testimony given by Dr. Malcolm Peterson on behalf of the Committee before the Joint Congressional Committee on Atomic Energy, January 29, 1970.

The tone from the first word is ominous. "At its present rate of growth, the electric power industry will exceed the physical capacity of the environment to absorb its wastes in the not-too-distant future. . . . Electric power production is now doubling about every ten years or so. It does not take many doublings before the physical space available for power plants is exhausted. At some point, we must stop increasing our power production. . . . Suppose, for instance, that all electric power is to be produced by modern, 1000 megawatt power plants and that each requires an area of only 1000 feet on a side. If all of the country's power needs were presently being met by 300 such large power plants, in less than 20 doublings — that is, in less than two centuries — *all of the available land space would be taken up by such plants.* (My italics) *Not the available fuel resources or water for cooling — just physical space. This does not leave room for transformers and transmission lines, let alone people.*"

The waste heat which power plants produce is already a serious problem in some areas. In the year 2000, if power consumption continues to increase at present rates, there will be enough excess heat produced *to raise by 20 degrees the total volume of water which runs over the surface of the United States in a year.* If we depend on fossil fuels or atomic energy, it will take only 30 years for the amount of carbon dioxide produced by the fossil fuels and/or radiation produced by the atomic plants to "have, in the case of carbon dioxide, drastic effects on the global climate, and radiation will have unforeseeable effects on the world's living things, including man."

Because of the time lapse in planning a power plant and its finally going into production, "orders (for new power plants) placed during the next ten years will account for nearly half the generating capacity which will be in operation by the end of the century." This is essentially the same prediction as that made by the pamphlet of the electrical industry. — *The plants must be built during the next ten years.*

What happens in this country is only a model for the rest of the world to whom we constantly hold out the promise that some day soon, they, too, can reach the high "standard of living" we have attained. If, indeed, they do by the year 2000, and the present population continues to grow at present rates, the amount of heat and carbon dioxide produced *by electric power plants alone* will have drastically changed our worldwide climate. "What this means is that the United States, if it wishes to be a model for the rest of the world, must quickly find ways of maintaining its standard of living less wastefully, with less power production per capita."

What does this mean — turning lights off if you're not in the room? Throwing away your electric razor and sewing machine? Possibly. But, to begin with, the Committee points out that the rate of increase in electric power is mostly determined by *industrial* uses of power — not the consumer's use of it. These take up 41 per cent of the total production of electric power in 1970.

The aluminum industry, for instance, consumes

about ten per cent of all industrial use of electric power. The industry plans much greater expansion — they are going to be making buses, cars, trucks and many more containers out of aluminum! As we have seen, aluminum cans are one of our biggest problems from the point of view of litter and solid waste. They do not degrade in the soil. They cannot be burned. They are all but indestructible.

Making cars consumes about one-third as much electricity as making aluminum. We all know what keeps the auto industry going is that they persuade us to buy the new model every year and to buy not just one but two or three cars for every family. Says the Committee on Environmental Information, "By designing automobiles so that they can be easily and economically reclaimed, and establishing some sort of national system for returning them to the manufacturers, energy requirements for the steel in automobiles could be cut dramatically, and one of the nation's worst waste-disposal problems could be solved at the same time."

A ton of steel plate or wire made from ore needs 2,700 kilowatt hours of electricity to process. *Reclaimed steel only 700 hours. A ton of aluminum requires more than 17,000 kilowatt hours!*

The electric power industry has predicted that, by 1980, 19 million American homes will be heated by electricity. Many new homes have an electric heating and cooling arrangement in one. In industry, too, the greatest increase in use of electricity is in heating and cooling. Says the Committee, "All these sources of the increased demand for electricity could be run on natural gas."

In another field — that of waste paper — the production of paper pulp is one of the largest consumers of electric power in many parts of the country. Disposing of the used paper is one of our greatest solid wastes problems. "Recycling of all paper, including paper packages, would solve about 80 per cent of the country's trash disposal problems and curtail another need for electric power," says *Environment.*

The production of nitrogen fertilizer, of which we have an over-supply, uses a great deal of electric power. It is also furnishing us with a monumental pollution problem. (See chapter 12). Cutting back on the use of nitrogen fertilizer would thus help to solve two urgent problems.

What choice do we have? The Committee says there is none. We simply cannot go on much longer increasing electric power production. "The simple law of physics determines that the waste heat and physical size of electric power plants will exceed the capacity of our country in the not-too-distant future. We are already running out of suitable sites."

There are other ways of producing electric power. The Committee suggests experiments with solar power, tidal power and geothermal power — that is, using the heat at the center of the earth's core. Coal, oil and gas should be used in place of electricity *wherever possible,* as in heating homes, water, cook stoves, and so on. "The Public is denied the opportunity to choose among the various paths before us if the assumption of unrestrained electric power growth is made. We believe this is not a necessary assumption."

It seems to me that, in this one article there are enough well-documented facts to at least enliven the discussion at a meeting to determine a site for a power plant — no matter what kind of power plant it is. But, more than that, in these facts you have the additional weapons to use in the fight against aluminum cans, useless and silly electrical gadgets, discarding paper rather than recycling it. Perhaps most important of all, the whole controversy around the place of the automobile in American life could be centered on the amount of electric power needed to produce the ugly chariots and the great saving that could be made by simply cutting down on production of them.

So far as the automobile is concerned, if we finally manage to recycle all cars instead of junking them, if we finally manage to convince people that one car or no car at all is the answer to the transportation mess, if we finally convince those who do buy cars that they should keep them as long as the things will hang together, we will have made gigantic steps toward coming to grips with the solid waste problem, we will have managed to save inestimable amounts of raw materials, and we will have cut down hugely on our use of electric power. Those of us who are vitally concerned with making a liveable environment have faced time and again the irrefutable fact that once you have damaged one part of the environment you have inevitably damaged other parts, for they are all related, they are all part of the same ecosystem. In the same way, once you have devised a sensible, practical, workable solution for one seemingly insurmountable problem, you will find you have solved or at least contributed to the solution of many more problems!

By cutting down drastically on the number of cars in use, we can save inestimable miles of highway construction and much of the ugly mess that goes along with cars — the gas stations, the garages, the tire dumps, the junked cars. And, of course, the air pollution, remember? But I thought we were setting out to solve the problem of electric power? We were. But in indicating one partial solution to the problem, which is simply to cut back on those industries which use the most electric power, we find that we have taken big steps toward solving many other problems as well!

The workbook prepared by Scientists' Institute for Public Information on *Environmental Cost of Electric Power,* written by Dean A. Abrahamson, is a valuable help for anyone facing a local problem with a power plant which threatens to, or already has, produced an environmental problem. Dr. Abrahamson describes the different kinds of power plants in a way that someone without technical training can grasp, if he works a little at it.

He makes it abundantly clear there are no simple solutions, if, indeed, there are any solutions at all. Both fossil fuel and nuclear power plants use up scarce materials. Both produce thermal pollution — that is, pollution by waste heat. Fossil fuels also pollute the air. Nuclear plants routinely release radioactivity to air, water and soil. Even if these releases are small at present, and considered generally safe by the AEC, production of many more such plants is bound to increase the total amount of radioactivity to which all living things are exposed. Plants concentrate this radioactivity, animals take it up and concentrate it. Hence exposure to radioactivity may be much higher in some areas and in some individuals.

We are eventually going to run out of coal, oil, and natural gas. What will we use for fuel then? The uranium used in present day reactors is also becoming scarce. Says Dr. Abrahamson, "today's reactors cannot operate for more than a very few decades without exhausting the total world reserves of uranium 235." The only two alternatives in the field of atomic energy are the controlled fusion reactor (based on the principle of the hydrogen bomb) and the "breeder reactor". Attempts to "harness" the fusion reactor have so far been unsuccessful. It appears they may never be successful. The breeder reactor (and power companies will tell you confidently that this is the hope of the future) has not yet been developed. This is an amazing kind of procedure that produces fuel as it burns — hence "breeds" fuel. Says Dr. Abrahamson, "If we are to derive our energy from nuclear fission it is absolutely essential that successful breeder reactors be developed *soon,* perhaps within the next ten years."

He suggests several other ways to produce power. First, the burning of garbage and other solid wastes. These have a heating value about one-third that of coal. Paris, France, has been solving its garbage problems for fifty years by burning solid wastes and producing electricity from the heat. "Three fourths of this is converted into electric power in four big plants; the largest sells enough power to serve a city of 50,000 and the excess steam heats hundreds of Paris buildings. Pollution controls have been installed which prevent dust and visible smoke from being emitted."

Research is under way in this country, chiefly at Palo Alto, California, where 400 tons of solid waste can, it is believed, be turned into power every day. The chief drawback to burning solid wastes for power at present is that certain plastics and other materials which make up much of our country's solid waste cause concern when they are burned. Air pollution hazards from this burning are almost completely unknown and believed to be potentially great.

Gas turbines are now being used by some power companies chiefly to satisfy peak demands. They are not very efficient, they do not require cooling so there is no thermal pollution of water, but all the waste heat is sent up into the air. And scientists are beginning to warn us that very much more waste heat released into the atmosphere will soon cause unpredictable and serious changes in world climates.

(Isn't it amazing how one group of engineers is forever concerned with how we will produce enough heat to heat our homes in the future, while another group of engineers pines away trying to figure out what to do with all the waste heat around, so that it won't pollute the air or the water. These two groups of engineers seem incapable of getting together and solving their two problems by devising a way to lead the waste heat into the homes and office buildings!)

Magnetohydrodynamic (MHD) plants — (a process where "a hot, ionized gas is passed through a magnetic field and electricity drawn off by means of electrodes placed in the field") that are efficient enough are not at present in existence, though they are possible. Dr. Abrahamson believes they will not be feasible until the next century.

If you want to dwell for a moment on the ultimate horror, it is the major accident at a major nuclear power plant at which an amount of radioactivity approximate to that of a 50 megaton bomb could be released, with all the injury that this entails, both immediate and eventual. Says Dr. Abrahamson, "although the probability for a major accident is small, the consequences could be catastrophic. . . . The damages could be several billions of dollars and the persons involved number in the thousands or tens of thousands." The insurance — the billions of dollars — would be paid by the taxpayers, of course. This has already been provided for by legislation. No commercial organization is willing to accept this kind of liability. If you want some pretty hair-raising stuff on what has happened at several nuclear reactors so far in our nuclear history, turn to Sheldon Novick's *The Careless Atom,* and read.

Most valuable for the activist is that section of the SIPI workbook which describes what happened in Minnesota over an atomic power plant, announced in 1968 near Monticello. Plans had been approved by the AEC, the U. S. Public Health Service and the Federal Water Pollution Control Commission. The Minnesota State Board of Health had tacitly agreed to go along. After construction of the plant was well underway the state agencies were consulted! Two University of Minnesota scientists became concerned lest the amount of radioactivity that would be released would threaten life in the water of the Mississippi River and human health in Minneapolis and St. Paul which get their drinking water from the river below Monticello.

The story is long, complex, and heartening. The committee that was formed to fight the power plant became the Minnesota Committee for Environmental Information. They forced the power company to appoint a specialist to make a complete study of the affair. They made a report to the Minnesota Pollution Control Agency themselves.

"In addition," says Dr. Abrahamson, "the Committee continued to question the proposed standards for radioactive and thermal waste disposal in the press, in public meetings, and in conversations with members of the Minnesota Pollution Control Agency." The company fought back in newspaper ads and press releases in which they claimed that the radioactivity released by the plant would be no more than any domestic tap water contains, that people living near the plant would receive only about half the amount of radiation the average American gets from watching television.

But the specialist made his report recommending *much stricter regulations of the amount of radioactivity* that would be acceptable and the Minnesota health and pollution authorities agreed with him. *Both Congress and the AEC maintained that no state has the power to set standards more strict than those set by the AEC!* Other states went along with Minnesota — Michigan, Illinois, Vermont, Wisconsin, Hawaii, Kentucky, Maine, North Dakota, Pennsylvania, Utah, Virginia and Guam.

Says Dr. Abrahamson, "If the proposed restrictions are put into effect and if they survive a legal test, Minnesota will have the strictest radioactivity safeguards in the nation and will have challenged the AEC's 24-year monopoly on standards."* (See chapter on radioactivity for more on this subject.) Because of all this furor in Minnesota, federal authorities are taking another long, hard look at standards of radiation protection. The

* In a history-making court decision at a late date, we were told that the federal government — that is, the AEC and the FRC — are the only bodies authorized to set radiation standards. The states are not legally permitted to set their own standards more strict than the Federal ones.

Congressional Committee on Atomic Energy has held lengthy hearings. The Federal Radiation Council and other groups at the federal level are re-evaluating their basic standards for permissible exposure to radiation.

Here are some more events of the same nature. A nuclear plant planned on Lake Cayuga, New York, has been indefinitely postponed as a result of the activities of a local group which fought it. Conservation groups in Maryland fought valiantly against two proposed nuclear reactors on Chesapeake Bay. Johns Hopkins scientists prepared a statement on the possible hazards. In spite of this the AEC licensed the building of the first plant.

The proposed reactor at Bodega Bay, California, invited a successful struggle against the AEC which had planned this nuclear reactor almost exactly *on* the famous San Andreas Fault in the earth which has been responsible for the West Coast's famous earthquakes. After years of exhausting controversy, the reactor today consists of a large expensive hole in the ground on which nothing was ever built. But the kind of mentality which will propose a nuclear plant on the very spot most likely to be struck by an earthquake is what you are up against in dealing with the building of nuclear power plants.

Dr. Abrahamson emphasizes the absolute need for private citizens, faced with a fight over a power plant, to engage, early in the affair, all the help they can muster from scientists — ecologists, geologists, fisheries experts, pollution experts, sociologists, and so on. The other important point to keep in mind is the necessity of making all the facts and all the arguments public. "The final decisions on hydroelectric plants — and on all forms of power generation — should come only after an open *public* discussion of the vital questions of environmental and health effects."

In a beautiful wooded corner where New Jersey and Pennsylvania meet lies a glacial lake, high on a mountaintop, pure, clear and unpolluted as the day it was formed — Sunfish Pond. For years the Lenni Lenape League has been fighting to keep Sunfish Pond out of the hands of a power company, bent on destroying the entire mountain top.

The lake lies in a plot of land deeded to the state of New Jersey by a conservation-minded family in 1954. Seven years later the state sold 715 acres to the power company, without approval of the legislature or a public hearing. The League has won concession after concession from the power company, but each new proposal of the company threatens more destruction, not only for the Pond, but for the rest of the mountaintop, including the famous Appalachian Trail. For three years, the New Jersey Assembly has passed a bill providing for buying back the land from the power company. For three years the state senate has buried the bill and refused to act on it.

The League fights with buttons, bumper stickers, letters to the editors of local newspapers and an annual pilgrimage to Sunfish Pond which has attracted conservationists from all over the nation, including Supreme Court Justice William O. Douglas. Pictures of the pilgrimage make all the local papers. They are followed by a spate of letters from devoted League members urging letters to the New Jersey Senate to take action on the Sunfish Pond bill. (A-517). You can help by joining the Lenni Lenape League, Brass Castle, Washington, N. J. 07882.

Joined with the Lenni Penape League in the struggle

to preserve the ecological integrity of the Upper Delaware is the Save-the-Delaware Coalition representing some 17 conservation groups. The Delaware Water Gap National Recreation Area has been authorized by Congress. Plans are proceeding to make of this incredibly lovely, historical river valley with its surrounding mountains a federally owned spot where some 10 million urban residents from nearby cities can come every year to "enjoy nature." But the fact that the area has been designated "recreation" rather than "park" means that commercial development is welcome.

A pumped-storage electric power plant is planned which necessitates a dam which will create a 37-mile long lake, drowning much of the historically valuable area, as well as wildlife, farmland, hemlock forests, and destroying 40 miles of free-flowing river, with all that this means in terms of fishing, canoeing and other recreation. The "draw-down" of water, especially during dry months, is bound to leave miles of littered mud flats around the lake, thus eliminating any recreational value. Fisherman predict an end to good fishing on the Delware. Ecologists point out that providing roads and accommodations, plus sewage and waste disposal for this many people will cost far more than the dam and will destroy most of the wild beauty which the tourists are coming to enjoy.

The Sierra Club recommends: write to Pennsylvania Governor Shapp and New Jersey Governor Cahill, opposing the dam. Write state senators, congressmen and senators of both states; write Russell Train of the Council on Environmental Protection in Washington. Donations can be sent to Sierra Club, marked "Tocks Island Fund" and to Save-the-Delaware Coalition, Box 264,

RD 1, East Stroudsburg, Pa. 18301. Trout, Unlimited at PO Box 71, Sparta, N. J. 07871 has free explanatory material available, as do each of the other groups.

In a pleasant corner of southeastern Pennsylvania lies an area which was recently designated a national landmark. It was the first soil demonstration site, 20 years ago. It consists of a watershed of five farms on rolling farmland, with Honey Hollow Creek flowing through the center. Houses are 18th century, land is carefully plowed and cared for in the best tradition of conservation farming. The five farmers, whose families have held the land for many years, have just been notified that the Philadelphia Electric Company is planning to build directly through the watershed an overhead transmission line desolating a 300-foot wide section of land with 100-foot high towers.

"How can you put a power line through a historic landmark when the purpose of the law is to preserve and protect the landmark site?" asked one of the farmers in a story in the *New York Times* for October 12, 1969. The farmers have formed the Honey Hollow Association and other groups have rallied to help: the National Audubon Society and various conservation, forestry and historical groups as well as agriculture organizations and schools.

The whole point to the Honey Hollow Watershed is conservation and preserving the ecology of the region, which, of course, the power line would immediately and permanently disrupt. Years ago the five farmers realized that their land was eroding, their stream filling with silt. They asked for help from the Soil Conservation Service. Since then, they have observed all the rules of good husbandry and good agriculture — contour plowing, natural hedgerows, tree clumps and groves and a variety of crops, rather than monoculture. The farms have been cited by the Department of Interior as "a model of soil and water conservation methods."

The farmers had planned to set up an educational center where young folks could come to learn about nature on nature trails, and to learn the basic facts about good agricultural practices. If the power company's plans succeed, the young folks will learn instead something about the threat of modern technological damage to all those things we do and should prize the most.*

And if you want one more cheerful story about a bit of direct action by somebody who is probably much younger than you are, how's this — from *Medical Tribune* for May 11, 1970. Franklin Gage, high school freshman interested in ecology, was worried about the thermal pollution of the Hudson River by the Con Edison nuclear plant near his home. Three weeks before Earth Day he decided to do something about it — quite on his own, without any help from any adult or any committee.

He would organize a short boycott of electricity in his hometown on Earth Day. He wrote a handbill pointing out that the Con Ed plant was raising the temperature of the river water about 3 degrees. A rise of as little as one or two degrees can kill certain kinds of fish. Fish are killed at the intake pipe where the water goes into the cooling system of the plant. The higher temperature

* A compromise solution was arrived at in mid-March, 1971 which had the "reluctant approval" of everyone involved. The wires will zigzag across the north corner of the watershed, rather than proceeding right down the middle — a small concession to historic, ecological and scenic values.

also breeds bacteria in the sewage already in the river.

If you want to do something about this condition, said Franklin, turn off all your lights and electrical equipment on Earth Day, from 7:30 to 7:45 in the evening. He borrowed a neighbor's duplicating machine, persuaded the township conservation group to finance the paper and printed up 5,000 handbills. He sent them to the newspapers and to Con Edison. He went from door to door in the community giving out handbills, sought out all commuters at the local station, visited the meeting of the village board, and gave the handbills to his fellow students to take home.

At Con Edison headquarters in New York City a public relations man admitted that they had received the handbill, said there couldn't possibly be any effect on the system as a whole, said he didn't think the boycott would happen, anyway. In any case, Con Ed can do nothing about the thermal pollution beyond what they have already done, said he. Although the PR man did not mention it, Con Edison is already planning two more nuclear plants in the same region, with a fourth in the works a little later on.

At 7:30 on Earth Day Franklin and his mother set out to see how effective the boycott was. They counted only houses with cars at home, meaning the family was at home. It appeared from his and other surveys that about 500 families had blacked out their homes to protest Con Ed and thermal pollution. There are about 2,000 houses in the community, so about one-fourth of all the residents observed the boycott.

At Con Ed headquarters in New York where all but one door had been barricaded against possible violence on Earth Day (!) the PR man said "We predicted there would be no effect and there wasn't." He was asked about the power failure that hit the same village about three hours later and said he had no information on that.

Interestingly enough, in this small village, some neighbors saw fit to find something subversive about Franklin Gage's efforts to save Hudson River fish. The family had a phone call from one irate resident who snarled "So you want us to go back to kerosene lamps!" On one street where American flags fly constantly to demonstrate the residents' devotion to their country, all the porch lights were turned on — something that had not happened since porch lights were used to indicate disapproval of Vietnam Moratorium Day.

In a letter to the editor of the *New York Times,* dated March 18, 1970, Ralph Lippman suggests that much of the demand for power is the result of sheer waste — a waste which Con Edison created "when it persuaded the Public Service Commission in 1952 to abolish the submetering of apartments in large housing developments." Without metering, a flat charge is made with the result that tenants think of electric power as "free" so that it is something to be wantonly wasted. Says Mr. Lippman, "The tenant who is presented with a bill each month for what he uses and wastes is sure to be more careful!" One wonders why such a basic obvious fact should have to be pointed out!

How are they dealing with the power problem in other countries — those poor deprived places less fortunate than we? Australia is making a study of the economics and technical problems associated with the use of tidal power for electricity. If there is a big enough market in the immediate area to make this production feasible there seems to be no doubt that tidal power could be used to produce electricity. No pollution, you see, no fuel to make air pollution. No thermal pollution to heat up all the water or the air in the vicinity. Just the ancient eternal tide going in and out as it always has and making free power for anyone who wants to harness it.

In France they have harnessed solar heat to make a giant furnace consisting of panels and 9,000 mirrors arrayed in ways to produce enormous quantities of heat by focussing sunlight. The whole operation cost about six million dollars — just about enough to buy the paper on which research grants are given out by our federal government.

New Scientist for March 5, 1970 tells us a proposed way to produce power almost without pollution of any kind by converting heat energy directly into electricity by sweeping charged particles through an electric field in a stream of gas. This is called an electrogasdynamic generator. The explanation is far beyond the reach of a non-scientist to grasp, but the conclusion is that "such a power unit would have a wide range of possible applications . . . the noise level would be very low and with continuous combustion the exhaust gases would be very much cleaner than those from internal combustion engines. . . . Because of higher efficiencies running costs should be less than most, if not all, alternative means of power generation."

In New Delhi, India an irrigation pump is now at the prototype stage at the Indian National Physical Laboratory. A solar reflector supplies heat to a hot-air engine (invented in 1816) to provide mechanical energy with no external fuel or electricity supply and no pollution.

In the book *Solar Energy Research,* Farrington Daniels states that in 1938 he would have predicted that development of solar energy would come before atomic energy as a source of power. However, many billions of dollars have already gone into atomic energy and almost nothing into research on solar energy.

Mr. Daniels points out that solar energy is inexhaustible so long as there are people on earth to use it, and that it could be a practical solution for people in underdeveloped countries which have much sunshine but little coal and oil. Solar energy seems to promise unlimited benefits with no risks at all, no pollution at all. The fact that almost everyone in the scientific community continues to ignore it seems to indicate either that those who sell some kind of fuel — oil, gas, uranium — are in absolute control not just of our country but of the entire planet, or else that we are simply a bunch of lunatics bent on self-destruction.

In the face of what appear to be problems that cannot be solved in providing electricity in the amounts in which it will be needed by the year 2000, one must take some notice of the electric automobile which, we are told by some experts, is going to solve all our problems of air pollution created by the gasoline motored car. "Engineer Sees Big Future for Electric-Powered Cars," said a headline in our local paper.

This engineer, from our local power company, was addressing a meeting of chemical engineers. "In 10 years we are going to see more of them on the road," he said. He brought a 15-horsepower car to the meeting. I wrote to this gentlemen asking for information as to where all the electric power would come from to power

100 million cars, which may be 150 million ten years from now, since we are even now experiencing blackouts and brownouts. He could not answer such a specialized question, but referred my letter to the expert on this matter who wrote me that I need have no fears on this score.

The cars will be plugged in at night, said he, when everybody is asleep and not using their power for other things. (Like air-conditioning? Like home-heating? Like industry?) This will spread out the demand for power and will even make things cheaper for all of us! "You need have no fear that a power plant will have to be built on every square mile of land if the nation converts to the electric car. Technological advances (yes, those were the very words he used) permit more power to be produced by fewer plants than was possible only a few years back. . . . It can be seen that electric plants are much better able to control pollution than is possible with millions of internal combustion engine cars crowding our highways." And so on.

This company, incidentally, features very frequently in all its display windows the glorious idea that no American home is really a home without electric heat. And half-page ads in the daily paper hammer home the thought, while experts predict in large headlines that there will be a rise of 23 percent in electric heated homes in the next five years, locally.

A student at MIT who is more or less specializing in the electric car told me in a letter that he envisions the electric car as being originally only for city driving, to cut the urban pollution, or possibly as a "second car" to be used only for shopping and commuting. So, presumably, we will go right on buying gasoline-powered cars and will, *in addition,* buy an electric car, too, just for specific uses.

Applying the principle of "tolerable inconvenience", what can you do to make certain you individually are not contributing to the present crisis which permits the power company spokesman to say "It's their fault — the consumers! They're the ones who demand all this electric power."

1. Observe all the rules suggested by power company authorities for preventing blackouts and brownouts and a lot more. Turn off all lights you are not using. Open freezers and refrigerators as seldom, and for as short a time as possible. Defrost them frequently to keep them efficient. Don't put in electric heat. Use electric appliances sparingly. I say, do without all the ones you can possibly get along without. Don't buy electric gadgets. Turn off your electric water heater when you're away from home. Don't air condition. If you live in some spot where it's impossible to survive without air conditioning, use it as seldom as possible. Don't turn on the TV or the radio and leave it on when you're not listening to it. Skip the Christmas lights from now on — and put up a sign instead telling people why you're skipping them. You can surely think of many more ways to save electricity, can't you?

2. Be alert to the first news about a power plant that's scheduled for your locality. The power companies are coming around to believing it's better to let the people know what they're planning to do to any locality, rather than doing it and then facing the fight. So chances are you'll have word in time to organize. Call in the experts fast. Get help from any friendly, interested scientist,

engineer or technologist who lives nearby. You'll be pleasantly surprised at how willing they are to help, for it's ever so gradually being revealed to them in their own publications that many of us laymen are blaming them for the dilemma we're in. If they had been sufficiently far-sighted and concerned to delay the development of this or that new technology, we might have had time to adjust socially to the change before it found us unprepared.

3. Read. Go to the library and get out all the books on environment you can find. Many contain helpful information.

"Do you want us to go back to kerosene lamps?" is the silly question asked of the high school boy trying to save the fish in the Hudson River. Can you give up your electric carving knife to save Sunfish Pond from the despoilers? Or did you make the decision the day you bought the gadget?

In case, like the cynic above, you are thinking that life would be completely intolerable without electricity, sometime, when you're in the area, stop off in Lancaster County, Pennsylvania and drive through the Amish country. In this lush valley carpeted with prosperous family farms, the religious sect, the House Amish, have no electricity, do not use cars or other gasoline powered machinery.

Whirling windmills pump their water from deep wells into cisterns. A hand pump inside the house brings it from the cistern. There is no indoor plumbing, hence no sewage problem. No radios, no TVs. You go to bed mostly when it gets dark and you get up with the dawn. Nothing you do all day causes any kind of pollution. You use lively horses and neat, shiny buggies for the trips to town or the neighbors. The horse manure, along with the leavings from the chickens, sheep and pigs are stacked up by the barn, later to be spread over the fantastically productive land. Planting is done by hand, harvesting with a horse or a team.

Clothing is simple and practical, carefully prescribed by religion. It lasts for years, is handed down from one generation to another, as are the farms, the furniture, and all the household goods. So there is no solid waste. Food is practically all raised on the farm, where it is stored or canned for the winter. The refrigerator is a spring house, deep in the ground, dripping with moisture and coolness.

The only noise is that of the birds and the farm animals. The air is pure, the water free from pollution or chemicals. There is no rush. You go about work in harmony with the seasons. Every moment of work has meaning — a meaning hallowed down through all the ages that man has lived on earth. You are raising food. You are storing or preserving it. You are making or repairing clothing or housing. Everything you do is related intimately to your own relationship with the earth and the living you take from the earth.

As you drive past these incredibly fertile farms, you watch the Amish faces for symptoms of some terrible deprivation because they are purposely doing without all the glorious benefits of technology that we have. The faces are happy, content, smiling, tanned. You compare them mentally with the faces you see in a subway in any city in the world. You compare their life with life in a modern city assaulted by pollution of all kinds, noise, strain, hurry, the TV turned on all night, the sleeping pills, the alcoholism, the dirty movies, the sterile, meaningless work in a harsh, sterile world of steel and concrete.

You wonder whether we made the wrong choice so many years ago when we left the farms and went to live in Utopia — the city.

CHAPTER 6

How to Save Trees for a Greener Future

"Indeed what ecology teaches us, what it implores us to learn, is that all things, living and dead, including man, are interrelated within the web of life. This must be the foundation of our new ethics.

"If you love your children, if you wish them to be happy, love your earth with tender care and pass it on to them diverse and beautiful, so that they, 10,000 years hence, may live in a universe still diverse and beautiful, and find joy and wonder in being alive."

Hugh H. Iltis
Botany Dept., University of Wisconsin,
Bioscience, Vol. 20, no. 14

"From time to time conservationists are bound to feel their position comparable to that of a man overly imbued with reverence for life, who decides at last that he must stay in his chair to avoid doing damage to the small unseen beings under his feet. But the untenability of that man's extreme position in no way negates the validity of his original reverence. In the same way, the impossibility of preserving either species or biological organizations completely intact in no way justifies our relaxing the effort to keep whatever can be saved, and to go on haggling with the forces remaking the Earth over each separate relic of the old landscapes."

Thoughts on Wilderness Preservation
Archie Carr, *Audubon* magazine,
September, 1969

In February, 1970, the community of Bedford-Stuyvesant in Brooklyn, New York, was declared a disaster area by 55 state senators. The social and economic problems of this part of the city boggle the mind and flatten the spirit. If you lived in Bedford-Stuyvesant and you managed to get through the day every day, surely nothing more should be expected of you. Certainly nothing should be expected of you in terms of kindness, foresight, appreciation of beauty. Furthest from your mind, it seems, would be such items as conservation of nature, reverence for living things, regard for historical monuments. In this concrete wilderness, one of the most downtrodden, neglected places in New York City, how could such qualities as these exist, let alone flourish?

The *New York Times* carried a story one day in December, 1969, about a tree growing by a row of old brownstone houses in Bedford-Stuyvesant. Unbelievably the tree is a southern magnolia which, as any horticulturist knows, cannot survive winters farther north than Philadelphia. This 40-foot marvel had survived for 84 years, sheltered, it appears, by the friendly old brownstone houses, its roots snuggled in beneath their cellars.

The urban renewal project going forward in Bedford-Stuyvesant arrived at the magnolia tree and announced that the tree, along with the brownstone houses, must come down. The children of the neighborhood, led by Mrs. Hattie Carthan, president of the Bedford-Stuyvesant Beautification Association, decided to sell chances to buy the tree. They made up attractive raffle sheets shaped like magnolia leaves, green and yellow paper in a fan shape, 25 cents a chance. Prizes were the usual radios, bicycles and so forth.

On a rainy January day, a delegation of 110 school children made a pilgrimage to New York City Hall in behalf of the magnolia tree. The City Landmark Preservation Commission listened gravely to their story and decided to make the tree a Landmark, preserving too the brownstone houses around it. I sent a donation to the Magnolia Tree campaign. I addressed it just "Magnolia Tree," with the name of the street. I suspect many readers of the *Times* did the same. In February, 1970, I got this reply from Mrs. Carthan:

> The community of Bedford-Stuyvesant in Brooklyn, especially the children, wish to thank you for your warm interest and support of our efforts to save the famous Magnolia Tree. Because of your kind response we surpassed our goal of $5000 and this has been matched by $5000 from the Horticulture Society of New York, with additional contributions of $2000 from Rheingold Breweries and $500 from Mobil Oil Corporation.
>
> The Bedford-Stuyvesant Beautification Association will make your generous donation part of a permanent fund which will first protect and maintain the Magnolia as a living landmark, expand our tree-

planting program to further create a natural environment throughout the community and, finally, help establish summer training and future employment opportunities in tree-care, botany and horticulture for our young people. Since the "Save Our Magnolia" campaign stimulated such a nationwide response, we plan to dedicate this tree as a symbol of reverence for life, and feel it now belongs to all who hold this belief. We intend to maintain continuous contact with our many new friends throughout the United States and consider them honorary members of the Bedford-Stuyvesant Beautification Association. You are truly a friend of Bedford-Stuyvesant and a very close one."

What are the elements of this touching success story that made it successful? First, the Tree; its doggedness and courage in persisting for so many years in a situation where it was a well-known scientific fact that it could not survive. The children's campaign and the Tree are the basic elements. The children love the Tree; most people love children. Children pleading for the life of such a rare and heroic tree have all the elements of a Hollywood story.

But note that Mrs. Carthan did not just get some excellent publicity for the campaign. She sent the children out into the wintry streets of Brooklyn with green paper magnolia leaves and a place to sign your name and give your quarter. The $5000 was raised by the children, not the publicity.

In Salt Lake City in January, 1970 there stood an 85-foot cottonwood tree labeled "Pioneer Tree Number 1". It was the first tree planted by Mormon pioneers when they arrived in 1847. The commissioner of city streets ordered the tree cut down because it interferred with drainage improvements.

The six members of the city's Shade Tree Commission announced that "If the tree goes, so do we." The tree was cut down. The commissioners resigned with a public blast at a system that would allow a single city commissioner to overrule the unanimous decision of a group of citizens appointed to conserve trees. They didn't save the tree, but surely that city councilman will give some serious thought to his decision before he orders another tree cut.

Here is a story from *New Scientist* for August, 1968. A report from the Boston *Globe* discovered that a $44,000 federal grant to beautify Route 3 across Massachusetts had been spent on uprooting the roadside trees. The local Audubon Society, always quick to an ecological hurt, followed up the story and discovered that the Bureau of Public Roads had decreed that millions of trees along America's highways should be cut down. They were reckoned to be dangerous, the Bureau's Traffic Safety Committee said, "when vehicles left the pavement." The coast-to-coast edict applies "to trees four inches in diameter or larger, located within a distance of 30 feet from the road, at the edge and within the median strip."

Asked to justify their action, a committee spokesman quoted a study of 507 fatal single-car accidents. 130 of them were due to banks and ditches, 107 to guard rails and curbs, 35 to information signs, 20 to traffic signals. Trees were apparently responsible for only 13 accidents of the 507. But the traffic officials said plainly that it was easier to take down the trees than do anything about other hazards!

"In Britain," says *New Scientist,* "Miss Sylvia Crowe, the queen of landscape planners, has pointed out that trees are dangerous if they obstruct road sign-lines, or if they are planted where they are liable to be run into. Fallen leaves sometimes cause skids. Boughs occasionally fall down and frost patches may be due to shading by trees on the south of the highway.

"But over and above all this, trees and shrubs relieve the physically deadly monotony of roadscapes; they stabilize soil and act as anti-dazzle devices. Foliage forms an effective sound barrier and, planted judiciously, shrubs, bushes and trees provide one of the best accident barriers known. Wild briars are reported to be able to stop a car travelling at 47 miles per hour with no injury to the driver and little to the car."

I wrote the federal highway department asking if indeed they had an ordinance forbidding all trees within a 30-foot area of a highway. They sent me — and you can get a copy if you write for it — the ruling which says, after the manner of many federal rulings that, well, maybe trees at a minimum distance of 30 feet from a highway should be cut down but on the other hand "the desirable width of clear recovery area may be greater or less than 30 feet . . . Highway safety and highway beauty can and must be made compatible." The ruling goes on to recommend that trees of special historic or scenic value (as if there were ever a tree without scenic value!) should be retained in their natural setting wherever possible." *They also recommend that shrubs and small trees should be planted close by the highway.*

In *Silent Spring,* Rachel Carson devotes much of a chapter on herbicides to roadside spraying of trees and shrubs. With the clarity and logic that characterize every page of that extraordinary book, she points out that, by indiscriminate spraying of everything at the sides of the roads, we are making worse the very conditions we are supposedly trying to remedy. It is quite possible, says Miss Carson, with careful spraying or cutting to eliminate those trees which present some hazard to the driver, at the same time planting and encouraging the growth of the many shrubs which will flourish at roadsides. Once the shrubs are established, the problem is solved, for they resist invasion of large trees, and there is no further problem of cutting or spraying roadside brush. You have also provided homes and food for wildlife and the many insects that must have the flowers of these shrubs for food. The simplicity and elegance of such a solution is apparently its undoing for all over the country roadside trees are being ruthlessly whacked down with such abandon that one wonders at the ferocity with which the operations take place. You can use Miss Carson's words and the words of *New Scientist* in your own fight against this kind of desecration.

"Slam-bang technology" is the word applied to the maintenance of our thruways by LaMont Cole of Cornell University in an editorial in *Bioscience* for November, 1969. He lists all the many advantages of tree-lined highways, including their wind-break capability, which prevents snowdrifts. Their leaves filter out air pollution, they prevent the glare of oncoming cars at night; they moderate temperatures and absorb noise; planted on median strips they would prevent accidents in which cars cross the strips and have head-on collisions. The bills for maintaining grassy strips instead of trees and shrubs would be eliminated, since the latter need little or no upkeep.

"Never underestimate youth power" is the headline over a story in *The Conservationist,* December–January, 1969–70. "I suggest", says the story, "that it is not very intelligent to claim that government and industry are self-propelled and self-sufficient. The individual can accomplish a goal — and in the face of great opposition."

"Recently at a town meeting in Dedham, Massachusetts, a motion under consideration called for widening a street by ten feet on each side. A resident of the street rose in opposition. He said his home had a tree, one of the few remaining at that end of the block, and he didn't want it cut down just to accommodate more trucks and cars. He wanted to preserve the grass against concrete, preserve elms and oaks against parking meters, preserve the breathing space against parking space.

"Here was a bare bone defense of environmental values. And the town meeting accepted his appeal and killed the street-widening proposal by a vote of 133 to 98. The hero who saved the street was a 15-year old boy."

Town meetings in New England are sometimes lively affairs. In other parts of the country, township, boro or city council meetings can be deadly dull. But there's something to be said for attending them. Nobody can get to every meeting. But somebody from your group should make a point of being there and of rising to question, object or applaud at appropriate times.

Out in San Francisco in February, 1970, a group of young environmentalists protested in a novel way to try to preserve 173 acres of woodland on a military establishment destined to be destroyed in new housing and freeway accesses. The picket signs said, "Isn't defoliating Vietnam enough?" and "At least make peace with trees." One young woman brought along a cake made in the shape of a tree which she tried to present to the commander of the post. A public meeting was held later by the young folks.

Time was when somebody cutting down trees around a city building would have aroused little concern. But officials of the Metropolitan Museum in New York City found themselves the center of a furious attack when they cut down 36 full-grown honey locusts in December, 1969. Protests were so loud, so violent and so urgent that the museum had to print 7000 circulars explaining that the trees had to come down because of a renovation. The architect just couldn't proceed with the trees in the way, said the circular, and besides, they plan to plant a lot more new trees to replace them. As a number of angry New Yorkers pointed out to a *Times* reporter, little new trees are no substitute for full-grown ones. Said the Chairman of the Atlantic Chapter of the Sierra Club, "I consider trees more essential than the damned new facade of that damned museum which has no business being in the park anyway."

Trying to save whole forests is complicated. Faced with a circumstance like this, the best idea is to get in touch with the "Save the Redwoods League" which knows all the tricks in the book. Since 1918 they have been working for a Redwood National Park, which they finally achieved when the President signed such a bill in 1968. But much more remains to be done.

One billion board feet of redwoods are cut every year and at present less than 250,000 acres remain of an original 2 million acres of virgin Coast Redwoods. Except for those preserved in California's state parks, these forests are privately owned and will eventually be logged. The league has many plans for saving parts here and there.

They use every weapon known in the conservation fight. They are fighting not only the lumber industry but many shortsighted plans for things like thruways in the forests. They use full-page newspaper ads, they have beautiful literature available; a bulletin for members, and obviously an efficient publicity and lobbying operation. The League says, "The task of saving Redwoods is far from complete. The map of the present Federal and State holdings shows the ultimate boundaries and the thousands of acres yet to acquired. It is hoped that matching funds both at the Federal and State level will be made available to assist in this large unfinished task. However, past experience has shown that the League must first raise very substantial private funds as a catalyst". You personally can help by joining the League. Send a card to this address for more information: Save the Redwoods League, 114 Sansome Street, San Francisco, California 94104.

And don't buy anything made of redwood, explaining to the lumberman or the furniture dealer why you are not buying. True, redwood lasts for many years when it is made into something that must withstand the weather. But isn't the cost too high? Here is one measure of tolerable inconvenience you can surely apply. It isn't all that hard to get along without something made of redwood, now, is it? If it's a redwood set of furniture for the patio that you are contemplating, forget it. Recover some old cushions and let people find out once again that it's fun to sit on the floor. Or paint your old chairs and tables and explain to your friends and neighbors why you decided against the redwood furniture.

We are reminded by a letter to the editor of *Science,* June 7, 1968 from Donald F. Anthrop that the total cost of a redwood park worth the name is 2 percent of one year's expenditure on space or equal to what we spend in Vietnam every 36 hours. "One can only speculate on what future generations will think of our system of priorities," says Mr. Anthrop.

The Sierra Club is trying to save a million acres of virgin forests in Alaska's Inside Passage. They have filed a lawsuit against the Secretary of Agriculture and the U. S. Forest Service who own the land, claiming that the sale of the land for logging was illegal since there was no public bidding. The spruce and hemlock forests are destined to be made into pulpwood to be sold to Japan! "There's no more beautiful country in the world," said the club's vice president, "Alaska is the last and perhaps our greatest challenge. It's potentially the richest state in the union. It doesn't need to export this priceless national heritage just to make a few dollars . . . It's incomprehensible to me why the government would destroy the very things that bring tourism to the area." The address of the Sierra Club, if you'd like to help in the campaign, is: 1050 Mills Towers, San Francisco, California 94104.

The bill that would have allowed increased cutting of timber in national forests went down to defeat (228–150) before the onslaught of conservationists who tackled the mighty lumber industry and got a postponement of floor action on the bill in February, 1970, meaning that the conservation interests had enough votes to defeat it.

The danger, of course, is only postponed, for there is little doubt that the lumber industry will try again.

In an analysis of the bill that was shelved, Michael McCloskey of the Sierra Club calls it a "crass raid" on a public resource. He points out that the lumber industry has not suddenly become tenderhearted about the poor housing in ghetto areas, only that it fears the competition of lower cost materials like aluminum and plastic in building the new homes called for in the Housing Act of 1968.

So the national forests could be raided, at federal expense, to provide lumber for the industry. "Intensive management" would be the watchword. New forests would be planted like agricultural fields — a thousand acres of spruce here, a thousand acres of white pine there — all "managed" to produce fast crops, in the exact sense of that word, a word so repugnant and so foreboding to anyone with knowledge of the importance of diversity of nature and the slow-gradual means by which nature maintains her ecological balances.

As Mr. McCloskey says in an article in *New Republic* for December 13, 1969, it is the height of folly to apply these managing techniques to the national forests. "These forests, found often on highly mountainous terrain, include many sites that are already ecologically fragile . . . Monoculture (planting only one kind of tree in one area) will invite increasing insect attacks, prompting repeated resort to insecticides damaging to wildlife, and fish. Fertilizers will leach into pure mountain supplies. Forest scenery will disappear as a large percentage of the canopy is removed to make way for young, row crops of conifers. The richness of a forest that is more or less natural will be supplanted by a relatively sterile and unstable ecology."

If you write to the paper and/or lumber industry

(yes, the reference librarian at your local public library can give you an address for these folks) on how you feel about "managing" a forest — especially these national forests which belong to you and other taxpayers — they will tell you that forests just love to be managed. It's better for them that way. Until modern man appeared to show the forests how to get along, they were unhappy and unkempt, not really knowing how to be forests. Yes, they really say outrageous things like that, not just in letters, but in full page ads in which they proclaim their dedication to making all forests into much better and more presentable places than they now are.

Ask them to read this statement from American Forests, December, 1969, and ask them if they can guarantee that their "managed" forests will affect people as the old-fashioned kind of forest affected F. Glenn Goff, when he wrote, "I consider it (the forest) to be a system possessing unfathomable artistic qualities encoded by the operation of laws through eons of time. The forest tells me — even more than the Mona Lisa or the symphonies of Beethoven — something about what I am, culturally and biologically. It gives me a glimpse of the processes that have produced me and function continuously to sustain me."

While one part of the country is wringing its collective hands over the disaster wrought on our Great Lakes and other waterways partly by intensive farming of the agricultural land around them, it seems almost impossible to believe that the lumber industry should be trying to wrest from us every acre of national forests specifically in order to commit the same terrible acts there and produce the same sterile and probably irreversible results.

We haven't seen the last of the raid on the national forests. Watch for the next piece of legislation to come along, thinly disguised as something beneficial for all. And then get busy with your typewriter or pen, writing your congressman and senators, getting your friends and neighbors to write. Write to the lumber industry, telling them how you feel about the national forests and their proposal to "manage" them. Speak with assurance, for all the disasters mankind has produced by "managing" nature are evidence enough that this procedure will not create more lumber, will not "save" the forests, will not contribute any final answer to anything. Let's leave the national forests alone, just as they are, forever!

CHAPTER 7

Saying No to the Land Developer

"The New York Constitution has included an environmental right since 1895 — the 'forever wild' protection of the State Adirondack and Catskill Forest Preserve lands. Many knowledgeable people claimed the right was too vaguely stated. 'Forever wild' was far too ambiguous. No court could rationally ascertain its real meaning, it was said. Our answer was clear: 'Forever wild' is vague; so, too, however, are 'due process', 'equal protection', 'unreasonable search and seizure', 'interstate commerce' and a host of other constitutional phrases. The court can apply to each the gradual and empiric process of inclusion and exclusion."

David Sive
Civil Liberties
April, 1970

"Woe unto them that join house to house, that lay field to field, till there be no room". . . .

Isaiah 5:8

SAYING NO TO THE LAND DEVELOPER

"What most men and women desire, particularly the young in our industrial society is . . . not more urbanism and industry but less; not a larger population but a smaller; not a rejection of agrarian values but a recovery of them; not a divorce from the natural world but a reunion with it. That's what the conservation movement is essentially all about. And if we have to destroy part of the technological apparatus in order to escape the trap the technocrats are setting for us, then that is exactly what we should do."

Edward Abbey, fire lookout at
Grand Canyon National Park,
author of *Desert Solitaire*
and other books.

"By overbuilding and by waterproofing the land man is turning much of the temperate, well watered northeastern United States into desert land. . . . We are now becoming aware of the fact that overcrowding humans intensifies detrimental characters of those humans. Should we continue to crowd? Should we not make every possible attempt to disperse, no matter how great the cost? A bit of open land has very great value, especially great value to children."

Dr. F. J. Trembley
Professor of Ecology
Lehigh University

"Man is a blind, witless, low-brow, anthropocentric clod who inflicts lesions on the earth."

Ian McHarg, Head of the Department
of Landscape Architecture and Regional
Planning, University of Pennsylvania

"My first job in the Department of Environmental Impact of the Federal Department of Transportation was to handle a case involving Beaucatcher Mountain near Asheville, North Carolina," said Mr. Oscar S. Gray who was head of that department for a number of years. "It involved a retired Colonel, his wife, and their home on that mountain. The state highway department was planning to cut a gash in the mountain and run an Interstate highway across it. The colonel and his wife asked the Federal DOT to stop the highway. Their home was an historical monument, they said, and the law forbade the destruction of an historical monument. The highway would destroy the surroundings of their home.

"I called the folks who make decisions involving historical monuments and they told me that the Colonel's house could not possibly qualify. I consulted with the highway people who told me that, if they did not cut that slash across the mountain they would have to build a tunnel through the mountain. They told me how much more this would cost. They pointed out all the disadvantages of tunnels and their propensity for creating traffic jams. Their case was so convincing, their arguments so sound, that I had to notify the North Carolina couple, reluctantly, that the highway would go through as planned.

"On my last day in the department years later I had one file still to close. The man who brought it to me told me that the Secretary himself had ordered a change in the highway design to put a tunnel through a mountain rather than a slash across the mountain. I asked him if it happened to be Beaucatcher Mountain near Asheville. He told me that it was.

" 'But that case was closed years ago,' I protested. 'The arguments against that tunnel are among the strongest I've ever heard in any case of citizen protest against a highway. What happened to change the Department's mind?'

" 'The Secretary tells me the Colonel and his wife came almost every day to his office to talk to him about the highway and the mountain, how much they loved their home, and how dreadfully ruinous the highway would be. Those days when he could not see them, they sat patiently on a bench outside the door. They brought their lunch with them in a paper bag. They made appointments whenever they could, to talk to anybody who would listen to them. They buttonholed people in the halls. If they couldn't persuade anybody from the department to talk to them, they just sat, waiting until somebody would talk to them. The Secretary has decided that such persistence deserves a reward and he has issued orders that a tunnel is to be put through the mountain.' "

Mr. Gray was making the point that persistence is probably your best weapon when you are fighting a superhighway. He was speaking at a meeting of the local Environmental Federation in our community where opinion was divided three ways in regard to a new interstate highway. Nobody really wants the highway, except the highway department and the many industries which make handsome profits laying down cement ribbons across the land.

Federal law requires that two public hearings be held on new highway corridors built with federal money, at which time local residents may present all their opposition to the proposed routes. The required two hearings had already been held on the eastern part of our proposed highway. The highway department thus considered this part of the debate closed. And since this decision brought the highway to a certain point on the landscape, the rest of us would have to go along with whichever route was chosen from that point on. "The salami technique", Mr. Gray calls it. You slice the proposed corridor into pieces and hold hearings on each piece. This seals the doom of the rest of the slices. The road *has* to go somewhere.

Mr. Gray told us there is a federal regulation, laid down in January, 1969, which makes it mandatory that these hearings be something more than window-dressing. The regulation is PPM 20-8, duly entered in the book of Federal Regulations. Highway builders must listen to protestations of the public concerning the social and environmental effects of their proposed route and must act accordingly. They cannot simply hold the two hearings as a formality and then go ahead as they had planned to. It's well understood by everybody concerned with highway building that this is how hearings have been treated by highway builders in the past. How else can one explain the relentless march of concrete across ravished lands, after hundreds of local citizens have turned out to meeting after meeting and hearing after hearing, to protest the laying of a single foot of cement?

Mr. Gray told us, further, that every one of our 50 governors objected to regulation PPM 20-8 when it was laid down. He said further that there is a determined effort by state highway departments to undermine it by whatever strategies they can use. The Department of

Transportation Act, which established this department and placed the building of Interstate highways in its jurisdiction, states clearly that, as a national policy, special efforts shall be made to preserve the natural beauty of the land, to protect parks, game and wildlife refuges, historical monuments, and so on.

It states further that the Secretary of Transportation shall cooperate with and consult with the Secretaries of Agriculture, Housing and Interior to develop measures which will enhance the natural beauty of the land. Furthermore, the act states that the Secretary shall not approve any highway corridor which will destroy a park, wildlife refuge and so on, *if there is a feasible alternative.* No court test has been made of this rule, Mr. Gray told us, although other similar environmental laws have been invoked in other cases of environmental protection. The legal action to prevent the jet airport near the Everglades was one such case.*

As probably everybody knows by now, the Interstate Highway program is funded with some five billion dollars a year which comes from taxes paid by car owners for gasoline, tires, batteries and anything else taxable which is needed by car owners. Its defenders, among them some of the most powerful lobbies in Washington and in every state capitol, insist that the money is sacrosanct, that it cannot be used for anything other than

* Later, in March, 1971, the Supreme Court ordered a review of D.O.T. authorization for an interstate highway to cut through a park in Memphis, Tennessee. The suit was brought by a Memphis citizens' committee, the National Audubon Society and the Sierra Club. Justice Hugo Black states that the record "contains not one word to indicate the Secretary (of Transportation) raised even a finger to comply with the command of Congress." It's a victory for all of us who are fighting highways, even if we must fight the battle over again, with every new occasion when a park is threatened.

highways. They seem determined to stick with this viewpoint, even if it means paving over the whole country with roads nobody ever uses.

As soon as wide, handsome roads are laid down in any state, there are, almost at once, more and more cars to fill these roads. This makes it essential, the highway builders say, to build still more highways, which automatically produce more cars to use them — and so on.

A. Q. Mowbray, in *Road to Ruin,* and Helen Leavitt, in *Superhighway-Superhoax,* devote much time to an analysis of just how the Highway Trust Fund works and the amount of destruction it has wrought on American landscapes and cities. The state provides only ten percent of the total cost of any Interstate highway. The Trust Fund provides the other 90 percent. The purse is too fat, too irresistibly big.

No matter whether you need the highway or not, no matter whether it will destroy the last patch of open land anywhere on your local map, the lure of that immense amount of money simply cannot be resisted by state governments or their agents, representatives in Congress and senators. How can you turn down this largesse on behalf of your constituents?

Gradually, as ribbons of concrete spread across the country, statistics pop up. You can drive all the way from New York City to California now without a single stop for a traffic light. This is "progress"? This is the purpose for which we are ruining our land, our water, our air? The dullness of travel on superhighways has begun to depress people who, supposedly, take to their cars in order to enjoy themselves and see the sights. Superhighways were supposed to decrease traffic fatalities. Fatalities continued to increase. Superhighways were supposed to decrease traffic jams. Instead they create more, as more and more cars jam the roads. Why should anybody ride a bus or a train if there is a brand new hundred million dollar superhighway to travel?

Superhighways were supposed to facilitate intercity traffic — provide 70 mile an hour speed for getting across country fast. Instead, local traffic entered at every cloverleaf, slowing down the whole mess while traffic jams piled up. So superhighways were taken *into* cities, climbed on steel and concrete ramps across the very heart of cities, cutting off one section from another, isolating whole neighborhoods, making slums of others, ruining merchants who found traffic whizzing past at 70 miles an hour with no customers stopping.

As the number of cars increased, more superhighways became necessary, more landscapes were ruined. Noise, pollution, destruction of wildlife, streams and mountains continued apace. Poor neighborhoods were considered most expendable because the cost of paying for destruction there was never so great. But some of the most opulent communities in the country faced the highway department's bulldozers with the same panic the slum dwellers felt. The battles fought in wealthy Westchester County, New York, the Georgetown section of Washington, D. C., and the Shaker Heights community of Cleveland are described in the Mowbray and Leavitt books.

Perhaps most depressing of all are the stories of what happened in some small pleasant communities — the kind of town Americans are supposed to have in the back of their hearts all the time as the ideal place to live and bring up kids — the dream home we all want to have eventually, after we've had our share of city life. The quiet, tree-shaded town of Morristown, New Jersey, was told at the one public hearing held that three percent of its total land area would be taken by an interstate highway which would also, according to Mr. Mowbray, "slice by a hospital, leap across a playground, plow under a hundred or so houses, some of them on the finest residential streets in town, and . . . cut open a 250-foot-wide swath between an elementary school and the pride of Morristown, Washington's Headquarters. By 1985, they were told, 70,000 cars a day would be racing through their town.

The Morristown residents launched an attack to save it. They went through all the heartbreak and frustration everyone has gone through who has opposed the building of an interstate highway. They were shifted from state to federal highway departments for answers to their pleas. Neither would give any final answer. They hired planners to map an alternate route. The highway department announced they would proceed with their original plans. Calls and telegrams to the governor, congressmen, senators brought equivocal replies. There was lots of money at stake, many influential moguls in the construction business who couldn't be alienated by any politician who wanted to be re-elected. The town organized almost to a man, with signs, bumper stickers, demonstrations. The Department of Interior, brought into the fray because the Washington Headquarters is a national shrine, protested vigorously, in vain. On the day the bulldozers approached, the courageous Morristown women marched out and sat on the bulldozer blades. They were moved forcefully and the town was invaded.

It seems that the highway builders believe in what they are doing. As Mr. Gray puts it, "They have an overdeveloped sense of their own rectitude." They are so devoted to their obsession with building highways that they just can't understand public objection. In some cases, state highway departments have abandoned projects rather than face litigation. They do this with a feeling that they are punishing local residents who will now not have this delightful, broad highway to use!

It is well to keep in mind that the state highway department, rich as Croesus with all that money available from the Highway Trust Fund, is really in a much more powerful position that the elected government of most states. Intrastate highways, which must be maintained, rebuilt or redesigned, can command only 50 percent of the cost from federal funds. The state must pay the additional half of the cost. So Interstate highway funds are prizes for any state government. Officials overlook the fact that, once these extensive roads are laid down, maintenance reverts to the state and bills may be very high. Recently we were told that interstate highways are crumbling fast, because of truck traffic. So highway bills will mount for state governments which have a lot of Interstate roads to maintain.

Mr. Gray believes that it is essential to put your case in the hands of a good local lawyer from the start, if you want to save some last remaining bits of loveliness in your landscape from the bulldozers. Most of all, he says, do not go into a hearing on a new highway without a lawyer, to help you build a record at the hearing which will stand up in court if you should decide to take the matter to court later. Judges are, he says, becoming more suspicious of hearings, coming more and more to understand that they are often only window dressing and lip service. Congressmen are aware of the deception that highway hearings often turn into. *No one has yet tested in court the provision which says the hearing must be genuine, must consider all objections made by the concerned public.*

The 1969 Environmental Protection Act, our most important piece of federal environmental legislation to date, requires that any agency of the federal government, preparing any kind of project in any state, must take into account the environmental impact of that project. The Wilderness Society is at present fighting the Alaska Pipeline, using these provisions as the basis of the suit.

The 1970 Highway Act provides that no more 90–10 percent contracts will be forthcoming for the Interstate network after 1973. So any Interstate highway project which can be held up until then cannot command such a big slice of federal money. Should any citizen of a state deliberately reject this kind of money? Won't it work a great financial hardship on the state to provide adequate roads if the Interstate network is incomplete? State governments are even now struggling with financial burdens that seem unmanageable.

It's another dilemma technology has brought us. It's another occasion on which we have to ask "Is progress, as we have formerly understood it, really what we want? Are more highways what we want or are they finally going to smother us in air pollution, noise and traffic jams? Isn't there some way to solve the transportation crisis without building more highways?"

Of course there is. The only possible answer is convenient, inexpensive, fast mass transportation systems in every part of the country. Fortunately Congress has finally come around to seeing the reasonableness of this solution. In October, 1970 the Rail Passenger Service Act of 1970 was passed and signed into law by the President. It provides for a corporation responsible for schedules, operations, connections, equipment, promotion and overall service. It is expected to include a corridor network connecting urban areas plus some transcontinental service.

In October, too, the Mass Transit Act was passed, providing money for mass transit systems throughout the country. This victory for commuters and everyone else who is unwilling or unable to spend a large part of every day getting to and from work or shopping, is due in large measure to Senator Harrison Williams of New Jersey. Secretary Volpe also supported both measures.

Until that happy day when Metroliners speed from city to city and clean, convenient buses pick you up at your door in the city, superhighways will continue to gobble up land. Where you are facing a superhighway which, once laid down, can never be taken up again to restore the land, the watershed, the forest, to its former condition, the best idea is to hire a lawyer from the beginning of the fight. Whether or not you sue, the lawyer can help and direct every detail of your fight, can investigate every possible loophole, every obscure regulation that may be relevant to your situation. Just the hiring of the lawyer and/or the announcement that you will sue may deter the highway department.

Your best friend in the Department of Transportation in Washington is the Associate Administrator for Right-of-Way and Environment. Write to him. Go to see him. Take a box lunch and stick around if you can. Be persistent. Take your signed petitions with you, and all clippings, statements, letters from state, local and federal officials relating to the highway. Most important of all, have the documents outlining the position of your local politicians if, of course, they oppose the route or the building of the highway.

What, besides highways, destroys open space? It's called "development" and it comes in many guises.

Nine thousand acres of salt marsh and 3000 acres of high ground on Bald Head Island off the coast of North Carolina are one of the last remaining spots of any size on the East coast undefiled by man and his developments. In July, 1970, the owner of the island sold it for five and a half million dollars to a developer who plans to erect a golf course, a yacht club and motels, and divide the rest in building lots. The state of North Carolina offered to buy the island with money from the Nature Conservancy. The owner refused and gave a mortgage to the developers.

The only course left for the state to preserve the island as a natural spot where sea birds, fish and marine life can live undisturbed, is to refuse a permit to the Army Corps of Engineers to dredge in order to build a bridge to the island. The state could condemn the island for a park, but they have no funds for this. *The New York Times* commented editorially, "There is no defense for this unconscionable deal. In years past, it was possible for private individuals to regard an ecologically valuable site such as Bald Head Island as just another real estate parcel to be disposed of as they saw fit. But the public has gained far deeper understanding of the fragility and importance of its physical setting.

For the protection of the coast against erosion, for the life cycle of fish, shellfish, and waterfowl, and for its inherent unspoiled beauty, a major salt marsh can no longer be regarded as one man's asset to be bartered for private profit. It is part of every man's natural heritage to be held in trust for the public good.

"The struggle to save Bald Head points up the wisdom of a law enacted in Connecticut last year which requires that an owner of any tideland, marshland or other land in the estuarine zone cannot do anything to alter its ecological character without obtaining prior state approval. A law of this kind would give every coastal state in the nation the sort of protection it needs."

From the *New York Times,* October 5, 1969, comes this story, by-lined Bayard Webster.

Rowayton, Connecticut. For 180 young girls, students in this quiet tree-shaded town bordering Long Island Sound, the month of October is a glorious one. It is the month when Connecticut State Senate Bill No. 419 becomes effective. The new law in force on October 1 calls for the survey and preservation of Connecticut's coastal wetlands which, up to now, had been unprotected by law from the ravages of indiscriminate dumping and filling.

The passage of the bill by the legislature was primarily the result of a campaign by the 180 students of the Thomas School here, a private girls' school for grades 6 through 12. For several years the girls had used a tidal marsh near their school as an outdoor classroom for the study of biology and wildlife. When they arrived this spring they found it was being used as a dumping ground by contractors.

They also found that Connecticut had no law prohibiting the filling-in of ecologically valuable bog areas, which provide spawning ground for fish and are rich sources of shellfish. That was when the girls determined to get such a law passed.

"It all started when we went out for our first class in the marsh last spring," said Susan Middleer, a 17-year old senior as she pointed to a filled-in section of Farm Creek Marsh, about a half mile from the school. "This is what we found. There is very little life here left to study," she added, looking at the small houses, built on dumped fill, that hemmed in the once-spacious marsh.

"The first thing we did," said Mary Cabral, a petite 16-year old senior, "was organize a mourn-in. We made black crepe-paper sashes, had an early breakfast at the school and led a silent march to the swamp." A dozen legislators were invited but only two showed up. The students were discouraged, but with the help of two science instructors, Mrs. Joy Lee and David L. Cherney, the class organized the whole school into a conservation group known as PYE (pronounced pie) for Protect Your Environment. Susan and Mary, aided by their art instructor, designed the club's emblem, a circle of yellow (sunlight) with triangles of blue (water) and green (the earth) inside. At first they fashioned home-made bumper stickers and lapel buttons showing the PYE emblem. Later contributions and money from the sale of the emblems enabled them to afford machine-made insignia. Their campaign to convert the legislature got underway in earnest.

How do you "convert" a legislature? Bombard all 213 of them with a total of 800 hand-written letters.

Invite them to breakfast for talks. Sell or give away more than 20,000 bumper stickers — to anyone, not just the legislators. Distribute and sell 25,000 lapel buttons.

Get up at 4:30 in the morning, go down to the train station and tell sleepy-eyed commuters about the threat to the scenic wetlands in their area. Hold conservation seminars in the community, talk to civic groups, Girl Scout meetings, garden clubs, League of Women voters chapters — anyone who'll listen.

After you think you've got everyone aroused, get your area legislators to introduce a bill. Nurse it out of committee. Cross your fingers as the State Senate passes it, hold your breath when the House does, too. Then breathe a sigh of relief when the governor signs it.

Representative Edward S. Rimer, Jr. of Wilton, who helped the girls with the legislation, said "Those kids were just great. Their sincerity and youthful exuberance were what won everybody over. There's no question that the bill wouldn't have passed without their efforts."

. . . . Before the effective date of the bill, there were no restrictions on the dredging or filling-in of tidal marshlands in the state. Connecticut is one of the last states to pass such legislation.

"Many people think a salt water marsh isn't good for anything — they don't understand its value," said Mr. Cherney, the biology instructor. He explained the importance of a tidal marsh: "It's a great source of food — it has mussels, clams, oysters — and it's the place where fish spawn and the young fish grow up before going out into Long Island Sound.". . .

As the girls returned to their science laboratory at school, Mrs. Edward T. Fabe, a science instructor who has also worked with the students this fall on the PYE program, sat on a stool and talked of her enthusiasm for her students' accomplishments.

"I think the whole movement is just fine," she said, as the school janitor walked in wearing the familiar yellow, blue and green button on his shirt. "It not only gives them a chance to learn biology and ecology but it enables them to become political activists — to see what the political process is all about. They lost a marsh," she added, "but they gained a broader vista of life."

Here are some figures from a 1969 study of open space in Pennsylvania. Your own state probably has done a similar study. Ask your state assemblymen.

Nearly one-half of Pennsylvania's farmland has gone out of food production since the turn of the century. This includes 420,000 acres *of some of the state's best farmland.* An average *of 115 acres of agricultural land, including 99 acres of cropland, is lost to food production and turned to other uses EVERY DAY.*

At present, only about 25 percent of the state's land is used for agriculture. Urbanization has claimed 13 percent. Of the eight million acres now in farmland, less than 40 percent is classified as "good" for agricultural purposes. The rest is submarginal. "Once agricultural land goes into nonagricultural use," warns the committee's report, "it will remain generally unavailable to the people . . . for the production of food and fiber."

You can't pave over land for highways, supermarkets and parking lots; you can't bulldoze thousands of acres for housing developments, skyscrapers, condominiums, country homes, racetracks, landfills, factories; you can't drown thousands of acres of land for manmade lakes for state parks or flood control and then, some fifty years from now, when the folly of destroying farmland wholesale becomes evident, you can't decide to tear it all up and make farmland out of it again! It simply won't work. Farmland isn't created that way. Nature requires thousands of years to manufacture topsoil, quarter-inch by quarter-inch. It cannot be created overnight.

The 1970 Handbook of the U. S. Department of Agriculture, *Contours of Change,* tells us that we are losing four billion tons of "sediment" every year — washed into our lakes, streams and rivers. And what's sediment? Topsoil mostly — irreplaceable, far more precious than any other one substance in the world. It runs off whenever a new highway is built. It floods off when houses are perched on towering hillsides or cuddled in the flood plains of streams. Just as forests, crystal pure lakes, plains, mountains are irreplaceable, once they have been bludgeoned and "conquered" by man's technology, so farmland and, with it, the pleasant, restful countryside, once destroyed by bulldozers, is gone forever.

How can we keep it? How can we keep it especially in the heavily populated areas around our great cities — in the megalopolis that already extends from Boston to Washington, D. C., from Pittsburgh to Chicago?

A state law (515) passed by Pennsylvania in 1966 gives any Pennsylvania county the privilege of adopting the plan of "covenanting" for preserving open space, forests, farmland and watersheds. Bucks County, nine-tenths "undeveloped", a pleasant area on the northeast edges of Philadelphia, has had an increase of 100,000 residents in the last ten years. Commissioners believe they can save from development about half the land by the end of the century. With this in mind, they feel it is imperative to save large areas of land now, in their present state as permanent open space. So Bucks County is considering the implementation of 515 to keep the county green.

Because of the new population growth, all the land in Bucks County will soon be reassessed for tax purposes. Taxes are bound to go up and up. Most of the money from county taxes goes for schools, some for roads and other services. Farmers will be especially hard hit by the new taxes. While other businessmen need almost no land, the farmer must have a great deal of land to stay in business. On the other hand, his land creates the need for no services. The county does not have to provide any more schools, roads or other services for a farmer with 500 acres than for an apartment dweller who owns no land.

Real estate taxes, which support most local services in our country, are relics of the time when land was almost the only measure of a man's wealth. So they were fair at that time. Today they work such hardship on farmers that, all over the country, farmers are selling out to developers, as taxes go so high they can no longer afford to farm. Since many people will probably not be able to keep their land under the new taxes in Bucks County, "covenanting" may be the instrument for keeping them there and keeping their land "open" — that is, undeveloped by either housing developments, industrial or commercial buildings.

The way 515 works is this: a landowner who decides to covenant for himself and his heirs agrees to keep his land in open space, as it now is, for a period of five years, without altering it in any way or selling any part of it. The county agrees that the property tax assessment will reflect the fair market value of the land, as restricted by the covenant. In other words, the present owner will continue to pay taxes on the basis of his land being open rather than paying what he would owe if the land were developed, which is, in essence, the assessment that will be placed on land which has not been covenanted.

If the landowner breaks the covenant and alters the use of his land to any use other than what is designated in the covenant, he pays to the county the difference in taxes which have been forgiven, plus five percent interest. The covenant can be renewed from year to year, or cancelled by either the landowner or the county with proper prior notification. In principle, 515 keeps the farmer on the land by reducing his taxes so long as he continues to farm. It keeps the large landowner on the land, so long as he keeps his land open and does not sell any part of it for housing developments, industrial or commercial purposes.

At a recent meeting, close to 1000 Bucks County folks gathered in the impressive new school auditorium for a hearing on the implementation of 515. Opinion ranged all the way from speakers who unalterably opposed 515 as useless, to many others who favored adoption as a "holding action — not perfect but all we have", to others like a spokesman of the Bucks County Audubon Society who urged the implementation of 515, saying that there is no hope for keeping any open land in the future if it is not held now.

As with any new idea, there are many complications which were brought out by one speaker or another. The act specifies that only designated lands can be covenanted: farmland of 50 acres or more; forest land of 25 acres or more; water supply land of 10 acres or more, or open space land which abuts on some area already open, such as parks, historical sites, game lands and so on. It was pointed out by several speakers that people who own less land also suffer from high taxes. Why should not they, too, have the right to covenant?

Someone reminded the taxpayers that, the more land you remove from tax rolls, the more everybody else has to pay in the way of taxes. One speaker thought a dangerous precedent might be set; soon people may be forced by law to covenant, he said, as land becomes scarcer. A spokesman for the Farmer's Association challenged the assumption in 515 that Bucks County is an "urban area" which is the only kind of area where 515 permits covenanting. He questioned, too, how assessors would decide upon "fair market value" without proper guidelines. He thought the farmer should be allowed to covenant for all his land including forests and streams, not just that part of the land used for farming. He wanted a better law, a clearer law.

A spokesman for a township civic association foresaw the loss of all agricultural land, if the proposed tax assessments go through. He thought 515 might slow down the loss of farms and open land. But he pleaded for more amendments and improvements in the law.

The speaker who won the most applause and agreement (representing a local Open Space organization) stated firmly that present housing laws permit only a given number of people per room in housing. She asked why we should not limit in the same way the number of people legally permitted to live in given areas. We do not know, she said, how many people can safely live in an area the size of Bucks County without unbearable pollution and stress. She pointed out that all the Bucks County streams are now polluted. Spinach and other leafy greens cannot be grown commercially — too much contamination by air pollutants. Last year petunias were blasted by air pollution at the famous Dupont Longwood Gardens nearby. The signs are ominous. Trees, grass, streams, hills, marshes must be preserved in order to preserve human life and an environment in which it can prosper.

Bucks County is deciding which way it will go in regard to covenanting for open space. Maryland, Connecticut, Delaware, New Jersey, Texas, California and Hawaii have laws similar to 515, with varying provisions in regard to time limits. Oregon, like Pennsylvania, favors a five-year roll-back on taxes for the covenanters. An excellent discussion of this highly controversial and important way of saving open space by manipulating tax assessments is available in chapter 6 of the pocket book, *The Last Landscape,* by William H. Whyte, listed in the bibliography. Mr. Whyte deals also with many other ways that have been tried in other communities. Any of them has serious faults. But there seem to be no methods that are faultless.

CHAPTER 8

Oil: The Environment Pays

"Our second great task is to control the American bureaucracy. As the problems of the nation and the states multiplied, the laws became more prolix and the discretion granted the administrators became greater and greater. Licenses or permits are issued if the agency deems it to be 'in the public interest'. Management of national forests and national parks is left to federal agencies which in turn promulgate regulations governing the use of these properties but seldom allow a public voice to be heard against any plan of the agency.

"The examples are legion and they cover a wide range of subjects from food stamps, to highway locations, to spraying of forests or grasslands to eliminate certain species of trees or shrubs, to the location of missile bases, to the disposal of sewage or industrial wastes, to the granting of off-shore leases."

Justice William Douglas
in *Points of Rebellion*

"Upon the motion of the Indiana State Board of Health, thirty-three of the principal citizens of Whiting, Indiana have been arrested under an indictment for maintaining nuisances prejudicial to the public health; in addition a summons has been served upon the Standard Oil Company in an action alleging that it allows impurities to flow into Lake Michigan, thus polluting the water supply of adjacent towns and cities."

Journal of the American Medical Association
August 4, 1894 (Yes, way back then!)

In the winter of 1970 the *San Luis Obispo Telegram* printed a resume of the situation in Santa Barbara, California, where in 1969 oil leaking wells in the Santa Barbara channel fouled the beaches in that affluent community.

Here is the story:

"Every major state officeholder or officeseeker who knows the facts of political life will be here next Wednesday for a big blowout marking an even bigger blowout — the first anniversary of the great oil spill.

"Speakers will talk to the children in every public school about getting the oil wells out of the Santa Barbara Channel lest another massive leak drench the magnificent coastline again.

"Former Secretary of Interior Stewart Udall, who approved leasing the oil tracts in federal waters and has since called it his own 'Bay of Pigs,' will be on hand for the official presentation of 'The Santa Barbara Declaration of Environmental Rights.'

"This drowsy town, something of a Palm Beach of the Pacific, has raised such an outcry against oil that there are signs it is finally being listened to in the Nixon administration.

"On the last day of 1969, Fred L. Hartley, president of the Union Oil Co., announced plans to install a third giant drilling platform in the channel. Hartley said that Platform C would be put into operation as soon as possible.

"A few days later, the Interior Department in Washington ordered Union Oil not to install the platform. The $7 million rig still sits in Vancouver where it was built and there is reason to question whether the federal government will ever approve its installation.

"The drive to close down all oil operations in the federal offshore waters has become such an emotional matter and the whole question of environment and anti-pollution is such an 'in' issue politically that two basic points tend to be forgotten:

"— The federal government invited the oil companies to undertake drilling in the channel. It received $603 million for the leases. Adding the investment made since and the expenses of removal, it would cost more than $1 billion to halt operations and it would come out of every taxpayer's pocket.

"— A special presidential panel of scientists and oil technicians studied the Jan. 28 spill and recommended that the best method of preventing continued leakage was to pump out the huge pool of oil as quickly as possible.

"— There are 14 other platforms being operated inside the three-mile zone under the jurisdiction of the state of California but no clamor is discernible for their removal. The State Assembly did, however, vote 64–0 for a resolution calling on the federal government to halt oil operations in its waters.

"The subject of oil has become such a hot issue in Santa Barbara that it is difficult to get straight answers to rather simple questions.

"On one point there is agreement. The shoreline of this gleaming Spanish-styled town was an unholy mess last January and February. A sheet of glob coated the beaches, blackened the rocks, stuck to the hulls of 1,000 boats in the harbor and gave off a nauseating stench.

"An estimated 800,000 gallons of oil came from a break in the ocean bed at Platform A where a new well was being drilled by Union which is doing the actual operations although the tract was leased in conjunction with Gulf, Mobil and Texaco.

"At one time, the spill covered an area of roughly 200 square miles of ocean before the well was finally capped with tons of cement Feb. 5.

"It killed thousands of birds, most of them western grebes whose feathers and wings became doused with oil when they dived into the water. Commercial fishing came to a halt because nets became fouled with goo when thrown into the sea.

"From that point on, it is difficult to find agreement on virtually anything.

"Union Oil acknowledged its responsibility for the debacle and undertook a cleanup job which eventually cost about $5 million. The tremendous rainstorms of the winter compounded its task because torrents from the coast mountains had swept an enormous amount of debris into the ocean and it had floated ashore, hundreds of trees and logs and other vegetation with an oil coating.

"Union estimated it removed 30,000 tons of debris. At one time it had approximately 2,000 men working on cleanup including many of the unemployed fishermen. The most effective method proved to be spreading straw on the sand to soak up the goo and then removing it. Rocks were subjected to various detergents and blasting.

"The visitor to Santa Barbara today will find the beaches and shoreline with no more trace of oil than any other section of the Southern California coast. There are many who contend that when the winds come in from the ocean at full force, the seas uncover a layer of oil that still lies about 10 inches beneath the surface, but you can find just as many others who say the beaches are no more affected by oil than they have been for years.

"The publicity given to the spill resulted in a sharp jolt to tourism. Stanley C. Lowry, general manager of the Chamber of Commerce, estimates the number of visitors was down about eight percent last year whereas Santa Barbara had anticipated an eight percent increase.

"Robert G. Kaneen, inspector for the California Department of Fish and Game, says that approximately 3,500 birds died. Members of the Audubon Society say that was the number of bodies of birds found and contend that the actual loss — as indicated by the smallness of migratory flocks this year — was thousands more than that.

"There is particular controversy over the effect of the spill on the unique seal and sea lion population of 30,000 to 40,000 animals on San Miguel Island, about 45 miles from the site of the break. First reports were that hundreds of seals, particularly pups, died after being covered with oil. One reporter who went there at the time contends that is absolutely correct.

"Donald M. Robinson, superintendent of the Channel Islands National Monument, says that autopsies have failed to establish that a single animal died because of oil. Robinson says there is always a high infant mortality rate among the seals and that there were no more carcasses than are to be found there any year.

"Robinson also says that, in view of prevailing wind and sea conditions, he believes the oil which washed ashore on San Miguel did not come from the Union Oil leak. It is worthy of note that Robinson is an employe of the Interior Department and that Secretary Walter Hickel has taken a dim view of all the bad publicity surrounding the Santa Barbara incident.

"Fisheries expert Kaneen says the pollution did not cause any long-range damage to fishing in the area.

"The anti-oil people say these discrepancies are not the important thing, anyway. Their stand is that there was a disaster and that it will occur again if oil drilling is not halted, particularly should there be an earthquake in the channel area.

"The most vehement of the protesters is an organization known as GOO (Get Oil Out) which has about 1,200 members and says it has collected 175,000 signatures to a petition calling on the government to reverse itself on the decision to drill in the channel.

"Harold Beveridge, wealthy head of a large research firm here, is first vice president of the group.

"Beveridge says the oil interests must be bought out no matter what the cost, perhaps by giving them leases on other federally owned oil land in return. Beveridge also is highly skeptical of the theory that only by continuing pumping can oil leakage be contained. He contends that state or federal technicians should test that finding by taking over the wells and halting operations for a trial period.

"Sen. Edmund S. Muskie, the 1968 Democratic vice presidential nominee, announced in Washington last week that he would introduce legislation in this session of Congress to authorize the federal government to buy back all the oil leases.

"But in Santa Barbara, it boils down to one slogan — GOO (Get Oil Out)."

January 20, 1970 two hundred students at Santa Barbara, California blocked access to the city's main pier overnight in a sit-in demonstration protesting the oil operations in the channel. The students sat down across the road. Picket signs said, "We don't water your gas, so don't oil our water," and "We're sick of breathing garbage."

January 20, 1970, the Santa Barbara County Board of Supervisors fired the county petroleum engineer because of published reports that he had been involved in real estate dealings that put him under obligations to the operators of the offshore drilling job that caused the oil spills.

Those of us who worry about oil pollution were something more than horrified when we learned (August, 1969) that Standard Oil of New Jersey was fitting a tanker (the *Manhattan*) with special ice breaker equipment and sending it to the Arctic to prove that all that fabulous oil treasure beneath the ice up there could be hauled back through the frozen waters with no risk. No risk at all!

The invincible ship, the *Manhattan,* ran into trouble ten miles off the coast of Delaware on a trial run, when she "limped back to port using only one of her two screws because of damage to the port power train," according to the *New York Times* for August 4, 1969. But she took off for the Arctic in August.

We followed her progress through the ice. We watched her crew members when they landed, when they appeared on TV talk shows and game shows. We read in ecstatic prose in full page ads in the *New York Times* and goodness knows how many other newspapers that the voyage of this well-equipped ship was a total magnificent success, a flawless achievement which went exactly as planned and proved that no harm could possibly come to the Arctic environment through such voyages. Let's have a whole fleet of tankers, was the cry. The *Manhattan* has showed us how!

It developed, after the *Manhattan* returned, that there was a hole in its prow through which two trucks could be driven. This was the "flawless" engineering feat! The Conservation Advisor of the oil company told me in a letter that, of course, such a hole might be expected! The *Manhattan* was an existing tanker, not specifically designed for this service. "New tankers . . . . would have hulls of high strength steel capable of operating in these cold waters." The steel ring that had been added to the *Manhattan* to prevent its being shattered by the ice had held and the hole had nothing to do with all this! "No, the holes were not planned," he wrote, "but we understand why the ice punctured the *Manhattan*'s hull. A new ship would be able to resist the ice pressure throughout its hull."

On March 4, 1970 the *Wall Street Journal* reported that the *Manhattan* would once again be sent into the Arctic oil fields. Not a newly designed tanker, you understand, "able to resist the ice pressure throughout its hull", but the same tired old *Manhattan* which had just taken this terrible beating. The *Journal* went on to say that the Canadian government had reached "general agreement" on the second voyage. . . . "The hole has been repaired but time hasn't permitted any extension of hull strengthening . . . the Canadian government will likely ask that oil be stored in the most protected parts of the vessel."

All anyone can do, apparently, is to sit and wait for the unspeakable accident that will occur. It seems inevitable that eventually an oil tanker will crack in the ice and millions of gallons of oil will be dumped into the Arctic waters. No one has the slightest idea of what the total environmental effect will be. Considering the delicate ecological balance of that part of the world, the total effect may be the end of all life on the planet. Literally, no one knows. Whether polar ice caps would melt, whether devastating floods would occur throughout the earth, no one, literally, knows. We are not fooling around here with a little oil slick that may mar some pretty beaches. This is the Arctic, whose ecology is almost entirely unknown and unexplored. In centuries of study, scientists might not be able to give all the answers to all the questions that arise from such a venture as this. Yet the oil company is proceeding on its way, its publicity department churning out full page ads in color on the magnificent technological achievements of the Manhattan and the complete safety of the entire operation.

Does the Arctic Ocean belong to the Standard Oil Company? Why is it not possible to convoke a meeting of representatives of every country in the world to protest the outrageous chance that is being taken on possible catastrophe for all of us? There is a group circulating a petition to the United Nations asking for a Population and Environment Council which would take up things like this. If you want to help collect signatures, send to this address for copies of the petition:

> Volunteer Coordinating Center, United Nations Petition for the Human Environment, P. O. Box 869, Adelphi, Maryland, USA, 20783

Perhaps even more horrifying is the plan to bring oil from Alaska through a pipeline which will run through or over the Alaskan tundra carrying 2,000,000 gallons daily of hot oil over or through a frozen land.

Wallace Turner in the *New York Times* for July 5, 1969 outlined the reasons why such a proposal was an invitation to certain disaster. The tundra — the vast, treeless Arctic plain — is underlaid with frozen ground. The oil pipe will be sunk somehow into the frozen mass. The oil coursing through it will be hot. No one knows what the consequences will be — to the Arctic tundra, which is an extremely delicate ecosystem, or to the rest of the world in terms of climate, if all this delicate balance is disrupted. If the covering carpet of lichen and mosses is broken and the ice beneath exposed to the sun, it melts.

The fragile nature of the tundra is obvious in traces of what has been done to it already. Mr. Turner says, "The ice highway created tracks on the landscape now being pointed to by scientists and conservationists as illustrative of their concerns about upsetting the delicate ecology of the Arctic region. . . . The road becomes a barrier to movement of animals, scientists say. It is a potential source of heavy erosion by creating ditches and a source of stream and lake pollution . . . in the area where the . . . . highway can become a gradually widening scar . . ." Any scars left on the tundra by man do not heal, you see.

There is concern, too, about the Arctic animals which will, it seems, certainly meet the fate of all wild things once man begins his invasions. Grizzly bears, which are extremely rare, are shot when they approach camps of workmen. Any pipeline may inhibit the migrations of the caribou and other migrating animals. It is impossible to imagine what a break in the line, spilling millions of gallons of oil, will do to the surrounding countryside in the way of immeasurable and uncontainable pollution. The right-of-way for the line will be 100 to 200 feet wide. Even now there are thousands of empty 55 gallon oil drums "scattered across the tundra like beer cans at a picnic — 'Alaska's state flower', a writer called them in *Alaska Magazine.*" Garbage and sewage will be burned, the workmen say, or hauled to a spot on the Arctic Ocean where they will be dumped. The pipeline will cost an estimated 900 million dollars.

On April 2, 1970 a federal judge issued a restraining order which would prohibit the Secretary of Interior from issuing construction permits for the pipeline and the road. Five Alaskan villages have sought permanent injunction against both. On Earth Day, April 22, 1970, Former Secretary Hickel, speaking at the University of Alaska, announced that the permit would be granted, just as soon as terms and conditions had been agreed upon and all requirements of the law have been met. He said, further, that he "will make certain the pipeline can never become an environmental hazard."

The mind boggles at even commenting on such a

statement when one reads in the *Times* five days later that William T. Pecora, director of the U. S. Geological Survey, told a group of 120 prominent Alaskans, in Washington to promote the pipeline, that his agency was in unanimous agreement that it was unsafe to bury the hot line in the permafrost for 90 to 95 per cent of the 800 miles across the Arctic tundra. The U. S. Geological Survey is, of course, part of the Department of Interior.

Mr. Pecora told them further that for months his experts had been telling the oil people that the pipeline could not be buried and had urged them to put it above ground. If they insist on burying it, he said, they must choose another route, for the survey will not permit them to do it on this route. According to the *Times* "he was highly critical of the way the oil companies had handled the plans for the pipeline. They had chosen the route without prior consultation with the Department of Interior of the State of Alaska and had refused to consider a piecemeal right-of-way, insisting on a grant of the entire right-of-way. And they have submitted no design plans — only route maps.

"At one point," he said, "the consortium's engineers had conceded there was a 50–50 chance of their proposed line's breaking because of the melting of the permafrost under the pipe." Some of the Alaskans were upset, says the *Times*, at the indifference to environmental damage by both the oil companies and some of their colleagues.

What can you do to protest this high-handed, ruthless exploitation of an entire state — our last remaining wilderness — as well as a project endangering all the surrounding waters, possibly all life on earth? You can boycott all products sold by Standard Oil. Read labels.

Don't just carry out a quiet boycott without telling anyone. Write to Standard Oil. Tell them you are not buying any product of theirs until their unforgiveable activities in regard to the Alaska oil have ceased. They will probably send you a lot of elegant promotional material designed to convince you that what they are doing will be beneficial in every way to every living thing in Alaska. Throw this away without reading it, unless you feel equipped to answer it.

A note in the *New York Times* for May 13, 1970 stated that the American Heritage Society, whose members include readers and editors of *American Heritage* magazine, announced 12 conservation awards totalling $50,000. The top prize, $25,000 was awarded to the Alaska Conservation Society. This group is working to protect the state's natural environment, which it rightfully believes to be threatened by the recent discovery of oil in Alaska. This is not much money for fighting Standard Oil and, apparently, the Department of Interior as well. But it will help.

Keep in mind, when you are planning conservation work, that money is available from a number of organizations and from some government agencies if your project impresses them as worthwhile.

Oil slicks and oil spills are not just the result of accidents. Most of them are caused by deliberate dumping of oil or plain carelessness in the operation of wells, tankers, ships at sea or installations on land.

Here are some of the stories of oil spills I collected from several papers over a few months around the end of 1969 and the beginning of 1970. Each one represents a local tragedy of immeasurable dimensions. Each adds its little or its lot to the worldwide pollution of waterways with oil which has grown, in the past few years, into one of the major problems confronting us. A broken oil pipeline killed more than 10,000 fish in a Carbon County, Pennsylvania stream in an oilslick that covered about five miles of the water. The line was broken by a bulldozer clearing trees from a dam construction. In the newspaper report nobody appeared to think that any damage would be collected or any fines imposed. The stream is a favorite trout stream, stocked with 13,200 trout that spring. Dead muskrats, turtles and snakes were also found in abundance.

A fuel tank leaked oil into the East River in New York, leaving a coating of oil across New York Bay and as far as the Staten Island shore. The state of Florida filed a 250-million dollar suit against the Humble Oil Company and the owners of a tanker which spilled oil into Tampa Bay. The state estimated the loss in dollars in the neighborhood of a billion dollars.

An oil slick in the Schuylkill River, Pennsylvania, coming from a reclamation pond near the river on which migrating birds alight, brought damage and death to Canada geese. Oil from a damaged barge flowed down the St. Johns River near Jacksonville, Florida, threatening one wildlife refuge and, across the state on the Gulf side, a tar-like substance rolled along the St. Marks River in another wildlife preserve.

From England came news of five big oil slicks contaminating the waters of Southeast Scotland. An article in *New Scientist* tells of fruitless efforts to get authorities even to look for the source of the slicks, while conservationists and wildlife experts worked around the clock trying to save the lives of sea birds. It was estimated that possibly 11,000 had died.

The *New York Times* reported that the source of the oil slick that killed nearly 1,000 waterfowl off Martha's Vineyard will probably never be identified. A spokesman for the Federal Water Pollution Control Administration said that, since 1966, there have been no successful prosecutions for water pollution under the 1966 provisions which require proof of negligence.

An Oakland, California oil spill came from a small amount of turbine fuel that seeped into a creek from a Shell Oil Company pipeline. The break, we are told, was caused by additional movement in the sliding East Oakland hills where several homes have already slipped away.

Here is a news release from Harrisburg, Pa. "Every day oil flows out of railroad yards and shops at Enola and dribbles into the Susquehanna River where it floats south into Chesapeake Bay. Every day a county fish agent takes a sample of the oily waters and files another criminal charge against the Penn Central Railroad for violating Pennsylvania's Clean Streams law. The oil spill has been polluting the river for 20 years. In these 20 years the railroad has paid a total of $1200 fine."

Thousands of dead birds were strewn over a southwest Alaska shoreline as agents sought to find the source of the oil slick that had caused the destruction. A twenty-mile square area near St. Petersburg, Florida, was devastated by an oil spill from a tanker which ran aground. The Coast Guard decided against using chemicals which might make the situation worse.

Another oil spill near Alaska destroyed tens of thousands of birds, whales, otters, seals and other wildlife. The source of the spill is unknown. One hundred miles of blackened shore line off Nova Scotia are the permanent legacy of a tanker aground. Thousands of sea birds died.

In February, 1970, 12 oil wells owned by Chevron Oil Company went out of control near New Orleans, spilling 600 to 1000 barrels of oil a day and resulting in an oil slick some 85 square miles. The company dumped barrels and barrels of chemicals that cause the oil to sink below the surface of the water. The U. S. Geological survey had given permission to use the chemicals, although a pollution expert from the Department of Interior said that the chemicals would probably cause more loss of life in the sea than the oil would. The Director of Louisiana Wildlife and Fisheries Commission agreed with him.

Thousands of gallons of oil a day poured from one well because the well was operating without a small device called a storm choke. The gadget costs $500. Federal regulations require that oil wells have them.

On March 2, 1970 former Secretary Hickel announced that federal inspection of the 12 oil wells disclosed 147 violations of federal regulations. No word was said as to whose responsibility it is to enforce the regulations. Presumably the Department of Interior. Hickel announced that he might ask the Justice Department to bring suit against Chevron.

The oil threatened 400,000 acres of oyster beds and a wildlife sanctuary sheltering some 6000 seabirds. Oystermen filed a law suit against the oil company asking for 31½ million dollars in damages. The state of Louisiana planned to bring suit against both the oil company and the federal government which had not given proper supervision to the operation. In May, 1970 a federal grand jury indicted Chevron Oil Company on charges of "knowingly and willfully" failing to install safety devices that, according to some federal experts, could have prevented the fire and subsequent oil spill. The grand jury stated that the oil company had failed to install safety devices on 90 of the 178 wells in the block. This is the first time legal action has been brought against anyone for oil pollution, although the law under which the action was brought was passed in 1953.

The grand jury charged Chevron Oil with 900 separate offenses. If convicted, the company could, under the law, face fines up to $1.8 million. The regulations which have been in effect since 1954 were further tightened on August 22, 1969 because of the Santa Barbara oil spill. Six days later, the Geological Survey's supervisor for the Gulf Coast region made the new regulations even more rigid and specific. Most of the alleged offenses involved violations of that Gulf Coast order.

The President of Chevron Oil was quoted by the *New York Times* as saying, "We are confident that when the case is tried, we will be completely vindicated."

These are stories collected in casual reading of several newspapers and magazines. What the final total must be each month staggers the imagination for, of course, only a small number of spills make any headlines. The rest just ooze away, contributing every day a little more death and destruction — not just to wildlife and birds, remember, but to everything that lives, for we are all bound together in an ecosystem. When one part of that system becomes so befouled with any contaminant that it cannot function, all the rest of us suffer. The idea of all the oceans of the world becoming so polluted that they can no longer produce food for us to eat or oxygen for us to breathe seems impossible. Yet it is a very real possibility — right now.

You sense it when you walk a white sand beach in New Jersey and find, when you come home, that your feet are slippery with oil which must be scrubbed off with soap before you can put on socks. This is not the site of any accident or calamity. This is just the average day's quota of oil that washes up on the white resort beaches of New Jersey. Where does it come from? No one knows. Presumably every ship that passes, every little local fishing boat and pleasure boat dumps oil into the water whenever and wherever its owner pleases.

According to an editorial in the *New York Times* for February 21, 1970, "far more damage is being done by casual and deliberate violations than by dramatic spills from wrecked vessels. Ships routinely, but unobserved, discharge their oil wastes into the sea, and tankers, cleaning out their cargo space after a haul, dump the oil wash into the ocean."

On January 16, 1970, a leading authority on the origin and fate of oil slicks said that the spillages have reached the point where the entire world ocean is affected. Petroleum constituents, some suspected of being cancer-causing, are entering the ocean food chain and eventually could reach dining room tables. Dr. Max Blumer of Woods Hole, formerly with the Royal Dutch Shell Oil Company, said that we are facing the loss of food from the seas — just at the time when our rising population makes this fine high-protein food essential.

He said further that it is quite possible, by analyzing the ingredients of the oil spill, to determine whence it comes.

He told of a research trip by Woods Hole scientists who dragged the Sargasso Sea for plant and animal life to study. Within two hours their nets became so fouled with oil that they had to be cleaned with a strong solvent. "Oil-tar lumps more than 2 inches thick were there. In an area 500 miles south-southwest of Bermuda the oil was so thick that towing had to be suspended." No accidents, no dumping. Just oil floating around on the open ocean.

Dr. Blumer said that annual world oil production is about 1,800 million metric tons *of which at least 60 per cent travels the sea in tankers.* The total spillage, from accidents, flushing of bilges and tanks is, he estimates, about a million tons. Since this does not include spills like that at Santa Barbara and industrial dumping into harbors and rivers, the total amount of oil on all the waterways of the world is probably *10 to 100 times more than that!*

On April 4, 1970 President Nixon signed a bill which "sharply increases penalties for oil spills and extends the liability for cleaning them up." Senator Muskie was the chief author and proponent of the bill. As Mr. Nixon signed it, he carefully noted the names of everyone who had been concerned in its passage and said, "If the environment doesn't improve, then you're to blame."

The new law introduces a new principle — absolute liability "without regard to whether any such act or omission was or was not negligent." The owner of the vessel is liable up to 14 million dollars. And any owner of any onshore or offshore facility who knowingly discharges oil is liable to a fine up to $10,000 for each offense, and is subject to the same fine if he fails to notify the appropriate federal agency that a spill has occurred. The new law authorizes a 35 million dollar revolving fund to finance government clean-up activities.

If the enforcement of laws to restrict air and water pollution appears to present formidable difficulties, what can be said about this law to prevent oil spills? Who, except for the ship's personnel, will know whether or not any ship at sea is dumping oil? Who will know whether small private boats are dumping or leaking oil? If a big oil slick comes drifting in, it may be possible, as Dr. Blumer states, to identify the kind of oil and fix the blame. But what of oil that coats the shores of every country in the world coming from heavens knows how many vessels in how many seas?

How do we begin to enforce the law as it pertains to the leaking railroad yards of the Penn Central Railroad? If the oil spill has been polluting the river for 20 years and nobody has done anything much about it, what hope is there that a new federal law will suddenly be invoked in Harrisburg, Pa.? And what of all the criminal charges already filed against the railroad? If there is no intent on the part of state authorities to pursue any of these charges, why should we expect that federal agents will decide to crack down on a small railroad yard and begin to levy fines?

The fines, which appear to be very large, but which are negligible compared to the figures being mentioned in damage suits, will be used by the federal government to "clean up" the damage. But how do you clean up damage from an extensive oil spill? How do you resurrect the birds, the seals, the otters that have died? How do you reconstruct the infinitely delicate and complex web of life that exists on and beneath the surface of the water, which is shattered? We know almost nothing of what goes on beneath the sea, almost nothing of the effects of oil on all this ecosystem. Oceanography is a step-child among the sciences. Money for researches goes to disciplines where some profit will soon be seen as a result. Just sitting around studying what goes on in the water is obviously not very profitable.

Unless, of course, it means life or death. And apparently it does. As long ago as 1968, Dr. LaMont Cole, Professor of Ecology at Cornell University, told us that marine organisms suspended near the surface of the water produce 70 percent or more of the world's oxygen which comes from green plants. We are now adding carbon dioxide to the atmosphere more rapidly than the oceans can assimilate it. "The carbon-oxygen relationship is essential to photosynthesis and thus to the maintenance of all life. But should this relationship be altered, should the balance between the two be upset, life as we know it would be impossible. Man's actions today are bringing this imbalance upon us", said Dr. Cole in the *New York Times,* March 31, 1968.

We are dumping vast quantities of pollutants into the oceans. Said Dr. Cole, "According to one estimate by the United States Food and Drug Administration these include a half-million substances; many are of recent origin, including biologically active materials such as pesticides, radioisotopes and detergents to which the ocean's living forms have never before had to try to adapt. No more than a minute fraction of these substances or the combinations of them have been tested for toxicity to life — to the diatoms, the microscopic marine plants that produce most of the earth's oxygen, or to the bacteria and microorganisms involved in the nitrogen cycle.

"If the tanker Torrey Canyon had been carrying a concentrated herbicide instead of petroleum, could photosynthesis (the process of a plant's producing oxygen) have been stopped? Again, we don't know, but Berkner is said to have believed that a very few instances of herbicide pollution, occurring in certain areas of the ocean that are high in photosynthetic activity, might cause the ultimate disaster." Human life would disappear from the planet in the space of time it took for each of us individually to run out of oxygen. There is no way of knowing how long the oxygen produced by land plants would last. We are destroying trees and other green things on earth just as fast as we can pave over large areas into shopping centers, highways and housing developments.

On December 16, 1969, at a conference of government officials and oil industry men, it was generally agreed that there is just no way to clean up oil spills. One industry spokesman said that present methods were "primitive." The best idea anybody has had is to strew the stricken waters with straw, let the oil collect on it, then rake up the straw and burn it. No one at the conference had any better idea. One man from the Federal Water Pollution Control Commission suggested the possibility of turning the oil into a jellied state when an accident occurs. This would prevent its spilling out and would make it easier to collect whatever had spilled out. The cost of such a process would be 10 cents a gallon, or slightly more than the cost of the oil itself.

Unfortunately nobody knows how to turn the jellied oil back into liquid oil again, after it has been collected.

In the midst of this fantastic kind of conversation the experts have on the subject of oil spills, it is somehow not surprising — but it shakes you to the core — to find a beautiful full-color ad headed "How to keep America beautiful — plant a lawn in a deep freeze". The ad goes on to say, "The North Alaskan Tundra is topped by a fragile mat of green growth. If you break it, heat from the never-fading Midnight Sun slowly turns the frozen mud into a swamp. Water runs. And irreparable erosion could occur. For that land has little ability to regrow its ground cover. This year, ARCO began an experiment to allow the Tundra to heal itself. Thirteen strains of winter-hardy grass have been seeded into a 20-acre Arctic lawn. And a special fertilizer, developed and made by an ARCO plant, will help it grow — all so that the tracks of man, as he searches and develops the riches of the wilds, will not mar or destroy as well. It's just one of the many steps ARCO is taking to see to it that the world we live in is just a little bit better than when we started." ARCO is, of course, The New Atlantic Richfield Company — ARCO.

You read it and then you re-read it. Yes, there's no way to misinterpret what it says. Engineers at Richfield have decided to "improve" the Arctic tundra, in the name of all of us. To make the world just a little bit better place to live in, they have undertaken an experiment involving special grass and a special fertilizer which will make over the tundra into a nice, simple, agreeable place where oil pipelines and highways can crisscross the continent without disturbing a thing! It seems incredible that anyone — even a child — could make such a lunatic proposal at this moment in history when the word ecology is rapidly becoming a household word, and the Arctic tundra is well known as the most delicate, most easily unbalanced ecosystem on the planet. Never mind, we'll plant a nice lawn there and "civilize" it!

The oil company not only makes this proposal. It goes right ahead with the experiment, spending probably millions of dollars that might instead be spent to determine some harmless sure-fire way of getting the oil out of Alaska *without disturbing anything in any ecosystem!* It does all this without asking permission or (apparently) advice from anyone. And it announces this as a glorious technological achievement in an expensive, full color ad!

The citizens of St. Petersburg, Florida published in the *New York Times* for March 12, 1970 what I believe to be one of the most effective and heart-breaking ads ever published. Illustrated with a photograph of a benevolent pair of hands cleaning the oil from an oil-soaked duck, and the headline "Don't die, ducky, don't die", it told the story of the oil slick catastrophe at St. Petersburg and of the help that came from all over the community as the entire population rallied in an effort to save the sea birds and the beaches.

Says the ad, "The beaches didn't die, though many birds did. Some beaches were scarred by the black slick, but not deeply or permanently. But we were. We the people of St. Petersburg. And we vowed 'Never again'. Never again to take for granted all the beauty Nature has given us with our birds and our beaches. It hurts us that so many birds had to suffer and die to open our eyes. But the pitiful picture of water fowl dying in the very same waters that they had fished so peacefully just the day before brought us face-to-face for the first time with the full meaning of pollution — showed us how very quickly man's carelessness can change all the natural beauty we take so very much for granted . . ." There's much more.

Single copies of the ad or quantity reprints are obtainable from: *Don't Let the Ducks Die,* Office of Public Information, City Hall, St. Petersburg, Florida 33701.

Although the ad talks about the oil spill at St. Petersburg, it is aimed at all pollution everywhere. You can use this ad locally when you are fighting other kinds of pollution. Or maybe you're fighting oil pollution in your locality, too! The other night I mentioned to a friend (an ardent conservationist) the difficulty I had writing this chapter because there seems to be no hope on the immediate horizon for anything at all to prevent or alleviate oil spills. He said well, it's good that we live inland and there are no spills here to worry about. He left me wondering when was the last time he looked into the Lehigh River, or the Susquehanna or the Delaware.

CHAPTER 9

The Half-Life of Plutonium Is 24,000 Years

". . . . the design and construction of a nuclear reactor epitomizes all the skills of modern science and technology. However, once it begins to operate, it threatens rivers and lakes with its heated waters and human bodies with radiation. . . . Unless we learn to match our technological power with an increased understanding of what it is doing to the natural world, we may stress the living environment to the point of collapse, and find that it will no longer support us . . . We are still in a period of grace. In that time, let us hope, we can overcome the myth of omnipotence, and learn that the proper use of science is not to conquer the world, but to live in it."

Barry Commoner
Environment
March, 1969

"Of all our natural resources, minds are the most precious. Two-thirds of our trained minds available for exploring scientific and technical frontiers, we are told by the President, are absorbed by the space, defense, and atomic energy activities of our country.

The rest of America's needs are relatively impoverished, neglected and starved."

David Lilienthal
former head of the Atomic Energy Commission

"The governor (Rockefeller) added he's been told by his science adviser, Mr. Edward Teller, the nuclear physicist known as 'the father of the H-Bomb' that 'someday one of these places is going to blow up' in an atomic explosion."

New York Post
March 29, 1967

"We have become reluctant to make moral judgments, to impose restraints on those who would wreck society, to accept any self-restraint on our own behavior."

Vermont Royster

In the July 16, 1970 issue of *Environmental Action,* published by the group of young people in Washington which sparked Earth Day, appeared a desperate letter to the editor from Mr. and Mrs. Kenneth Leslie, Jr., of Tunkhannock, Pennsylvania. They wrote in part, "We in this area of Wyoming Valley are trying frantically to oppose a 100 megawatt nuclear reactor plant, the largest under construction and the first of a new fast breeder reactor series. In this respect, we need your help. Our Environmental Control Committee is trying to do their best, but face financial and other difficulties, the majority of these being ignorance on the part of the communities involved in regard to the risks such a plant could cause. We have a number of colleges and institutions nearby willing to help but we do not know what course of action we can take or how to organize such a 'teach-in' for this purpose."

That was in July. In October we heard that Dr. John Gofman, Professor of Medical Physics at the University of California and Research Associate at the Lawrence Radiation Laboratory, was scheduled to speak at several colleges which turned out to be the ones the Leslies mentioned. Dr. Gofman, currently at the center of a controversy over what official limits of radiation exposure should be, spoke on radioactive pollution and health. He was in the area for two days, giving press interviews, speaking everywhere a meeting could be organized, and appearing on a panel discussion on the local TV station, with an adversary from the University of Pennsylvania, a radiologist who pooh-poohed Dr. Gofman's fears for human health, if present official levels for radiation exposure are retained.

The Citizens Committee for Environmental Concern was organized at Tunkhannock in October of the previous year to study the effects of nuclear power plants on the environment. The Committee came to the conclusion that they should oppose the building of the reactor planned for a location near Tunkhannock and recommend a moratorium on the entire nuclear power program "until the technology is developed to the point where all risks we are now asked to tolerate will be eliminated."

"We probably have the most extensive compilation of reference material on nuclear reactors in the state. Much of this literature is available . . . to anyone interested in learning more about the problem — the long term radiation effects from nuclear power plants," said an article in the newsletter of a local conservation group, H.E.L.P. (Help Eliminate Life Pollutants). The Committee goes on to say, "During the past summer, we have also secured over 5,200 names of citizens in the immediate area on a petition opposing the construction of the . . . reactor. We are now in the process of distributing this petition anywhere within a 60-mile radius."

In one year the concerned committee in this very small community (about 3,000 people) became a fighting force, able to help others faced with a reactor project, collecting signatures on petitions and arranging excellent, provocative community information programs with speakers of Dr. Gofman's caliber.

They started out, these Pennsylvania folks, without any more knowledge than the rest of us have of the vocabulary of radiation pollution or nuclear reactors. Can you, the reader of this book, define and state that you clearly understand the meaning of words like megawatt, fast breeder reactor, long-term radiation effects, to say nothing of what you get into later: words like radioisotope, radionuclide, rad, rem, millirem, fission, fusion, mutations, DNA, gamma rays, alpha rays and so on?

If the folks in Tunkhannock mastered this difficult terminology and came to understand the extraordinarily complex concepts that go with radiation and nuclear power plants, then the rest of us can, too — if we care enough to do it. Certainly those people who are told unceremoniously that the new nuclear power plant will be only a few miles from their home have a greater incentive than the rest of us for learning as much as they can about nuclear reactors real fast

But, we might as well face it, the power utilities and the AEC have decided that future electric power will be produced by nuclear power plants. Remember the estimate we gave in chapter 5 that, in 200 years, if we continue to double the rate of our use of electricity, as we are now doing, the entire land area of the USA will be covered with power plants — with not even one spot remaining — for people to live. If there isn't a nuclear power plant within 50 miles of your home at this moment, it seems safe to say that sometime in the near future there will be.

The basic facts are these. Power plants which burn fossil fuels (coal, gas and oil) cause air pollution and thermal or heat pollution. The air pollution comes from the burning process. The heat pollution arises because these plants must be cooled either by air or water. The heated air or water — in the vast quantities in which it is used — may change the climate or may heat up waterways to such an extent that aquatic life becomes impossible. In addition to these environmental objections to fossil fuel plants, we are told we are running out of these fuels and must eventually turn to new ones.

Nuclear power seems full of promise. (Remember how exultant we all were when the president announced the beginning of the era of the "peaceful atom"?) Nuclear power plants produce power by fission. This is the process by which the nucleus of an atom is split, producing radioactivity and great energy. "Fission products" are the split parts of this atom, including almost 200 different radioactive materials. It's the fission products we worry about, in terms of radiation pollution.

There is no debate about the fact that any nuclear power plant produces radiation pollution. The AEC admits this and goes on to point out that the amount of this pollution is so small it poses no risk to anyone living in the vicinity of a nuclear power plant. The radiation may be in the air or in the cooling water which, after it has cooled the plant reactor, flows back into the river, lake or bay from which it was pumped.

It is immediately obvious that aquatic animals concentrate the radioactive pollutants. The small plants and animals take it in with their food, larger fish and shellfish concentrate it when they eat the smaller ones, and so on. It is also obvious that an accident at a nuclear power plant can result in such horrors as only science fiction stories ever relate — from a slight leak of a highly dangerous or a less dangerous contaminant, to a fire, an act of sabotage, or an explosion which could devastate the country for many miles around and make it uninhabitable for possibly thousands of years, depending on the nature of the radioactivity released.

The figures given, even by AEC experts, on the possible damage such an accident could cause, are too overpowering to be grasped by the non-scientific reader. Suffice it to say that AEC experts said at the beginning of their work that no nuclear power plant should ever be placed near a center of population. The danger is too great. In the years that followed they proposed nuclear power plants in the center of New York City and — it seems almost impossible to believe — directly on the earthquake fault in southern California which has produced all of California's earthquakes. Dr. Edward Teller, who promotes nuclear energy possibly more enthusiastically than any other expert, believes that all nuclear power plants should be underground. It is too dangerous to site them above ground, he says.*

There is general agreement among most radiation experts that all radiation is harmful to some extent, that is, that there is no threshhold below which we can confidently say "Well, any radiation below this level can't possibly hurt anybody." We have no basis on which to form such an assumption. So we must assume that we should avoid all exposure to radiation, if that were possible.

There is something called "background radiation" which always comes up when you get into a discussion on radiation pollution. This is the radioactivity naturally present in the world — all the radiation all our ancestors have been exposed to for ages before man discovered how to split the atom. Part of background radiation is cosmic rays, from outer space. You can think of them in terms of x-rays. The earth is constantly showered with these rays, so, ever since the beginning of time, every living thing has had its share of radiation from cosmic rays.

Certain kinds of rocks contain small amounts of radioactive material. In some areas of the world there are radioactive substances in drinking water. People who spend a great deal of time outdoors may get more radiation from cosmic rays than people who live mostly indoors. The sea-going man gets less background radiation than the mountain dweller, for cosmic rays are more intense at high altitudes.

* The *New York Times* reported on April 1, 1971 that the Air Force has used a nuclear power plant on Lake Michigan as a practice target in simulated low-level bombing runs. The planes fly at 500 feet, raising the possibility, or should I say the probability, of a crash into the plant. In January, 1971, a bomber, on such a run, crashed only 10 miles from the Michigan plant.

It's a good idea for the environmentally-minded to remember that the supersonic plane, flying at the altitudes which would make it economically feasible, will expose personnel and passengers to more damage from cosmic rays than those of us who stay nearer to sea level.

There is no way to avoid background radiation. Speakers refer often to certain levels of radiation exposure as being such-and-such a percent of background radiation. This does not make these levels safe. There is no reason to believe that background radiation is harmless. But there is nothing we can do about it and we just live with it.

Speakers and writers who defend the position that present permissible radiation levels are safe customarily tell us that human beings lived all these centuries with background radiation and it didn't hurt us, did it? So how can a bit of additional radiation — only a small percentage of background radiation — do us any appreciable harm?

Those experts who believe we should cut down sharply on present permissible levels of radiation put it this way: humanity and other living things have survived *in spite of background radiation, not because of it.* There is plenty of reason to believe that many, or perhaps most, of our diseases are the result of background radiation — that is, the injury by radiation to genetic material in our cells which controls heredity.

Some scientists are now convinced that our commonest diseases — cancer, hardening of the arteries, coronary heart conditions, diabetes, arthritis, schizophrenia — are inherited. That is, damage has been done to the genetic material in earlier generations which causes these disorders to appear in this generation. And — this is the most horrendous fact of all — *such damage to genes can never be repaired.*

Any set of parents who carry the damaged gene or genes which produce these aberrations, is bound to pass the inherited damage along to a given number of their children. And these children, if they live long enough to reproduce, are bound to bequeath the same damage to their children, and so on — *for all of future time!* We are not talking here about some contemporary plague that can be wiped out with a vaccine or a pill. *This damage is forever — unto all generations.* The only circumstance which can prevent future damage in the case of inherited disability is for the carrier of such damage to die before he or she can have children, or to take great pains and make great sacrifices to see that he or she does not have children. Which among us would ever be in favor of increasing our present burden of ill-health, in terms of human suffering? At this date, one out of every four Americans will have cancer at some time during his life. The figures on heart and circulatory conditions, diabetes and schizophrenia are equally appalling.

Now think in terms of economics. All these future sick people must be taken care of. We cannot increase the world-wide toll of illness without at the same time providing vast new amounts of money for hospitals, drugs, doctors, convalescent homes, nurses — and of course, the loss of manhours and productivity that goes with debility and illness. Unless we intend to turn over the largest part of our national budget to caring for the increasing numbers of sick people, we simply cannot afford to take steps which may cause these numbers to increase. The next time you read or hear that nuclear power plants will lower costs for us all because nuclear energy is cheap, add mentally the costs outlined above — the financial costs, and those of human suffering.

Professor Joshua Lederberg, Nobel prize winner geneticist of Stanford University, refers to the government as "the most dangerous genetic engineer". He believes that average exposure to the Federal Radiation Council allowable dose can ultimately result in an added burden of medical and health care costs due to genetically determined diseases which may range from one billion to 100 billion dollars annually.

Generally speaking, the harm done by radiation accumulates as the individual experiences greater exposure. That is, the potential harm of background radiation *is added* to the potential harm of dental and medical x-rays, plus the potential harm from the medical use of radioactive materials in diagnosis and treatment of disease, plus exposure to defective color TV sets, and microwave ovens, and every other exposure one has experienced to this most potent and still quite mysterious force.

When you are told that radiation from a nuclear power plant poses no threat to anyone in the surrounding community, keep in mind that no one knows how much exposure to radiation any one individual of that community may have had in his lifetime, from x-ray, from cosmic rays or from some other purely individual exposure. In other words, no one has any way of measuring what unknown burden of harm from radiation any one of us may already be carrying.

Each of the more than 200 radioactive elements involved in nuclear fission may present a hazard to a different part of the body if it concentrates there because of the way that particular substance behaves in the body. Strontium 90, which worried us during the bomb tests years ago and which is still present in small amounts in our food, seeks out bones once it is taken into the body. Radioactive iodine goes directly to the thyroid gland where it is a special menace to children because of their small size. Strontium 90 stays around for quite a long time. Its "half-life" is 28 years. The half-life of iodine 131 is only eight days. The half-life of plutonium is 24,000 years.

By "half-life" we mean the time that will elapse before half of any given amount of this radioactive substance will decay and disappear. It does not matter where the radioactive substance is — in the soil, air or water, in one's bones, teeth, thyroid gland or kidney, the radioactive material does not disappear until the time decreed for its disappearance, which may be hundreds of thousands of years.

In addition to the harm that may be done by exposure of one organ like the thyroid gland to considerable or small amounts of one radioactive substance, one must consider the overall radiation to which we are all subject, simply because we live in this world and our physicists developed new sources of radiation when the atom was split. In 1950 the International Commission on Radiation reviewed all the facts and defined the "permissible dose" of radiation as "that dose which, accumulated over a long period of time or resulting from a single exposure, which, in the light of present knowledge, carries a negligible probability of severe somatic or genetic injury (that is injury to the individual or to his descendants through heredity); furthermore it is such a dose that any effects that ensue more frequently are limited to those of a minor nature that would not be considered unacceptable by the exposed individual and by competent medical authorities."

A great many assumptions are made in this early definition which leave the individual out of it. How can any group of experts — international, national or local — decide for you what is the extent of personal physical damage you would consent to, for yourself and your descendants, for the sake of continuing with the peacetime use of atomic nuclear energy? How can any official body decide "Well, it's permissible for a given number of people to get cancer as a result of using nuclear power in peacetime, for the benefits that will be achieved make up for all this". Benefits to whom? The man dying of cancer really doesn't care very much whether he has the latest electrical gadgets arranged around his bed, or whether the Christmas tree lights are burning, now does he? Yet this seems to be, in essence, what we are told every time some expert from the AEC or the power companies tells us that "the risks are worth the benefits". What risks? To whom? What benefits? Whose benefits?

The Atomic Energy Commission is in the peculiar position of being a government bureau, charged with promoting to the utmost the use of nuclear energy and at the same time policing its own activities, its own safety standards, its own provisions against accidents, sabotage, and pure ignorance of what new complications may arise from any new nuclear technology. It has large appropriations of your money and mine to develop, in conjunction with private industry, an extensive, countrywide nuclear power industry. Huckstering is the word sometimes used by people who don't like the way the AEC goes about its job. And certainly speeches of the AEC hierarchy (and they make speeches all the time, everywhere) are remarkably like the insistent propaganda the advertising industry spreads around for cigarettes, cars, clothing, breakfast cereals and everything else.

They are the experts, they tell us, everything is under control, nobody needs to police their activities or lay down any regulations. They will regulate themselves. Certain fission products, the radioactive debris from power plants, are the most toxic substances in existence. So it seems to many of us that someone who is not employed by the AEC should be monitoring AEC installations and activities, to insure their perfect safety. *This is not the case.* The AEC itself monitors its own activities — in some cases in complete secrecy — and tells us cheerfully that everything is under control, no cause for worry about a thing.

Depending upon these same arrangements in other aspects of life, we would have no air pollution or water pollution abatement bureaus, no police, no FTC, no FDA, no Public Health Service, no Bureau of Standards. Everybody would be on the honor system to keep his part of the community safe, honest, unpolluted and ideal. It seems fairly obvious this would not work. The industry frantically promoting its own products seldom does much about banishing pollution from its operations until it is forced to do so by some separate, objective monitoring or policing agency of the government.

It's not that AEC scientists are vicious or evil or wish us any harm. But institutions involving professional careers must be protected from attack from without. No human endeavor can exist without errors, carelessness, slip-ups. But an institution as well funded and as important as the AEC has become does not intend to let criticism from outside hinder its activities. So they continue to tell us they are perfectly capable of monitoring their own activities in regard to safety and at the same time do their utmost to push the idea of nuclear electricity, all over the country, as fast as it can be produced.

When you are faced with a nuclear power plant next door, you probably will find yourself flattened with a barrage of promotion, publicity and impressive leaflets from the power company involved — all aimed at making you feel good about the whole thing. Atomic energy is "clean" — not "dirty" like the coal-burning power plants. As for radioactivity, they will tell you, no industry in the history of mankind has such a record for safety as the nuclear power industry. And no matter if the water in the river has higher levels of radioactivity, and no matter if trucks bearing highly radioactive waste and spent fuel rods roar over our crowded highways every day (with the chances for accidents rising with every additional car on the road), and no matter that there is, of course, a slight chance of accident or sabotage, both in the plant and in disposal of the waste — never mind, they will tell you. The Federal Radiation Council has set the limits below which we are all perfectly safe.

And they will hold before the eager eyes of your governing body the promise of lots of jobs and prosperity, plus lower taxes, for you will have this huge, expensive plant right there to help pay the taxes. Some short-sighted communities have fallen for this propaganda and are delighted, they claim, to welcome this glorious new industry which will so greatly improve the community. The propaganda usually works best in small communities where there are no experts on nuclear energy, no colleges or university specialists to help puzzled citizens straighten out their feelings and facts in regard to the proposition.

The strategy is further to make the community — a town, a county, several counties — wholly dependent upon the nuclear power plant for their electricity. What happens when something goes wrong? As AEC Commissioner Theos Thompson puts it, "there may be at one time or another increases in these levels (of radiation pollution) due to such things as a few faulty fuel pins in a fuel loading, a loss of stored coolant from some tank, holdup and discharge of effluents in batches . . . or other factors. . . . If the State arbitrarily lowers the levels which are permissible in a given state until they are barely above normal levels, they run some risk that at some time they will either have to require the shutdown of this plant, or else find some graceful way to back off from their own regulation." If or when something happens at the plant which may raise the radiation levels, your community, county or state will be asked, "Do you want to do without electric power altogether, or take a chance on a bit more radioactivity?" That will be your only choice.

Possibly the first question you should ask any power company which announces they plan a nuclear power plant in your community is how much insurance they provide for any future accident of whatever magnitude. They will have to tell you that insurance companies refuse to accept more than a tiny part of responsibility for the immense costs of a nuclear accident. Insurance companies consider nuclear power plants such poor risks that they refuse to guarantee indemnity for the costs of damage.

So American taxpayers take the financial risk, as well as the health and property risk. Under the Price-Anderson law, the government is required to pay indemnity on nuclear accidents, the maximum liability being approximately $560,000,000 for any one disaster. Dr. Gofman says of this law, "If the Price-Anderson Act were repealed, as it assuredly should be, it is extremely doubtful that any future nuclear electric plants above-ground would even be contemplated by the electric utility industry."

The "fast breeder reactor" which the people of Tunkhannock, Wyoming County, Pennsylvania, are fighting, produces plutonium-239, which sticks around for hundreds of thousands of years once it is released into the environment. This is what Dr. Gofman said about plutonium in testimony before the Select Committee on Nuclear Electricity Generation of the Pennsylvania State Senate, August 20, 1970: "Plutonium creation can justifiably be regarded as one of man's most immoral acts. It is surely regrettable that military preparations worldwide should have led to the manufacture of huge quantities of what may well be the most hazardous single radioactive substance imaginable. Plans to create a civilian electrical energy economy built around the use and transport of tons and tons of plutonium-239 (24,000 year half-life) not only may be properly regarded as extreme immorality, but also as an unmitigated nightmare for the human species. The fast breeder reactor program is a giant step forward in creation of this nightmare. It is, to me, unbelievable that serious consideration is apparently being given to an above-ground fast breeder reactor in Wyoming County, Pennsylvania. This is not only potential disaster for Wyoming County, but for a large part of the Eastern Seaboard for periods like 100,000 years."

"Plutonium in the form of plutonium oxide particles is one of the most powerful lung cancer producers known. One-millionth of a gram is the order of amount required to produce lung cancer. Release of *any* plutonium upon the surface of the earth irreversibly increases lung cancer hazards for periods measured in 100,000's of years. Any mishap in handling of the ton quantities of plutonium associated with fast breeder reactors can compromise the future of countless generations of humans. Who assures that absolute perfection in such handling will exist? Who assures that fast breeders, notoriously less likely to be safe than current reactors, won't have that *one* irreversibly disastrous accident?"

He went on to suggest to the State Senate that they set a moratorium of five years for all new nuclear power plants above ground and that they declare an injunction for an indefinite period against fast breeder reactors or any other nuclear activity associated with even the possibility of release of plutonium to the environment.

A bill was introduced into the Pennsylvania legislature on July 28, 1970 providing that "Until the General Assembly determines that radiation sources, devices and equipment utilizing such radiation sources connected with fast-breeder atomic energy plants are safe, and not injurious to the health of the public, consistent with the purpose of this act as expressed in section 2, no license or permit for any new fast-breeder atomic energy plant shall be issued or granted in this Commonwealth under this act or any other law."

Dr. John Gofman, who came to Tunkhannock to help the people there in their fight against the "fast breeder reactor" planned by the AEC, is Professor of Medical Physics at the University of California and Research Associate at the Lawrence Radiation Laboratory. His other professional qualifications make him one of the most distinguished scientists in the world, where nuclear science is concerned. *He believes that permissible levels for radiation of entire populations should be set at zero.* He says that, by setting a definite level for permissible radiation, our official bodies are saying, in essence, "Here is a license to poison us, but only to such and such a degree." Dr. Gofman's projections of what the harvest in illness and death may be as a result of present official radiation standards have been sharply challenged by the AEC which persists in presenting its activities as wholesome in every way, free from any threat to human life.

Dr. Gofman and his colleague, Dr. Arthur Tamplin, are called by Philip Boffey in a *Science* article (August 28, 1970) "a rather unique thorn in the side of the AEC", but he points out that "as concern continues to mount over the social consequences of scientific undertakings, there are bound to be additional scientists ready to proclaim misgivings about government policies."

The two researchers have conducted a fiery campaign in support of their views. They issue technical papers, they speak at scientific meetings, they testify at congressional hearings, talk to the press, appear as witnesses at hearings on the siting of nuclear power plants. The Congressional Committee on Atomic Energy had the AEC prepare an answer to their charges that the AEC is hampering them as they try to criticize the agency and its standards. Ralph Nader asked Senator Muskie to look into the matter. Muskie asked the American Association for the Advancement of Science to look into the charges and countercharges.

The *Science* article concludes by saying that "if the AEC has really taken punitive action against them — and one must admit that circumstantial evidence suggests this may indeed be the case — then something must be done to right the situation, not only for the sake of Gofman and Tamplin, but for the sake of all future dissidents who want to challenge the agency they work for as well."

Dr. Gofman believes that permissible levels for radiation of entire populations should be set at zero. This is not unreasonable, since everyone involved in the debate on what the levels should be admits that all radiation is, to some extent, harmful. All radiation is poisonous. How then does Dr. Gofman propose that we use the power of the atom for industrial purposes?

Let's have a fair and open debate on the question, he says. Every time a new nuclear endeavor is proposed, let us invite all the local residents who will be exposed to the everyday radiation which is unavoidable near such plants and exposed to the potential hazards of an accident at the plant which may devastate the entire community and make it uninhabitable for thousands of years in the future. Let us give these residents all the information we have on what the risks will be *and let them vote on whether they consider that the benefits justify the risks.*

There is no disagreement about the fact that the proposed reactor at Tunkhannock is an experiment. There is no disagreement about the fact that plutonium is one of the most dangerous substances in the world which will be present in enormous quantities in a breeder reactor.

At the Rocky Flats, Colorado plant of Dow Chemical Company where nuclear bombs are being made, congressional testimony has indicated that radioactive contamination is widespread in the plant and many workers have been exposed to dangerous levels of radiation. Between June 14, 1957 and October 28, 1958, there were 24 explosions, fires, spills of plutonium and incidents of contamination at the plant. Oil contaminated by plutonium was loaded into a drum to be hauled to the AEC dumping ground for radioactive waste. Some of it leaked out on the road. The AEC paved it over with asphalt. After the asphalt disintegrates, the plutonium will still be there — *for hundreds of thousands of years!*

The only other "breeder" reactor we have any experience with is the Enrico Fermi reactor which was located 30 miles from Detroit and which in October, 1966, posed the threat of what one writer calls "a bit worse than the maximum credible accident." *Perils of the Peaceful Atom* describes the cause of the accident, which was announced about a year later. "It was one of six identical sheathing elements in the cooling system, elements not even called for in the original plans for the reactor, nor officially recorded after installation.

They'd been kind of thrown in, you might say, as last-moment safety measures during construction. "Unfortunately a workman had failed to secure one properly and it had been swept up by the sodium rushing through the cooling system and cast against cooling nozzles, blocking them. This caused several fuel subassemblies to overheat, warp, melt and shove a couple more out of kilter, making the meltdown."

Authors of this book tell us that the AEC seemed willing to take the lesson they had learned, but the nuclear power industry pressed harder than ever to proceed with building more of this kind of reactor.

As the situation is now, the Federal Radiation Council, the AEC and other governmental bodies set the regulations, determine the level at which it will be permissible to radiate whole populations, then say to the community, "We — not you, but we — have decided that the benefits of this power plant will justify the risks we are asking you to take."

Speaking at a discussion before an American Cancer Society's seminar, Dr. Gofman said it is sheer insanity to construct nuclear power plants near cities. They should be built underground so that discharges of radiation would not poison air and water in the vicinity and they should be located 100 miles from any population center, because of the ever-present danger of accidents and the daily discharges of radiation from the reactor.

Dr. Tamplin said at the seminar that there are ways to control radiation pollution. He also questioned the need for so much electric power, *which is increasing ten times faster than the population is increasing.* "What do we need all that power for?" he asked, "to run plants that turn out aluminum trays for TV dinners and beer cans. I question whether this benefit outweighs the risk of generating all this pollution into the environment."

He also believes that chest x-rays to test for tuberculosis are not worth the risk of cancer or genetic damage. He said that medical x-rays should be used more sparingly and x-ray equipment should be improved to minimize radiation damage. He thinks that physicians and dentists are much too quick to give patients diagnostic x-rays which in some cases could cause genetic damage, birth defects or cancer.

The Philadelphia Inquirer, reporting Dr. Gofman's speech on March 22, 1970, pointed out that there are at present three nuclear power plants within 100 miles of Philadelphia *and there are plans for 11 more to be operating by 1977. The New York Times* for March 16, 1970 quoted Dr. Gofman and his associate Dr. Arthur Tamplin as calling for a 10-fold reduction in the amount of radiation considered permissible for the public.

The two researchers state that, if the entire population of the United States is subjected to the present radiation limit which the AEC considers "safe", there will be 32,000 more deaths per year from cancer and leukemia — or, an extra cancer for every ten that occur for other reasons.

Drs. Gofman and Tamplin have been pressing hard and persistently for changes in the regulations. They are criticized for being "emotional" about their views. They recently wrote to the International Commission on Radiological Protection, "It has been said that we write on asbestos paper. Our endeavor is not to inflame. But there are some people, outside the ICRP, who are so asleep as to require awakening before they and the world are in flames."

Dr. Gofman says the only thing that would have to

be altered is the approach to the economics of the whole thing. Nuclear power plants *can present much less of a hazard than they presently do* — but it costs money. Radiation from x-ray machines, medical use of radioactive materials, disposal of radioactive waste and all other exposures to which all of us are potential victims from day to day, can be kept to a bare minimum, but it costs money. Nobody is willing to spend the money, so we will continue to play Russian roulette, not only with present world-wide health and longevity, but the health, in fact the very survival, of all future generations of human beings on earth, so potent is the poison with which we are here involved.

Dr. Gofman and Dr. Tamplin state that their studies have shown that, if everyone in the U. S. were to receive the amount of radiation currently allowed, there would be 32,000 more cancer and leukemia deaths per year. In 1969, Dr. Ernest Sternglass, Professor of Radiation Physics at the University of Pittsburgh Medical School, announced his belief, carefully backed up by extensive studies, that fallout from our nuclear tests had been responsible for a large number of deaths of unborn children, also infants and children who lived in the path of the radioactive debris which was carried on the wind over the USA in those days. His figures show that the effect of radioactive fallout may be about one hundred times greater than we had supposed.

Some other scientists disagree with his calculations. No one knows where the final truth lies, but it would certainly seem the better part of wisdom not to take any more chances until we know.

Dr. Linus Pauling, professor in the department of chemistry of Stanford University and twice winner of the Nobel prize, supported the views of Dr. Gofman and Dr. Tamplin in the *Bulletin of the Atomic Scientists,* September, 1970, by saying, in part, that his own calculations show that, if the American people were to receive the dose of "high energy radiation from peaceful uses of atomic energy allowed by the Federal Radiation Council the increased incidence (of all forms of cancer) would . . . be 96,000 additional deaths by cancer each year as the result of the damage done by the high-energy radiation from the peaceful uses of atomic energy."

Dr. Pauling goes on to say, "We may ask whether the sacrifice of some tens of thousands of people to save the money that would have to be spent to decrease the amount of exposure to high-energy radiation from nuclear power plants and other manmade sources of high-energy radiation is justified. People die, ultimately; if not from cancer, then from some other disease. Need we be concerned that some people are caused, by our decision, to die five or ten or 15 years earlier than they would have died if our decision had been a different one? I feel that we should be concerned; that the cutting off of a man's life in this way, by cancer, is undesirable; that we should try to decrease the number of deaths by cancer, rather than take such action as to increase their number. Also much suffering is caused by the birth of a grossly defective child; I believe that we should strive to decrease the number of such births.

"The arguments that have been presented by Gofman and Tamplin and that are supported by the calculations given above seem to me to require that a decrease be made immediately in the Federal Radiation Council guidelines for radiation exposure of the American people."

In spite of unrelenting attacks on these views by other

scientists, Robert Finch, then Secretary of Health, Education and Welfare, hence chairman of the Federal Radiation Council, in March, 1970, ordered a general review of radiation safety standards, the first since the mid-1950's. A spokesman of the AEC's Department of Biology and Medicine *(New York Times,* March 16, 1970) said he could "confidently predict" that the investigation would not change safety standards "unless there is irresistible pressure from the outside." If you and I don't put pressure on our legislators, pressure on the Department of Health, Education and Welfare, the Federal Radiation Council and everyone else involved in this review, the pressure exerted by proponents of the opposing view will determine what the Council does.

AEC officials say that, if radiation standards are tightened to the levels Gofman, Tamplin and Pauling demand, the effort to find peaceful uses for atomic energy will be over. The new standards will also, they say, limit the use of radioactive substances in industry and medicine, will change x-ray procedures, drastically alter work rules of the AEC weapons plants and research facilities, tighten restrictions on nuclear-powered electric generating plants and alter present methods of disposing of radioactive wastes. It seems to me we could not put our money to any better use than doing just these things — if by so doing we can feel even a bit safer about the highly controversial level of radiation exposure which our scientific experts think should be permissible for all of us to be exposed to, from birth.

When the local power company announces a nuclear power plant in or near your community, you will not be the first to cross swords with the AEC and a power company bent on producing this "clean" kind of electricity. Almost all such power plants built have been fought stubbornly and well by people living in the vicinity. The Fermi reactor near Detroit was fought by the entire trade union movement of that city.

A number of states are at present locked in battle with the AEC because they demand the right to set radiation limits within their own states, to protect their own people. In every case, they want the standards for exposure levels set much lower than the AEC requires — that is, they want much more strict safety precautions than the AEC wants. The outcome of this struggle is not yet determined, although the court decision decreed that only the Federal government could set the standards.

Your first step, when the reactor in your community is announced, is to get in touch with all your legislators. You will be surprised at how much they know about the subject. Many of them in Washington have been wrestling with the AEC and the Federal Radiation Council for years. Pennsylvania Representative Daniel Flood on October 14, 1970 made an impassioned speech in the House protesting the Tunkhannock nuclear plant. He used words like this: "This nuclear experiment is to have as its fissionable core a ton and a half of plutonium. If sabotaged and explosively compressed, which I am assured can be accomplished in a variety of ways, this neighborhood gem will instantly become a huge, incomparably dirty atomic bomb. The resulting permanent — and a couple of centuries is fairly permanent so far as I am concerned — poisoning of the Susquehanna Watershed from New York State to Chesapeake Bay would probably eliminate this large and heavily populated section of the United States as a habitable region. . . . As to the loss of credibility currently bemoaned by the hierarchy of the Atomic Energy Commission, I intend to examine on this floor the multitude of half truths and misleading statements which have contributed to this monstrous abuse of the public trust."

Call on your Federal and state representatives at once. Get them into the battle early. Then cast about for the best, the closest, the most courageous experts in this field that you can find to help you. Dr. John Gofman would be a good place to start.

Get in touch at once with the head of the biology department of the closest college or university. Someone there can give you names and locations of experts who will be eager to help. Call them on the phone. Don't be modest about your lack of understanding of the vocabulary and the workings of nuclear power. They don't expect you to have this information. That's their job. It is also their job to help you. These are dedicated, highly moral and altruistic men who are risking their professional futures, and putting their very lives on the line to fight what they are convinced is the most monstrous immorality of our time.

Once you have assurances of help, get busy arranging for some publicity. Ask the local newspaper to do a series of articles on the subject, if they haven't already planned one. Get the TV station and the radio station alerted to the speeches and the informational programs you intend to present. You might arrange a panel discussion between someone from the local power company and the nuclear expert you are bringing to town.

Perhaps they may suggest having a scientist who disagrees with the viewpoint of your expert. Fine. Arrange for a debate.

Call on the local colleges and universities to open their meeting halls, invite their biology students and faculty. They will welcome the opportunity to sponsor a debate on this very timely and controversial subject. Get somebody started raising money. You will need it for publicity, for expenses of speakers, for literature to give out. It is bound to be a long, hard fight. You must be steadfast. You and your environment group must be willing to accept the sharp disapproval of the local power company which, after all, has staked a lot of money on this new venture.

Go to your local library. Ask the librarian to make a display of everything in the library on this subject. Offer her literature from your group. Once you have arranged the meeting for your expert or experts, get all the publicity you can get. Work with the reporter who does the series on nuclear power plants in the paper. Work with the radio and TV stations. Get donations, if you can, for posters and flyers announcing the meeting. Local businessmen may be willing to give you the use of their copy machines or mimeographs. Local printers may donate their time and facilities. Put together a fact sheet on all aspects of the powerplant and what it may mean to the community. Circulate this with a petition.

The hardest part of your job is to educate people to the fact that there *is* another side to this question — apart from the AEC's side. Most people honestly believe government regulations will protect them from any possible harm from a nuclear power plant. You will have to tell them differently. And your job will be harder if they have been led to believe that the great new industry will bring prosperity to the region.

Many other groups and individuals are studying these problems and working to solve them. Many can give you help if you are just beginning your local fight. Even if they can't help, they'll be glad to hear from you. It's lonely, fighting out there. It's good to know there are others on the firing line. Here are names and addresses of some of these individuals and groups.

Citizens Committee for Protection of the Environment
71 Pine Avenue
Ossining, N. Y. 10562 Phone: 914–762-1362

Mrs. Joan Daniels, Co-chairman
Citizens Committee for Environmental Protection
71 Warren Street, Tunkhannock, Pennsylvania 18657

John K. Mustard, Ex. Director
Delaware Valley Committee for Protection of the Environment
Moorestown, N. J.

Sheldon Novick
Center for the Biology of Natural Systems
Washington University
St. Louis, Missouri 63130
(Mr. Novick is the author of *The Careless Atom*)

Larry Bogart
National Committee to Stop Environmental Pollution
214 Third Street, N. E., Washington, D. C.

Dr. Ernest Sternglass of the University of Pittsburgh

Dr. Arthur Tamplin of the Lawrence Radiation Laboratory
University of California.

Professor Joshua Lederberg of Stanford University.

Another Mother for Peace
Mrs. Dorothy B. Jones, Co-Chairman
407 N. Maple Drive
Beverly Hills, Calif. 90210

People's Lobby, Inc.
Mrs. Joyce Koupal
1524 N. Western Ave.
Hollywood, Calif. 90027

Mrs. Pauline Koch
1206 S. Gramercy Pl
Los Angeles, California 90019

Mr. and Mrs. Patrick O'Brien
109 Domingues St.
San Clemente, California 92672

Mrs. Dorothy Cope
203 Segre Pl.
Santa Cruz, California 95060

Mrs. Eleanor M. Galiardi
NHF, 4072 Winkle Ave.
Santa Cruz, Calif. 95060

Sierra Club
Attn: Michael McCloskey, Conservation Director
1050 Mills Tower
220 Bush Street
San Francisco, Calif. 94104

Colorado Committee for Environmental Info
Dr. H. Peter Metzger
2595 Stanford Ave.
Boulder, Colo. 80303

Morey Wolfson
Citizens Concerned about Radiation Pollution
3 S. Cook St.
Denver, Colo. 80209

Mr. Robert Kunz
Conn. Conservation Assn.
Mystic, Conn. 06355

Joseph Browder
Friends of the Earth
917 — 15th St. N. W.
Washington, D. C. 20008

Ed Chaney
National Wildlife Federation
1412 — 16th St., N. W.
Washington, D. C. 20036

Campaign against Pollution
600 W. Fullerton Ave.
Chicago, Ill. 60611

Richard Lahn
1775 Crofton Pkwy.
Crofton, Md. 21113

Charles Tucker
Chesapeake Envir. Protection Agency
Box 113
Harwood, Md. 20776

Dr. Eric Schneider
Box 205
RFD. 1
Prince Frederick, Md.

Mrs. Donna Smith
Upper River Rd.
Ipswich, Mass.

Mr. Roger Wilson
Sierra Club of Michigan
243 Boston
Grand Rapids, Mich.

Intervenors for Palisades Plant
POB 22
Kalamazoo, Mich.

Dr. Fred Brown, Pres.
Michigan United Conservation Clubs
488 W. Ashby Rd.
Midland, Mich. 48640

Saginaw Valley Nuclear Study Group
Editor: Kathy Bjerke
POB 1166
Midland, Mich. 48640

Mrs. William D. Sinclair
5711 Summerset Dr.
Midland, Mich. 48640

Shirley Hunt, MECCA
5600 Hillside Ct.
Minneapolis, Minn. 55435

Dr. C. W. Huver
5345 Woodlawn Blvd.
Minneapolis, Minn. 55417

Larry Bogart
Anti-Pollution League
77 Homewood Ave.
Allendale, N. J. 07401

Elisabeth Linch, Anti-Pollution League
Box 116
Collingswood, N. J. 08108

Delaware Valley Committee
for the Protection of the Environment
305 High Street
Moorestown, N. J.

Survival, Inc.
Attn: Walter De Young, Chairman
85 Hardwick Lane
Wayne, N. J. 07470

Independent Citizens Research Fnd.
for Study of Degenerative Diseases, Inc.
468 Ashford Ave.
POB 97
Ardsley, N. Y. 10502

Mrs. Susan Reed
N. Mountain Dr.
Ardsley-on-Hudson
N. Y. 10503

Mrs. William P. Carl
Lloyd Lane
Huntington, L. I., N. Y. 11743

Mrs. Dorothy Barnoux
Citizens Committee for Protection of the Environment
71 Pine Ave.
Ossining, N. Y. 10562

Citizens Committee for Radiation Control
Justus C. Poole, Secy.
549 West 123rd St.
New York, N. Y. 10027

Citizens Opposed to Nuclear Expansion
The Nature Conservancy
Attn: Daniel Smiley
Lake Mohonk Mtn. House
New Paltz, N. Y. 12561

Mrs. Mildred Kurtz
CLEAN
74 Mt. Tom
New Rochelle, N. Y.

Robert Fleisher
64 Perry St.
New York, N. Y. 10014

Mrs. Ruth Gage-Colby, Chairman
Citizens Committee for Protection of the Environment
155 E. 38th St.
New York, N. Y. 10016

Elise Jerard
115 Central Park W.
New York, N. Y. 10023

Mrs. Ann Margetson
515 W. 122nd St.
New York, N. Y. 10027

Helen Putnam
Metropolitan Coalition to Stop Nuclear Plants
340 E. 51st, Apt. 14D
New York, N. Y. 10017

Mrs. Mary H. Weik
166-2nd Ave.
New York, N. Y. 10003

Mr. E. Grant Pike
463 Helendale Rd.
Rochester, N. Y.

Mrs. J. M. Waller
153 Biltmore Dr.
Charlotte, N. Car.

Miss Vicki Evans
LIFE
c/o Dept. of Biology
Bowling Green State Univ.
Bowling Green, Ohio 43403

Dr. Irwin Oster
Prof. of Biology & Genetics
Bowling Green State Univ.
Bowling Green, Ohio 43403

George N. Kundtz
Nuclear Committee, Cits. for Clean Air & Water, Inc.
13167 Westchester Trail
Chesterland, Ohio 44026

Citizens for Clean Air & Water, Inc.
312 Park Bldg.
140 Public Square
Cleveland, Ohio 44114

Glenn Lau
Rt. 1, Box 126
Oak Harbor, Ohio 43449

Mrs. Chas. B. Stebbins
Citz. for Clean Air & Water, Inc.
705 Elmwood Rd.
Rocky River, Ohio 44116

Eugene Future Power Committee
POB 5274
Eugene, Ore. 97405

Larry Williams
Oregon Environmental Council
1238 N. W. Glisan St.
Portland, Ore. 97209

Delaware Valley Conservation Assn.
Joan Matheson, V. P.
Dingman's Ferry, Pa. 18328

Coalition on Nuclear Power
c/o Douglas Baker
Philadelphia Ecology Action
POB 1600
Philadelphia, Pa. 19105

Judith Johnsrud
433 Orlando Ave.
State College, Pa. 16801

Citizens Concerned for the Environment
Mrs. John Daniels
71 Warren St.
Tunkhannock, Pa.

Orion D. Hack, Pres.
S. Carolina Environmental Action, Inc.
Hilton Head Island, S. C. 29928

Wayne Usry
3414 Hawthorne Ave.
Richmond, Va. 23222

Terry James
RD. 3 Brattleboro, Vt. 05301

Dr. Irving Lyon
Bennington College
Bennington, Vt. 05201

Lake Champlain Committee
Attn: Blake Lawrence
Box 501
Charlotte, Vt. 05445

Esther Mattson
11328 N. Riverland Rd.
Mequoh, Wisconsin 53092

CHAPTER 10

We're Deep in Hot Water

"Unless we move energetically into space we will in time destroy the biosphere and, with it, ourselves. . . . This eventuality (of heating up the biosphere with more waste heat than it can absorb) can only be avoided if evolutionary processes can adapt the biosphere to higher temperatures during the time in which the heat addition is occurring. And the pacing of human activity is too rapid to permit such evolutionary adaptation . . . 50 years hence our energy output will be 40 times that of today and just one century hence, it will be 1,300 times that of today."

Robert B. Bathelmy
Aero Propulsion Laboratory
and
Capt. Howard A. MacEwen
Air Force Space and Missile Systems

"In a case brought by American Civil Liberties Union attorneys arising out of the Santa Barbara oil spill, plaintiffs' Fifth Amendment rights are pleaded as follows: 'The personal right is the right to live in, and enjoy, an environment free from improvident destruction or pollution; the property right is the right to the ownership, use and enjoyment of property, free from improvident invasion or impairment.' "

David Sive,
Civil Liberties,
April, 1970

One morning in July 1970 our local paper carried a short note announcing that hearings would be held by the Delaware River Basin Commission on two nuclear power plants proposed for our part of the country. One of them, to be located on the Schuylkill River would be "cooled" by water from the river. But since the plant will need 69 million gallons of water a day, of which an average 35 million will evaporate into the atmosphere, the plan is to pump water from the Delaware River some miles away.

Then another atomic power plant is planned for the Delaware River which will need 153 million gallons of water daily, of which 43 will evaporate into the air. These two rivers are in the heart of the megalopolis that extends from Boston to Washington, D. C. which, we are promised, will, by the end of the century contain so many people that there seems to be no certainty they can all be contained in this amount of space, without cramming them all into mile-high apartments which will probably cover every inch of land.

The announcement of the hearings caused not a ripple among the residents of my county. Of course not. No one knew what was being proposed, so most people probably did not bother to read the notice. More electric power? Sounded good. We need it, don't we? Can't put up with these brownouts. Have to keep the air conditioners on all day. And of course most people these days are putting in electric heat, so it's just as well we have some new power plants. On the next page you can read the local power company's half-page ad pleading for us to use more electricity — more, more, more! Electric heat is the cleanest, the best!

The hearings would not discuss radioactivity. That was reserved for a later hearing by the AEC. The chief problem to be discussed at these hearings was something called "thermal pollution", a fairly new kind of insult to the environment, about the total effect of which we know almost exactly nothing. Thermal pollution means heating up air or water by discharging into it huge amounts of waste heat. Waste heat, you will ask. Why are we wasting heat, then, to make electricity with which to heat houses and buildings? Why not use the waste heat? Why not, indeed? You will see why not as we get further into the subject of thermal pollution.

When you make electricity using steam a great deal of heat is produced. You have to get rid of it someway, so you locate your power plant near a body of water and you pump the water through the plant to cool it. Then you discharge the water back into the stream, river or lake. Naturally the hot water heats up the stream, river or lake.

If, because of what you are doing to the water, grave environmental results ensue, you could put up cooling towers instead, which are quite expensive. Here you expose the hot water to the air where it evaporates. So the air is heated instead of the water and, depending upon the amount of water evaporated, you will probably change the climate of the nearby region. This is thermal pollution.

During Earth Week celebrations locally, the man in charge of pollution knowledge at Bethlehem Steel spoke on the subject before a group of Lehigh University engineers. He was concerned chiefly with air and water pollution which he said he thought might be fairly well controlled only for the next ten years or so, if we manage to control the population explosion. But thermal pollution? There is no remedy for thermal pollution, he said, and in the foreseeable future no remedy can be developed, so far as he is concerned. He told us of a small area in Western Pennsylvania where a power plant with cooling towers evaporates millions of gallons of water daily into the air. Continual fog and mist hang over the place, he said. "The entire climate of the community has been changed". There is no way to avoid it.

Our local paper carried no story on the results of the testimony at the hearings. It was printed only in the editions that go to the two counties most concerned. The two rivers flow almost on the boundaries of my county. The Delaware flows through one of the most heavily industrialized regions of the world. Donald E. Carr in *Death of the Sweet Waters* states that the Delaware "serves the greatest concentration of people and industry of any watershed in the United States."

He goes on to describe the present condition of the river thus, "Since about 1900 this rather stodgy river had become a slowly swaying sewer so foul that ferryboats churned up enough hydrogen sulfide to peel the paint off shoreside buildings." In spite of this, the Delaware, which flows from the Catskills in upper New York State south, to divide New Jersey from Pennsylvania, is also one of the most fought-over rivers in the

East. As long ago as 1931 New York City began to tap the Delaware for drinking water — 400 million gallons a day. By 1965, in the middle of a drought, an emergency was announced. There was so little water left in the Delaware that salt was rising from the ocean farther and farther into the mouth of the river to contaminate permanently the water supply of Philadelphia. Water tables around the river fell and wells went dry.

The Army Corps of Engineers has recently gotten Congressional okay and money — lots of money — for the Tocks Island area on the Delaware which involves damming the river to create a recreational lake where New Yorkers and other metropolitan dwellers can bring their motor boats. This is in the area of the Delaware Water Gap, about 50 miles north of where the proposed nuclear plant will be built.

None of these facts is directly related to thermal pollution. I point them out to emphasize the demands on this river, the extremely precarious state of its flow already and the fact that everyone seems to think that, because the river is there, everyone can and should use it for any purpose at all, without any regard for what it does to the river.

Meanwhile a survey of water resources in the Delaware area, described in *Science in Agriculture* for Summer, 1970, found that the most critical future problem related to the Delaware area is water supply — that is, whether the river will be able to furnish all the water needed in this area ten years from now.

Ten years from now presumably the proposed power plants will be in operation, and millions of gallons of water will be pumped from the Delaware to the Schuylkill. The number of industrial plants along the

Delaware River which use its water for cooling and dumping of wastes will have increased proportionately, one presumes. And the number of people needing drinking water in both New York and Pennsylvania will have increased immensely.

What are the effects of thermal pollution? One of our most serious problems with water pollution at present is lack of oxygen produced by pollution of many kinds. Heating the water reduces oxygen levels still further. And fish need *more* oxygen, rather than less, as the temperature of the water rises. Low oxygen level reduces the water's ability to cleanse itself of pollution, thus killing off plant life which, in turn, is needed to sustain fish.

Donald E. Carr said in *Atlantic Monthly* that the Mahoning River in Ohio at one time reached a temperature of 140 degrees Fahrenheit, which forced local industries to slow down or shut off during times when the flow of water in the river was low. It is obvious that it takes a lot less heat to raise the temperature of a little bit of water than of a large amount of water. And in summer when, because of drought, the water in streams and rivers is customarily low, it is also heated naturally by the hot summer sun.

According to Dr. Joseph A. Mihursky of the University of Maryland, just a few more power plants and other industries added to the shores of some of our most exploited rivers will increase the temperature of the water to as much as 140 degrees in summertime — 40 or 50 degrees above the survival requirements of most water organisms. Along a crowded river the water is used over and over. Even today, says Dr. Mihursky, there are rivers in heavily industrialized areas where

150 per cent of the water passes through a succession of electric generating plants during the summer.

We are told that electric generating capacity doubles every ten years. "If that trend continues to 1980 — and there is every reason to believe it will — the power production then will require cooling water at a rate of 200 billion gallons a day. *But 200 billion gallons a day is one-sixth of the average daily runoff of all the surface water in the U. S.*", says an article in *Medical Tribune* for February 5, 1970. By the end of the century one-third of all surface water will be used for cooling purposes, *just to generate electricity.* The many other industrial uses of the same water generally return it to the stream, river or lake in much worse condition than it was before, in terms of thermal and all other kinds of pollution.

As of 1967, the response to temperature has been studied in less than 5 percent of the almost 1900 fish species listed in the American Fisheries Society's list. "Heated discharges may change an aquatic ecosystem in a number of ways," said the Assistant Professor of Fishery Biology at Cornell, "and our knowledge seems inadequate to precisely predict the degree of change which can occur without production of a serious ecological upset."

Writing in *Bioscience,* November, 1969, LaMont Cole, professor of Biological Sciences, Cornell University, explains thermal pollution, partly in relation to a proposed nuclear power plant on Lake Cayuga. As a concerned biologist should, he brings up all the known detrimental effects of thermal pollution in terms of the health of a body of water and its denizens. Here are some of his points.

1. Our burning of coal, gas and oil has caused a measurable increase in the carbon dioxide content of the atmosphere. Jet planes are releasing great quantities of both carbon dioxide and water at high altitudes. We have no way of knowing what effects all this will have on climate, but "they certainly have the potential for changing climates."

2. We are using "prodigious amounts" of water to cool industrial plants and this use will grow as our need for power grows. Nuclear plants release more waste heat than plants burning other fuels. "When heated water is discharged at a temperature above that of the air, we must expect an increase in the frequencies of mist and fog and, in winter, icing conditions."

3. Eventually, bodies of water may become so hot that nothing can live in them. Fish of any type are rare in water heated to 90 degrees F. "So far as animals are concerned, a body of water at a temperature of 30–35 degrees C is essentially a biological desert". The algae, which are most harmful in terms of eutrophication, are the only plants that flourish.

4. Oxygen decreases as temperature goes up. Decay of organic matter and other processes involving oxidation proceed more rapidly at higher temperatures. Salts become more soluble. Chemical reactions become more rapid. Evaporation may increase the concentration of dissolved salts.

5. Toxins have a greater effect at higher temperatures. Parasites and disease are more likely to be dangerous. Water at a higher than usual temperature places even greater strain on the life processes of the animals living there, so that it becomes ever more difficult to adapt. A certain kind of oyster, for example, can toler-

ate a wider range of salinity in winter than in summer when temperatures are higher.

6. The mixing of layers of water in a lake is disrupted when warmed water is dumped. Says Dr. Cole, "The effect of this addition of heat on the average temperature of the lake will be trivially small, but the biological consequences can be out of all proportion to the amount of heating. . . . The threat to the welfare of the lake is very real."

7. Many water organisms can adapt to higher or lower temperatures *when they have time.* But when water is discharged during peak generating hours, there are severe temperature fluctuations that will make it impossible for many organisms to survive. And if fish and other living things become accustomed to the higher temperatures near where the heated water is pumped in, and congregate near this, they will suffer from temperature shocks when the plant closes down for refueling or repairs and the water becomes cold again!

Dr. Cole says, categorically, "Man cannot go on increasing his use of thermal energy without causing degradation of his environment and if he is persistent enough, he will destroy himself. There are other energy sources that could be used, but no source can support an indefinitely growing population. . . . Man is on a collision course with disaster if he tries to keep energy production growing by means that will impose an increased thermal stress on the earth." He suggests an immediate effort to determine the level of population that the earth can endure without deterioration, then an effort to achieve this "steady state."

In *Scientist and Citizen* for October, 1968, John

Cairns, Jr., Professor of Biology at Virginia Polytechnic Institute and Research Associate of the Limnology Department of the Academy of Natural Sciences of Philadelphia, writes, "We're in Hot Water" in regard to thermal pollution.

Says Dr. Cairns, "The same pressures which are moving us toward the use of more electric power are also putting other demands on our rivers and lakes. As the human population expands, more intense use must be made of non-expanding resources, including water resources. He goes on to quote a *Science* article as saying "It seems that the real choice for the future is between 'thermal pollution' and a shortage of electric power."

The waste heat to be discharged from a proposed Monticello nuclear plant near Minneapolis in the winter *would furnish the entire heating for one hundred thousand Minnesota homes,* he tells us. And yet it seems to be impossible for the technologists trying to find economical, non-polluting ways to heat houses, to get together with the ones trying to find ways to dispose of immense amounts of waste heat which threaten to pollute the same community!

"At hearings on stream use for power generation or other purposes, biologists are often asked to prove that a particular discharge of heat or some other intended change will harm the area. They usually cannot do this because each drainage basin has its unique characteristics and extensive background data is frequently not available."

And "in view of the complex nature of the heat pollution problem, the need for consideration of existing information and the gathering of new information

— ecologic, engineering and economic — is urgent. The human population growth rate may have many disastrous present and future environmental consequences which are already beyond our control. However it is also possible that immediate action may prevent further ecological collapse and may even make possible the restoration of environmental quality."

Standards for thermal pollution must be set by federal authorities and state authorities. In May, 1970 the Federal Water Quality Administration announced that thermal waste discharges into Lake Michigan will not be permitted to raise any portion of the lake water more than one degree higher than the surrounding water. Enforcement officer Murray Stein asked that the states bordering the lake make the same provisions and hinted that, if they did not, the federal government would.

Power companies in the four states, Illinois, Michigan, Indiana and Wisconsin, plan 10 nuclear plants on the banks of the lake. All of them intend to discharge cooling water into the lake *and all of them say they could not meet this new standard if it is adopted.* A spokesman for Commonwealth Edison, which plans to put a $300 million plant at Zion, Illinois, said "if this policy is made into regulation, we would be forced to close both our fossil fuel plants on Lake Michigan. And at Zion we couldn't possibly comply." The standards are impossible to enforce.*

In an article on thermal pollution in *Power Engineering,* April, 1970 F. C. Olds reveals the results of a study

* The *New York Times,* March 26, 1971, announced that Michigan, Indiana and Wisconsin had agreed to a Federal standard of no more than 3 degrees F, which will mean upgrading all cooling systems of plants using the lake water. Illinois, however, still refused to consider the Federal standards.

this magazine did among 135 power companies. One hundred twenty-three of these are not now in compliance with the state laws on thermal pollution. The reasons are many. Twenty states do not yet have approved standards regarding thermal pollution. In some states which do, there is not yet any agreement on how far away from the plant the maximum permitted temperature can be registered. In some states the criteria change constantly. It may take five years to build a plant and in these five years the new requirements may have rendered the plant illegal!

As requirements become more and more stringent, expenses skyrocket. One company executive complains, "Huge expenditures are being called for, not to prevent fish kills, but to make fish more comfortable for a few hours per year." It seems apparent that public pressure will have a great deal to do with finally determining what the standards will be. Some pressure comes from conservationists on one side. But, on the other side, there is the pressure of power shortages, which influence lots of people to believe that, no matter what happens to the river, the lake, the bay, or the stream, we must have our air conditioning, must heat our homes with "clean" electricity, must continue to buy all the silly, useless gadgets that run up the electric bill, environmentally speaking.

In January, 1970, a Con Edison plant at Buchanan, New York was closed for three days because of a massive fish kill — perhaps 150,000 fish were sucked into the conduit which draws water from the Hudson River. Power company officials were puzzled, said the *New York Times,* as to why the fish had been attracted to the spot where they perished. The Scenic Hudson Preservation Conference said, "Con Edison's latest fish kills, which the company now admits, prove the emptiness of the utility's promises and assurances. If they cannot protect the Hudson River fisheries at Indian Point despite continuing promises to do so, how can any of Con Edison's statements regarding natural resources be taken seriously?"

Conservationists plan to use such arguments in their opposition to the building of other power plants farther up the Hudson. Con Edison contends that the chief reason for the power shortages which plague New York City is the opposition of conservationists to its plans for building ever more and more power plants.

The New York State Conservation Department made a study of the fate of fish near the proposed Storm King Pumped Storage Plant. Using all available knowledge and equipment in their study, the fishery experts found that probably a very small number of all the eggs produced by a typical fish would be drawn into the power plant. However, the conclusion of their article, published in *The Conservationist,* December-January, 1969–1970, stated that, if a lot more plants are located on the Hudson, near this spot, the cumulative effect could be disastrous. More and more studies must be done all the time, it seems.

Waterways which cross national or state boundaries intensify problems. Switzerland has proposed nuclear installations on the Rhine which will raise the river's temperature excessively before it flows into Germany. The Germans think this will impede their own proposed nuclear projects. But, the Swiss say, even if they and Germany agree to an even share of the possible waste heat pollution, Germany will still have to put up cooling towers on her part of the river.

According to the *Bulletin of the Atomic Scientists* for

March, 1970, a lawsuit has been brought by the Metropolitan Sanitary District of Greater Chicago against Commonwealth Edison. It asserts that condenser-heated lake water will "radically raise the temperature of substantial parts of the waters of the lake and cause thermal pollution severely and deleteriously affecting the ecology of the lake."

An official of the United Auto Workers and 13 others have brought a second suit, contending that 3 billion gallons of lake water a day would be heated to 18 to 20 degrees Fahrenheit above the lake temperature in surrounding water. Its discharge back into the lake would increase the toxicity of existing pollutants, stimulate the growth of aquatic plant nuisances and speed up the deterioration of Lake Michigan, already in jeopardy. Both suits also cite the threat of radioactive pollution of the water which is a principal source of drinking water for about eight million people.

Dr. Philip F. Gustafson, associate director, Radiological Physics Division, Argonne National Laboratory, says in the *Bulletin* article, that by 1975 the heat introduced into Lake Michigan from electric power generation will be about 2.2 times its present level. Taking up different eventualities that may occur to produce serious ecological effects, he says that closing down the plants at certain times may be necessary to avoid disaster. Or, cooling ponds and cooling towers may be necessary. Both of these may make *major weather changes,* leading to "periods of local fog, snowfall or even thunderstorm activity."

The Federal Water Pollution Control Administration has brought suit against Florida's biggest electric company to stop excessive discharge of hot water from a generating plant at Biscayne Bay. Federal investigators say the plant has done severe damage to marine plant life and fish in an area where the government is planning a national marine preserve. This is the first federal suit to prevent thermal pollution.

The power company in question discharges into the ocean 10,000 gallons per second of water heated to about 100 degrees. Ocean temperatures in the area may be raised to 100 degrees or more. In 1969 a peak of 103 degree temperatures caused a sizeable fish kill. The power plant's discharges exceed both federal and state limits on thermal pollution. Researchers have found a zone of more than one square mile of "biological degradation" in the path of the water pumped from the power plant. The only answer seems to be cooling towers which would require some 4000 acres and several million dollars. As we pointed out earlier, the cooling towers cause a different — and possibly just as destructive — thermal effect, as millions of gallons of evaporated water form into mists and fogs. It is hardly conceivable that the residents of Miami, near the location of the power plant, would appreciate this kind of climate.

In order to bring the suit, Secretary Hickel had to make use of the old 1899 statute against polluting water. Since no mention of thermal pollution occurs in this law, of course, the suit speaks instead of the destruction of small organisms which pass through the plant's heat exchangers and emerge as refuse. This is the "pollution" on which the suit is based. However, experts of the Federal Water Pollution Control Administration make it clear that what was to blame was the elevated temperature of the bay, not any material pollutant. The zone of destruction amounted to about 670 acres of bay bottom, according to *Technology Review* for June, 1970.

The AEC is doling out large sums of money to do research on the effects of thermal pollution: how to predict what the temperature will actually rise to in any given condition; how heat can be better dissipated, where power plants should be located, in order to avoid thermal problems; the biological effects of high temperature and of temperature changes on various living things in the water; and, finally, beneficial uses for what the AEC likes to call "thermally-enriched" water. When you speak of it as "enriched", somehow it begins to sound desirable, doesn't it?

A recent UPI story tells of a man-made lake in South Carolina where the AEC cools and recirculates water from nuclear reactors. A laboratory studies the effects of the heat. Alligators and turtles love the place, we are told, because of the nice hot water. The fish which were there before the thermal pollution began are flourishing. The article goes on to say that "none of these examples means that unlimited thermal pollution in the future would be anything other than calamitous."

In Oregon, a power company set up an experimental agricultural project to see whether heated water from a proposed nuclear power plant can be used to help farmers. Sure enough, when they buried pipes and released warmed water through them, strawberries ripened a few days earlier, corn grew a bit taller, and orchards sprayed with the warm water survived frosts. Conservationists say the experiment is a public relations gimmick. And they ask what is a power company doing in the agriculture field? How do they know enough about farming and orcharding to judge the results they get and the possible ill effects?

Professors from nearby universities point out that nobody knows much about how plants respond to warm water irrigation. What will the effect be on insect life and plant diseases? And an associate professor of biology is very concerned about the possible contamination of the food with radioactive isotopes. The water, which has passed through the power plant, contains radioactivity. "The possible dangers of directly providing for the accumulation and concentration of radioisotopes during plant and animal growth, followed by human consumption of such crops," he said, "should be carefully studied. This issue is exceedingly complex and may be of overriding importance." The story appears in *Science,* August 1, 1969.

Chemical Week for December 17, 1969 announced that The Swedish Association of Engineers is running a contest to find out what can be done with waste heat from a nuclear reactor. The winner gets a prize of $15,000 for answers best geared to Swedish problems — that is, presumably, just how do we go about using the waste heat to heat houses, factories or office buildings.

To someone with a non-engineering mentality, the problem seems a rather simple one to solve. Surely engineers who are capable of designing and constructing all the elaborate, highly technical apparatus which takes up so much room in the world these days should be able to figure out how to get a little waste heat from here to there without too much trouble. One wonders whether anyone really wants to do it.

A recommendation for what the average citizen can do to work against the possible ill effects of thermal pollution comes from a source from which one expects to get apologies and excuses for industry — not attacks on it. In an editorial "Electrical Heating and Thermal Pollution" (*Chemical and Engineering News,* June 29, 1970), Executive Director of the American Chemical Society F. T. Wall lays the facts on the line. *Heating anything by electricity which could be heated by some other means is expensive, in terms of environmental damage and waste of resources.*

Even the least technologically educated among us can easily see the sense of his reasoning. You can heat a house or a water tank directly with coal, gas or oil. What is the ecological or economic sense of using the coal, gas or oil to heat a power generating plant which will then manufacture electricity to heat the house or water tank? About two-thirds of the total heat produced by the power generating plant is waste which must be discharged unused into the air or the water, creating thermal pollution with all the possibilities of nationwide disaster which we have talked about.

Says Mr. Wall, "the conclusion is still inescapable that, from the standpoints of thermal pollution and fuel consumption conservation, we would be better off using directly the heat resulting from burning a fuel instead of going through an electrical intermediate." The power companies insist, in their ads on the "cleanness" of electric heat. At one's home there is indeed no pollution. All the pollution occurs instead at the power plant to which the house is connected by wires. These, too, provide another kind of desecration of the planet — destruction of landscapes.

"What can be done about this?" asks Mr. Wall, "In the first place, the use of electrical resistance heating should be severely restricted wherever electrical energy is generated by steam plants whose operations seriously affect the environment. Prompt action might give us enough time to determine more precisely what further measures, if any, must be taken to avoid serious, irreparable consequences." He emphasizes that he is talking only about heating — not electric light, motors, or small heating units, but the space and water heaters that cause so much pollution and so much waste of resources. "Finally," he says, "our people should be reminded that what they see and feel in their houses does not disclose all of the environmental effects attending living in those houses."

Early in June our local paper carried a notice from the local power company that we might expect some brownouts during the summer if we didn't turn our air conditioners down or out when the weather was hot. Nobody cares apparently if you keep the conditioner on when it's cool! In the same issue of the paper and in many later issues were half page ads for home heating, electrically — the only way, the best way, the clean way!

I wrote to the power company pointing out that this seemed to be contradictory and asking if those of us who put in electric heat might not in future years be asked to turn off our heat if the weather gets cold — too many people will be using electricity. The Coordinator-Customer Relations called me on the phone to set me straight. I dislike talking to people on the phone about controversial matters, so I told this gentleman that I would write him specific questions and would ask him to answer them specifically, so that I could not possibly misquote him in my book.

I asked the following questions and included a number of quotes from technological and consumer journals, most of which are dealt with earlier in this chapter.

"1. Is it your opinion that we can continue to expand the uncontrolled use of electric power indefinitely into the future without hazard to the environment?

"2. Does it not seem to you highly inconsistent to continue widespread advertising for installation of electric heat while you are cautioning us not to turn on air conditioners during hot spells?

"3. If you really believe that consumers are 'demanding' electric products, including heat, as you indicated over the phone, why then are you spending a great deal of money on advertising to convince them they should install electric heat? Surely if they are already demanding it, they need no more persuasion from you — right?

"4. Some time ago I asked your company why they were promoting electric cars, since these, too, are bound to use a great deal of electricity if they are widely used. Your Mr. R. H. Lichtenwalner told me that no one is the least worried about providing the power. The electric industry plans to double its capacity by 1980 and quadruple it by 1990, just as Dr. Malcolm Peterson predicts. He told me further that electric cars will be recharged at night when everyone is sleeping — an off-peak period. This means, I assume, that, when the time comes that we must use electric cars, we will then be told by the PP & L to cut off our air conditioning, our freezers, our refrigerators, our electric heat and whatever other equipment you have persuaded us to buy by then — so that all the thousands of electric cars can be recharged every night. It just doesn't make any more sense than anything else being told to us, by industry or government, in relation to the future. Can you tell me, please, whether PP & L believes that they can still provide plenty of electricity for all the electric cars, *once we have most houses heated electrically?*

"5. Can you give me some very general idea of how PP & L expects to expand in order to double its capacity in ten years? Where will the power stations be and how will they be powered?"

One month later I received the following reply from the same gentleman:

"It is indeed gratifying that there are people such as yourself who not only express a concern for the environment but are willing to back-up their concern with action — in this case, your research and effort involved in writing a book on the subject.

"In this regard, the attachments to your letter would seem to support your deep concern about utility operations. However, most of what is written on those pages extrapolates present ways of doing things and their impacts on the environment to a future date when energy needs are forecast as such and such and, therefore, the impacts of producing that energy will be of a horrendous magnitude. This would be equivalent to a study of the transportation industry in the past age of the horse which forecasted a day when the four-legged animals would stand shoulder to shoulder and nose to tail on our streets and highways.

"Obviously, such an equestrian catastrophe was headed off by an accelerating technology which developed a 'better way.' And implementing this better way has involved heavy use of electric energy. Throughout this letter and your earlier letter about the electric car your concern about the increasing use of electricity appears directed at individual consumer applications — home heating and the potential of electric vehicles. In 1968, of the total-electric energy sold in the United States, only 31 percent was consumed in the home. The remainder was used in producing and providing goods and services for all of us.

"So you see, when a curtailment in the use of electricity is suggested — a position which we do not agree with — the matter of 'doing without' has a much broader and deeper reach than merely cutting back on home air-conditioning, heating and other direct individual consumer applications.

"I believe the answer to your questions are (sic) well covered in the enclosed material with, in most cases, the most pertinent passages marked. For what we consider a good round-up of about what PP&L is doing to maintain the quality of the environment, I should like to direct your attention to the olive-colored folder with the ecology symbol. This folder is the reason for the small delay in replying to your letter. We had it in production and it was just delivered today.

"Responding to your closing paragraph, I should like to conclude with the last two paragraphs of remarks made by Mr. Austin Gavin, PP&L's executive vice president, at this year's annual meeting of shareowners.

'There are some who are saying that one solution to the environmental problem is reduction in the use of electricity. This is part of a broader position that we should have zero economic growth or even a reduction in gross national product. This is one alternative. But we suggest that all the consequences of such a policy be identified and evaluated before it is promoted as a solution. Are we ready to reduce our standard of living? What effect would such a policy have on our doing all the other socially desirable things such as rebuilding our cities, providing better methods of mass transit, reducing poverty and providing jobs for the additional young people coming into the work force? We will need 30 million more jobs by the end of this century if our population continues to increase at present rates. If we are to control population growth, can we do it without taking away individual freedom? These and many more gut issues need to be faced up to if we are to solve our environmental problems.

'It seems to us that all the qualities that have made possible our past achievements can be used to reduce the burdens on our environment to an acceptable degree without sacrificing our high standard of living. We, at PP&L, will do our part to attain this goal. As John Gardner has written " 'The prospects never looked brighter and the problems never looked tougher.' " "

Apparently the same thoughts I voiced to the power company had occurred to other people, for some time during the summer the power company announced the appointment of an environmental specialist, an able, dedicated young man who had headed the local cultural center until it closed for lack of county funds to maintain it.

Whether my letters and those of other concerned citizens brought about this very welcome addition to the power company staff I do not know. I like to think they did. At an August meeting of our conservation group we had a letter from the power company offering us the use, for a bird sanctuary, of a three-acre plot of land on which they have a sub-station in our township. We could maintain this fine marsh with all its birds and wild flowers and keep it forever free while the power company pays the taxes on it. An excellent idea, we thought. And we accepted gratefully.

On June 1 the local paper carried a statement by the president of the power company that the power company had not promoted the sale of air conditioning or major appliances for the past four years.

In August our conservation group had a "booth" at the local fair — a great institution visited by hundreds of thousands of people. Across the hall from us was the power company booth. They were distributing a handsome full color booklet entitled "Live Better Electrically," with the motto, on the cover "The Wedding veil cleanliness of total electric living."

This little magazine carries story after story of attractive, smiling people whose asthma has been cured when they put in electric heat, whose family colds have been eliminated with a dishwasher (!), whose self-cleaning electric oven is so efficient that presumably this housewife has lots of time to stand around, getting photographed for the power company magazine. On another page you are urged to "paint the night with light" — that is, plug in your electric skillet, corn popper, blender, warming tray, etc., etc., outside as well as inside, for you should have your entire garden, patio, pool as well lighted as the house!

Another family, says the booklet, gained another room in their basement by taking out all those ugly old fuel tanks and boilers and installing electric baseboard heat. Each individual room has a separate control. The words are not spoken but the implication is there — "isn't it worth destroying all our waterways so you can have perfect fingertip adjustment of temperature of every little corner of every teensy little room?!" *Well, is it?* Is this what technology has brought us to?

There are three pages of refrigerator-freezers, two on electric water heaters, a page of recipes, naturally, then a page of appliances. There's a hair dryer, (how can anyone possibly afford the time to dry one's hair without an electric dryer, even though every other page of the booklet suggests that the average housewife has at least 15 hours of complete leisure every day, because of her time-saving electric appliances.) Then there's an electric can opener and knife sharpener. An electric casserole (Cook the carefree way!). An electric mower. And finally — who would be without it? — an electric fruit ripener! I am not making this up. To "do the work of the sun" you just buy this attractive gadget for about $17, turn on the "Gro-Lux" fluorescent lamp and put your unripe fruit under it. The sun continues to be available, right outside the window, but who wants to bother with old-fashioned sun-ripening of fruit, when, for just a little money and a bit more destruction of the planet, you can have electric sun! Other booklets promote electric water heating with astonishing figures on how much cheaper it would be to rip out your old gas heater and put in a new electric one.

All this promotional material was given out at the Allentown Fair in the summer of 1970 when the newspapers had been full of warnings of power blackouts and brownouts all the way from northern New York State down to Philadelphia.

I plan to write a few more letters to the power company and I think you should do the same locally. It might not be a bad idea to ask the power company to take out your electric water heater and stove, if you have them. You're changing over to gas. Letters to the *New York Times* during one of their summer brownouts pointed out that, with all the furor over the brownout, with city employees going home early, subways curbing their speed, elevators not running all over the city, every city street and bridge still blazed with electric signs, every skyscraper burned lights far into the night. Another reader pointed out that the city could perhaps cut its electricity consumption in half by raising the temperature in air conditioned offices, theaters and restaurants to a bearable level, so that occupants would not have to sit bundled up in sweaters. Another reader, from upstate, queried very logically just why people who live quietly upstate with no air conditioners, no Broadways with millions of electric lights, no subways, no skyscrapers, should be asked to defile the integrity of their environment, pollute their rivers and lakes, tear down their mountains, change their climates and perhaps bring the entire environment to total ruin, just so that New Yorkers can enjoy looking out at millions of lights ablaze. Why indeed?

CHAPTER 11

QUIET — People Zone

"If . . . there is a (constitutional) right to an unquarried mountain, to a river that is not buried with millions of cubic yards of fill, or to an urban neighborhood not torn apart by an expressway, the denial of that right is substantially irrevocable. We are generally unable to restore what we have destroyed. We can more easily reform our own human institutions than we can restore a bulldozed landscape.

"There is special reason, therefore to require more deliberation and less speed in connection with projects that destroy the environment. . . . We have only one earth and, according to many politicians, scientists and college students (whose rare unity may be some evidence that they are right) not much more than 14 years to save it. I hope that the courts will act accordingly."

David Sive, *Civil Liberties*
April, 1970

"A falling off of outrage is the beginning of paralysis."

Morris Renek
New Republic
September 9, 1967

". . . in almost all of the court struggles for environmental rights to date, citizens' groups and conservation associations have been pitted against administrative agencies."

David Sive,
Civil Liberties
April, 1970

This was to have been a chapter devoted chiefly to the supersonic transport plane and the weapons conservationists have used in the battle against it.

It seems to be unnecessary, so this chapter will be, instead, a victory celebration for our side. We won! We won the fight against the biggest boondoggle of all time, the monstrous plaything nobody wanted except the company manufacturing it. Beginning with a small questioning murmur about ten years ago, the clamor against the SST had risen to a roar by the end of 1970.

On a memorable day in December, the Senate voted to reject the 290 million dollar appropriation for building prototype SST's. On December 6, the *New York Times* had this to say about the Senate's action:

"Specifically the 52–41 Senate vote deleted from an overall Department of Transportation budget a $290 million appropriation to press on with the building of two SST prototype planes. The issue now goes to a House-Senate conference, where SST proponents hope to salvage enough money — perhaps $100 million or more — to enable the program to limp along at a slower pace.

"But Senator William Proxmire, the Wisconsin Democrat who engineered the Senate action, appeared confident that the momentum built up against the SST would ensure its end.

"The SST, designed to carry just under 300 passengers at 1800 miles an hour (about 400 miles faster than the French-British Concorde and Russian TU-144 now undergoing test flights) has been in trouble before in the decade since the government advanced the first installment of an anticipated $1.3 billion investment in its development.

"It came close to disaster in 1968, when Boeing ran into horrendous technical difficulties with the swing-wing design that had won it the initial competition. Boeing saved the project by switching to the conventional fixed-wing approach, which has been going very well technically. But never has the plane seemed so close to oblivion as it does now.

"The Senate vote was also, however, a triumph for many forces. Chief among them were conservationists, who had warned of threats to the environment, and political figures, who bought the conservationists' argument and also questioned the order of national priorities.

"For many months the anti-SST groups have charged that the SST would spread atmospheric pollution, could cause cataclysmic climatic changes and would bombard the world's population with sonic booms and objectionable subsonic noise during take-offs. They also contended that it was shocking to pour money into what they considered a transportation frill when those funds were urgently needed to help relieve social distress. And they marshalled an impressive group of economists to derogate the argument of pro-SST forces that sacrifice of the SST market would cause serious economic damage, particularly by undermining the United States balance of payments position.

"The Senate vote was a shocker for many government and other figures, who fear that erosion of the nation's leadership in aviation would present a long-range danger to United States power and prosperity. But SST advocates were also bitter about some of the arguments presented by SST opponents."

The *Times* goes on to describe the rebuttals of the pro-SST forces. The noise of the SST would hardly be noticed! There isn't a chance that it could threaten a major change in climate! Etc.

The *Times* continues, "Some observers think the Senate vote might have gone differently if the White House and the industry had responded earlier and more vigorously to the concern of the determined anti-SST coalition. On Wednesday, the day before the big vote, the pro-SST Senate bloc put through amendments providing a legal ban on boom-producing flights over land and a legal requirement that SST's be as quiet at airports as subsonic jets.

"That was much too late to stop the anti-SST avalanche."

Possibly one reason why it was possible for conservationists to stop the SST juggernaut was the sheer idiocy of this project obvious to all from its inception. If ever there was a project which Had to be Done Just Because It Could Be Done and the hell with what effects it had on the earth and its inhabitants, this was it. From the beginning it has been apparent that the only advantage which could accrue from building this monstrosity was that a few — a very few — rich businessmen might be able to get across an ocean or a continent a few hours earlier. The plane has absolutely nothing else to recommend it!

Everyone admitted this could not possibly save anybody any time, since the amount of time needed to get from the airport to whatever city one wished to visit would still require the long, endless hours jammed into traffic messes. Everyone admitted that the damage done to the human biorhythm by flashing across half the world at 1800 miles per hour would require several days or perhaps a week or more of adjustment to bring the passenger back to normalcy.

Everyone agreed that the sonic boom was wholly unendurable and unacceptable. A number of cities banned the proposed plane from their airports. A number of countries banned or threatened to ban it from crossing their land area. Everyone agreed that building the SST would eventually necessitate larger airports farther away from cities, resulting in even longer, more traffic-ridden trips to wherever one was going. Almost everyone agreed that we do not have any final idea of the extent of damage that might be wreaked on the environment. Damage suits for destruction already wrought piled up. We, the taxpayers, footed the bill for these, of course. And we were expected to foot the bill — already close to two billion dollars — for building two prototype or sample planes for this Frankenstein monster which nobody wanted! Airlines frankly admit they cannot afford it and predict it will prove to be an economic bust.

Jacques Ellul in *The Technological Society* theorizes that the problems we are having with technology occur because of the very nature of technology. It is running along by itself, he says, evolving as living things evolve — a process which, once begun, cannot be stopped or controlled. If You Can Do The Thing, It Must Be Done, and your doing of it creates a vast circumference of other measures that Must Be Taken — economic, social, political. By the time these have grown into powerful forces, it is impossible to withdraw from the technological project itself, even though you find it is impossible, impracticable, unwise or completely defenseless from the point of view of common sense. You must proceed, nevertheless, because all the economic, social, political events you have created force you on!

The SST illustrates perfectly what Ellul means. Nobody — or hardly anybody — ever talks about it in terms of convenience or usefulness any more. We must build it because of the balance of payments! We must build it because we must retain our position in leadership of world aviation. We must build it because all those folks at Boeing will lose their jobs if it is cancelled!

The Citizens League Against the Sonic Boom was founded in 1967 under the directorship of Dr. William A. Shurcliff, Senior Research Associate at the Cambridge Electron Accelerator at Harvard.

His book *SST and Sonic Boom Handbook* lists 21 other organizations in this and other countries whose chief or parttime occupation is fighting the SST. The battle which culminated in the December, 1970 Senate rejection of an SST appropriation was fought with letters to the editor and to congressmen and senators, articles in the public press, meetings, newsletters, demonstrations, proposed lawsuits, appeals to government bureaus concerned with environmental protection, books, editorials, testimony before congressional committees, personal visits to congressmen and senators and masterful persuasion and political finagling by those Senate giants who steadfastly stood for common sense and protecting the environment in the midst of all the decade's hoopla over the SST. Senator Muskie alone is credited with bringing ten fence-sitters down on the side of the opponents. Senator Percy and Senator Proxmire, other movers and shakers, could not have won the victory without the help of the Sierra Club, the National Wildlife Society, Environmental Action, Friends of the Earth, Citizens Committee Against the Sonic Boom and many more such groups.

A *Times* reporter called the Sierra Club office the morning after the Senate vote and asked about the background din — the noises and cheering. He was told "We're not exactly having a wake here."

We won! We won at least the first battle in the campaign. The enemy forces are re-grouping and, with the probable encouragement of the administration, they will soon be proposing even more outrageous and idiotic steps in regard to the SST.

But we won the first battle! We proved conclusively for the first time on a national issue which has been gathering momentum for ten years, that we *can* protect this fragile earth and the people on it from at least one cruel and expensive assault by technology. Let's take heart from the victory over the SST and press on along all the other fronts! And, of course, let's keep an eye cocked over our shoulders to catch the first gestures toward revival of this gigantic imbecility which has, for the moment, been controlled.*

Stop watch in hand a New Yorker recently timed a trip from his home in Long Island to the General Post

* The final, March 24, 1971 vote in the Senate refusing funds for the SST appears to have scuttled it forever. But don't become too confident. Such is the nature of technology that we may have to fight this battle again in a few years.

Office Tower in London, England. The time in flight over the ocean was 6 hours, 7 minutes. The time spent getting from his home to the New York airport and from the London airport to the Post Office was 3 hours, 38 minutes 7–7/10 seconds. More than half as much time was spent covering several miles on the ground as on the 3,500 mile flight across the sea!

He timed another trip from New York City to Fort Lauderdale, Florida. From the moment he pushed the elevator button on West 43rd Street to take-off at Kennedy airport was 2 hours, 51 minutes, 34–6/10 seconds. Flying time to Fort Lauderdale was 2 hours, 20 minutes.

Let's press on to keep all those hundreds of millions of dollars from being misspent on the SST and let's somehow get them spent providing some kind of acceptable ground transportation for all of us!

CHAPTER 12

Not Bread, But a Stone

"Or what man is there of you, who, if his son shall ask him for a loaf, will give him a stone?"

Matthew 7:9

"In less than 20 years, the use of synthetic chemical pesticides has increased from a level of a few million pounds a year to nearly one billion pounds annually, according to the Public Health Service. Almost 60,000 pesticide formulations are now registered in the United States and each of these contains one or more of the approximately 800 different pesticide compounds."

Public Works
June, 1970

"I think it is bad that the TV networks make an annual profit of about 20 million dollars from Saturday morning children's programs; I am appalled to learn that 50 percent of all the nation's 2 to 11 year olds are in place before their TV sets every Saturday morning instead of in parks, woods or beaches or doing something intellectually stimulating; and I think it terrible that three companies spend over 42 million dollars on TV advertising of dry breakfast cereals in 1969. One is inescapably led to think how the money of these firms and the time of American children could be put to better use."

Dr. Michael Latham,
Professor of International Nutrition
Cornell University
in testimony before a Congressional Committee

In the March, 1970 issue of *FDA Papers,* the official publication of the federal Food and Drug Administration, an officer of that bureau, Leo Friedman, Ph. D., stated that American food contains "as a conservative estimate" about 10,000 chemical additives. Some of these are added deliberately in the processing of the food, others migrate there from the wrappings, others are residues left from the soil, water and air in which the foods were grown.

Dr. Friedman said, further, that "Many food additives have a long history of apparently safe use. Nevertheless it is becoming increasingly clear that untoward effects in people, stemming from food additives, are exceedingly difficult to recognize or even establish with any degree of certainty once suspicion has been aroused. It has been amply demonstrated . . . that subtle and long-range chronic effects are real events which can be related to specific external causes."

He pointed out further that the magnitude of the task is increased when you realize that it is not enough just to test the toxicity of one chemical substance in an animal or a man. What happens to the man or the animal who is exposed to some other chemical before the test has a great deal to do with the results. "Man is usually exposed to many (chemical) agents simultaneously or in close proximity. The need to understand the interactions among these agents becomes more and more obvious." He goes on to say that in other countries the law forbids the use of a new chemical in food where the safety of one in long use has been confirmed. In our country, on the other hand, any chemical manufacturer may sell to the food industry any new chemical which performs the same function as an old one, and all the tests must be done over again, all the chances taken once again by everybody who eats this new additive at their meals.

It's perfectly true that every individual has a different reaction to any potential poison. A food additive should be tested in regard to its effect on every organ of the body under every possible combination of circumstances that might increase its potential for harm, says Dr. Friedman. Now, just consider this statement for a moment. It is a well known fact in toxicology (the study of poisons) that when you add one poison to another, the total effect may be far more than just twice as bad. If you add three poisons, the total effect may be much more than just three times more poisonous than the effect of one poison. Again, it may not. You don't know until you test. This is called "potentiation." One poison "potentiates", or renders more powerful, another poison.

These toxicological facts make it readily apparent that even if the Food and Drug Administration were interested in testing chemical additives in food, and even if they had the vast financial and personnel resources necessary, they could not possibly perform this task. Just how could you go about testing the possible effects of any two additives on a large number of animals over a period of years, then, after you had apparently proved the safety of these two additives, adding still a third additive and testing the safety of this, in combination with the other two, and so on — until you have tested all possible combinations of 10,000 chemicals? It is, of course, patently impossible.

But this is not all. Any resident of a modern industrialized country is exposed every day to hundreds of thousands of other potential poisons — in air pollution, in water pollution, in cosmetics, in drugs, in household cleaning compounds, in industrial pollution at jobs and so on and so on.

Contemplating this dizzying array of possible combinations of poisons that can do you in, one begins to wonder how any of us have survived up to now, and how long we have a chance of surviving into the future. We actually understand very little about all these things; most modern hazardous chemicals have been introduced within the past 20 years or so.

Dr. Friedman reminds us that, in the past, animal tests have been done on newly weaned animals. Recently, in the furor over the flavoring agent, MSG, it came to light that newly born animals (and of course children) are developing the cells of nonregenerating tissues (kidney, brain and muscle) very rapidly during these early days. Once damaged by some chemical additive in food, these cells cannot repair themselves later on. So, he says, testing must now begin at birth, since the MSG incident produced damage in newborn animals, but not in older animals.

As time goes on, researchers find that old tests are no longer reliable, for new equipment is developed which can reveal damage which the old tests were not sensitive enough to show. "Our only hope of finding and plugging up these holes in our safety evaluation screen (of which we may be currently unaware) lies in new and innovative studies and approaches," says Dr. Friedman. He goes on to suggest that we may uncover the causes of degenerative diseases, cancer and all the metabolic diseases (diabetes, heart and circulatory disorders and so forth).

It is commonplace for nutrition scientists who work, directly or indirectly, for the giant food industry, to scoff at such prediction of harm from food additives and call anyone who points them out a "faddist". It's rather difficult to apply this contemptuous term to Dr. Friedman, who is Acting Director of the Division of Toxicology, Bureau of Foods, Pesticides and Product Safety, FDA. So far as I know, his history-making article in *FDA Papers* went completely unnoticed by the press. There is no way of knowing how much of the reason is just ignorance of what is going on at the FDA and how much is the result of concern for food advertising which pays a large part of the bills of almost every publication of general circulation in this country, from the daily newspaper right up to the slick weeklies and the gaudy women's magazines.

The fact remains that the present America food supply — the most abundant, the most beautiful, the most inexpensive food supply in all of history — *is teetering all the time on the very edge of turning out to be the one most potentially dangerous substance in our total environment.*

What are some of the additives we should be concerned about? Let's talk first about what gets into food while it is being raised. Stock animals — cows, chickens, calves, lambs, ducks, turkeys are no longer the product of homestead farmers who raise the animals in their pastures and meadows, woodlots and barnyards. No, indeed. Stock animals these days are raised in what one writer has called *Animal Machines* (Ruth Harrison is the author, the book is published by Vincent Stuart, Ltd. of London; the foreword is by Rachel Carson.) Don't glance at this book unless you have a strong stomach and a hard heart where animals are concerned. The pictures alone are enough to turn any humane person into a vegetarian. You view hogs jammed together in such concentrations that it is utterly impossible for them to move, hens crammed into "battery cages" where the sole object is to keep the eggs rolling out at any cost to the animals in health and comfort. Calves are confined in utter darkness in tiny stalls with bars and tethers to keep them from moving. They are deliberately starved of minerals so that their flesh will be "white". It seems that gourmet cooks demand "white" veal, God only knows why. The torture endured by these animals is unimaginable. Their bodies caked with manure, they are unable to rid themselves of the flies which torment them. Dying from lack of minerals and lack of roughage which all ruminant animals must have, these miserable creatures end up on your butchers' counter as "veal."

The raising of pigs, sheep and beef animals is almost as barbaric, though why should we use the term "barbaric"? No "barbarian" would ever treat animals like this! It is only modern technological man who has developed the best, the fastest, the most economical way to produce food. And this is it. Skip over the unimaginable horrors of slaughterhouses and consider for a moment just how any producer of food can keep animals alive under conditions like this until time to butcher them.

The natural habitat of any animal is the outdoors. Cows should roam over pastures, getting plenty of sunlight, lying in comfort to chew their cuds. Pigs should be free to root in the ground, chickens to scratch and peck worms and grubs out of the grass. Calves should be free to wander about as young things do, getting every bit of nourishment they can get from their mothers and from their pasture. Diseases can be easily controlled under such conditions. Animals which are ill can be separated from the rest until they recover. But, most of all, the healing virtues of sunlight, fresh air, nourishing food and the happy knowledge that there is plenty of room and companionship will keep almost any creature from becoming seriously ill.

What would happen to human beings under conditions like those in what stock raisers euphemistically call "intensive farming"? Concentration camps give us a good idea of what happens. Living things simply cannot survive under conditions like this unless they are drugged constantly, and hopped up with every imaginable kind of pill, potion, food supplement, injection and, in many cases, poison which holds off one disease or another or causes more rapid growth or some such condition desirable *from the point of view of the farmer, not the animal.* So this is precisely what happens in all those places on the face of the earth where "intensive farming" is practiced.

The Food and Drug Administration has come under some sharp criticism for its permissive attitude toward antibiotics in animal feed. In England strict rules have been laid down governing many of these drugs. If you are on the FDA mailing list, every few days you receive through the mail a new list of antibiotic combinations permitted for use in food or injections for cows, chickens, ducks, sheep, etc. Instructions are given for how the drugs are to be fed or injected, how much is to be used and how long a period must elapse before the animal is slaughtered after the drugs are given. How much attention any individual farmer gives to these instructions is a matter between him and his conscience. Certainly no FDA inspector is standing by his side all day as he goes about his work. To be sure, spot checks are made of meat and milk to determine the amount of antibiotics they contain but certainly the vast majority of all stock animals are never tested before they are sold.

Antibiotics have come in for special concern because there is considerable evidence that bacteria develop resistance to certain antibiotics and this resistance may be transferred from one group of dangerous bacteria to another. This resistance may carry over to human beings who eat the meat. There are, too, human beings who have such exquisite sensitivity to certain antibiotics that they will die in an allergic crisis if they ever get a tiny amount of, let's say, penicillin. Such people are taking a chance with their very lives every time they eat a piece of meat or drink a glass of milk.

The February 10, 1970 issue of the *Wall Street Journal* carried a headline "Chicken Cancer Called Widespread Enough to Pose Nightmare for Poultry

Industry." Avian leukosis is a disease — a poultry form of leukemia. After a great deal of fuss, the Department of Agriculture (this kind of decision is theirs rather than that of the FDA) decided against allowing cancerous chickens to be sold. For the present, that is. Of course, it was conceded that practically all poultry carry the virus in their bodies, so we are getting it anyway, but not in the quantities we'd get from sick chickens.

Ludwik Gross, M.D., a cancer specialist, writing in the *New York Times* in January, 1970, said "nobody can foresee the possible long-term effects on human health of the ingestion of large quantities of leukemic organs. . . . Only a few years ago cancer investigators were under the impression that a well-known chicken tumor . . . could be transferred in the laboratory only to chickens and certain related birds, such as pheasants and ducks, but not to other animal species. Unexpectedly we have now realized that this particular tumor can readily be transmitted to many other animal species. . . ." Final word from the Department of Agriculture states that they are not changing their ruling. Chickens afflicted with leukosis may not be sold for human consumption. It's safe to say that hullabaloo raised by Ralph Nader and a lot of consumer groups all over the country had a lot to do with this decision.

In September, 1970, the FDA announced they had decided to allow farmers to feed a certain hormone to cattle *at double the levels formerly permitted.* The hormone is diethylstilbestrol. It fattens the cattle in less time. Farmers are supposed to stop feeding the hormone to their animals two days before butchering. An AP dispatch pointed out, "The regulations depend heavily for enforcement on the voluntary cooperation of farmers and feed mills." An Iowa State University Professor who raises cattle himself said, "Within 12 hours after a farmer decides the price is right, his cattle are likely to be at the slaughterhouse." And cleaning out elaborate feeding machinery already stocked with food supplemented with the hormone is too much trouble for most farmers. The FDA action was taken at the request of a drug company which manufactures the hormone.

Why should we be concerned? Diethylstilbestrol is suspected of causing cancer. Don't we have some protection against additives which may cause cancer? We do, indeed — the Delaney Amendment to the 1958 food protection law which states that no additive is permitted in food if it is found to cause cancer in laboratory animals *at any level of feeding.* The regulation is under heavy fire at present from the food and additive industries, bulwarked by the AMA which feels that the amendment is unrealistic, unenforceable and so on. It is, it appears, seldom enforced in the spirit of the law, although sometimes, as in the celebrated cranberry case, the FDA makes a great show of protecting us.

Well, then, let's all be vegetarians. Shall we take a brief look at what happens to fruits, grains and vegetables at the hands of the growers who are out to send you, remember, the best, the finest, the most perfect and the most beautiful apple, orange, turnip or lettuce leaf! We have been educated unfortunately to equate beauty with wholesomeness. The bigger and more perfect the apple, the most toxic spray has probably been used in its production. Lettuce that is crisp, so crisp, and completely free from any holes or worm-nibbles has been raised under conditions where sprays are applied as often as anyone can get around to it, until the soil is soaked and drenched with them.

In 1965 *Science and Citizen* estimated that there were approximately 500 pesticide compounds in use in a total of 56,000 different pesticide formulations registered with the government. This number has undoubtedly increased greatly since then. The U.S.D.A. *Handbook* for 1966 states, "Insecticides are important to agriculture and in general they are effective, safe and cheap. However, the great good derived from them can sometimes be partially offset by adverse effects. The chlorinated hydrocarbon insecticides may leave toxic residues. Some of these insecticides turn up in meat and milk, persist in the soil and under certain conditions may harm beneficial insects, fish and other wildlife. Another problem is the resistance that builds up in certain species of insects. . ."

Science and Citizen, October, 1966, tells us that DDT came into widespread use in the early 1940's. The first resistant houseflies were reported in 1946. There were 12 insect species in which resistance to organic insecticides had been reported by 1948, 16 in 1951, 25 in 1954, 76 in 1957, 137 in 1960 and 157 in 1963. By 1966 there were more than 165. "Resistant" means that they are no longer harmed by the chemical. So they swarm back in ever-increasing numbers, year after year, so that ever higher doses of ever more toxic chemicals must be developed to destroy them.

In the April, 1965 issue of *Science and Citizen,* we are told that scientists are relatively ignorant about the chemical alteration of pesticides by the action of plants, soil organisms and various physical aspects of the environment. After the introduction of one pesticide, for example, it was discovered that it was converted, through the action of weather, into a much more toxic form. It was also discovered that one chemical can react with another to produce a substance more dangerous than either of the first two. Malathion, for instance, is more toxic in the presence of EPN, another insecticide. There is evidence that parathion, a highly toxic insecticide, becomes more dangerous in the presence of certain tranquilizers.

What about the cancer-causing possibilities of pesticides? Says *Science and Citizen,* "Some of the chemical characteristics of dieldrin, endrin and heptachlor are the same as those that in other compounds are known to induce mutations and cancer . . . Toxic doses of chlorinated hydrocarbons are known to cause liver damage, alterations in brain wave patterns and cancer in some experimental animals . . . One of the hydrocarbons, DDD, is used to induce cancer in animals for experimental purposes." DDD, incidentally, is characterized as of "low to medium" toxicity to human beings in the U.S.D.A. book, *Safe Use of Agricultural and Household Pesticides.* Not nearly as toxic as parathion, phorate, phosdrin, Tepp — and so on!

Is it likely that anyone is going to drop dead from eating produce as contaminated as the available FDA figures indicate? It seems unlikely, for this is not acute exposure, but rather chronic exposure. And, says *Science and Citizen,* "The doses in chronic exposure may be far below those necessary to produce the symptoms of acute toxicity, but this does not necessarily imply lack of hazard, particularly if the exposure involves an entire population and the entire lifetime of individuals . . ."

In the United States more than two and a half billion dollars are spent annually on weedkillers. Why do weeds pose such a threat to the commercial grower of food? They compete with the food plants for available moisture, soil, minerals, light. They interfere with harvesting machinery. And some of them may show up in the final crop and have to be removed after the harvest. All this is expensive for the grower.

From 1944 the use of weedkillers or herbicides has increased rapidly in this country. By 1964 more than 260 million pounds of herbicides were produced. By 1962 they were applied to more than 70 million acres of cropland. It may cost as much as two million dollars just to develop an effective weedkiller, so the producer has a big investment in it and wants to be sure of a profit. *Chemical Week* reported in 1963 that the sales of all pesticides by 1975 are estimated to hit the two billion dollar mark. Weedkillers will make up a large part of this volume.

What do we know about weedkillers and their effects on the soil? Very little actually. Says the *USDA Handbook for 1966,* "The complexity and variation of the soil system makes the study of herbicide residue complicated, expensive and time consuming . . . Weed researchers want to know more about persistence or carry-over of herbicides under different environmental conditions so they can establish safe rotation practices . . . Often a number of herbicides are used during a single crop season . . . when used according to instructions on the label they have never caused a reported injury or death of any person through contamination of food (as of July 1, 1965). No safety system, however, is infallible." Exactly.

Most of us remember the day when the Food and Drug Administration removed from sale a big part of the cranberry crop in one area of the country because it was contaminated with a weedkiller. The incident occurred because the growers used the herbicide at the wrong time of year. Government spokesmen were quick to point out that the herbicide had been misused, that this could not happen if directions were followed to the letter. But so far as the consumer is concerned, it doesn't much matter to him how the contamination happens. He risks being just as badly injured no matter whose fault it is!

Doesn't the FDA have inspectors who check on this kind of thing all the time? The FDA has a pitifully small group of inspectors who spot-check shipments of produce that cross state lines. They have no jurisdiction over food raised and sold inside state boundaries. Every month's issue of *FDA Papers* carries notes on produce seized: celery from Louisiana contaminated with parathion, a chemical so toxic that several drops on the skin can produce death; squash from Florida contaminated with endrin; wheat from Minnesota contaminated with mercury; cabbage from North Carolina containing too much toxaphene; celery from Wisconsin contaminated with parathion; shelled corn containing captan which is not permitted in any quantity, however small; popcorn from Iowa contaminated with aldrin, an insecticide, and 2, 4D, a weedkiller; butter from Illinois contaminated with dieldrin, an insecticide.

These were some of the shipments that were stopped. How many others were not checked? No one will ever know, of course. The amount of food moving across country is impossibly immense for even a very large staff of inspectors to check every shipment. Most states have a staff of inspectors to check on produce sold within the state borders. How good a job they do is anybody's guess. When did you last check with your own state board of health to find out how large their staff of inspectors is, and how much of all produce sold in the state is inspected?

Pesticide Residues, published by the Food and Drug Administration, says that the inspector "collects samples of crops he thinks most likely to contain unauthorized residues." This booklet also points out that the harmful effect of one chemical may increase when it is taken along with residues of another.

They cheerfully tell us that people may be much more sensitive to poisons than the laboratory animals on which the effects of the poisons are tested, and that some people may be more sensitive than others. They tell us firmly that no chemical known to cause cancer in animals is allowed in any food. Of course, DDT is the most widespread of all pesticides and scientists are now beginning to discover that it may cause cancer in animals. DDD, as we have seen earlier, is used in laboratories *specifically to induce cancer in animals!*

As this book goes to press, Michigan studies the legal steps to permanently ban DDT for farm, garden and household use. Sweden recently outlawed DDT and all its derivatives pending further scientific study of its effects on higher forms of life.

A one-year ban on the use of DDT and DDD pesticides has been in effect in Arizona since mid-January, 1969. New York and Pennsylvania authorities are among those states considering a DDT ban similar to Michigan.

"Several organic phosphates that act systemically (the plant absorbs the insecticide and moves it to the leaf or stem) can be used to control certain insects attacking cotton, vegetables and forage crops. Seeds are treated with the chemical, or granules containing it are placed in the furrow at planting time. The chemical is taken up by the plant and when an insect feeds on the leaf or stem it dies."

This is the story of the systemic insecticide, told so casually in the U. S. Department of Agriculture Handbook, *Protecting Our Food.* This chemical makes the entire plant poisonous, so poisonous that any insect even nibbling on it is killed. When such poisons were invented, alarmed farmers and gardeners protested. How could they poison their entire crop just to kill insects! They were assured by the chemical makers and the Department of Agriculture that such poisons would never be used on food plants. They were for ornamental plants only, and things like cotton which is, of course, not eaten.

But somehow, over the years, more and more systemic insecticides have been used on food and today they are spread all over the landscape almost as casually as those which are sprayed on. Any effort you might make, any small gesture you might perform toward getting rid of insecticides by washing your fruits and vegetables thoroughly, even scouring them with soap might help a little in removing chemicals on the outside of the food. But it will obviously achieve nothing for chemicals which are inside the plant which produced the food, hence inside the food itself.

Were systemic pesticides used on the vegetables you bought at the supermarket yesterday? Who knows?

Where were they grown? Did the farmer observe carefully all the precautions listed on the label of the pesticide which supposedly give the consumer some protection against them, or did he just proceed according to his own ideas? Who knows? Do you?

A government publication totally concerned with protecting you from pesticides is the *Pesticides Monitoring Journal.* In a recent issue an article told of pesticide residues in seed foods and the products made from them: salad oils, margarine, salted peanuts and so on. "A total of 1,230 residues of 20 pesticide chemicals were reported in 641 positive samples of the 2,389 samples of raw products . . . DDT . . . dieldrin, lindane, toxaphene, endrin, BHC and chlordane account for 95 percent of the residues found in oil seeds . . . and refined oils."

There are legal limits to the amount of such pesticides that may be present in foods, although everyone concerned agrees that the ideal situation is to have no residues at all. But such a situation is apparently not possible. With one exception, no foods in the above list had more toxic residues than the law allows.

The government also conducts what they call a "total diet sample" based on what a presumably very nutrition-conscious teenage boy might eat in the course of a week. Periodically, samples of such foods are tested by government chemists to see how high the level of pesticides are this month, generally speaking. The cold objective facts and figures chill the bones, although the chemists conclude cheerfully that "residues remain at low levels".

In March, 1968 *Pesticides Monitoring Journal* the following were reported:

In garden fruits a total of eight chlorinated organic chemicals were detected, DDT being the most common. Ten were found in orchard fruits, DDT being the most common. Leafy vegetables were found to contain DDT, DDE, TDE, aldrin, BHC, chlordane, dieldrin, endrin and lindane. Parathion was found, as was arsenic. Potatoes showed DDT, dieldrin, CIPC, lindane, TDE and PCP. Grain and cereal products were contaminated with DDT and eight other toxic chemicals, meat, fish and poultry contained a total of ten chlorinated organic pesticides; dairy products thirteen.

"The presence of chlorinated organic residues was confirmed in 224 of the 360 composites examined . . ."

Now, you might go away thinking that there's not much to be concerned about here. The amounts of all the chemicals were within the "legal limits," weren't they?

We remind you that many pesticides like DDT accumulate or pile up in body tissues. The total damage they do is the total amount to which you are exposed over a lifetime.

Your children come into the world with measurable quantities of DDT in their bodies. They get more DDT from milk, either breast milk or dairy milk. One very concerned Swedish scientist, Dr. Goran Löfroth of the Institute of Biochemistry at the University of Stockholm, wrote in the December 5, 1968 issue of *New Scientist* that DDT has been found to cause cancer, that most people in countries where the use of DDT is widespread already carry from 5 to 27 parts per million in their body tissues. He says further that breastfed babies in European countries are consuming about 70 percent above the maximum acceptable amount of DDT, while breast-fed babies in the United States have a still higher intake. In respect to dieldrin, another highly toxic pesticide, forty percent of the babies in Sweden ingest at least twice the amount maximally acceptable to officials and *breast-fed babies in America consume about ten times that recommended limit!*

Dr. Löfroth states that . . . "Man himself is the potential victim — not just those birds and beasts for whom these chemicals have already proved disastrous. There is at least the possibility of a human tragedy occurring if our present practices continue unrestrained. Must we demand the evidence of a catastrophe before we act? . . . Summing up, we see that we are exposing coming generations to amounts of organochlorine pesticides which are greatly in excess of those to which we are exposing ourselves."

If there is any doubt in your mind about the toxic quality of the chemicals we are talking about, send for a copy of the government publication, *Safe Use of Agricultural and Household Pesticides.* Here are 65 pages of pure horror. You are told the safe way to open the bags of poison; how to dress when you apply them, how to dispose of the empty containers so that they will not poison anyone who happens to pick them up! There are pages of urgent instructions on how to wash your clothing if you happen to spill any of the poison on you; how to care for the rubber gloves and gas masks you must wear. If your shoes become contaminated with pesticide, you must burn or bury them!

Pictures show farmers and gardeners as well as the pilots who fly the spray planes completely covered in protective clothing, with glass face masks, rubber shoes, special gloves. Then follow ten pages of first-aid instructions for perhaps saving your life if you happen to expose your eyes, face, skin, hands, lungs to these shockingly deadly poisons. The last 20 pages divulge the "relative toxicity of chemical pesticides". Here is the record for the pesticides whose residues were reported on practically everything tested in the *Pesticides Monitoring Journal.* The pesticides are graded according to whether they have low, medium, high or very high toxicity for human beings. On every page the reader is urged to read pesticide labels carefully and do exactly what the label says.

Finally, there is the massive study conducted by the National Cancer Institute involving 50 out of 130 widely used pesticides, which turned out to cause tumors in animals tested. Results of this study were announced early in 1969 in abstracts for a scientific meeting. Suddenly the Institute decided that they would not present papers on this subject, after all, "until the study had been re-examined." *Federal officials even refused to reveal the names of the products that had produced the tumors.* Some of them are bound to be finally declared to be cancer-causing, but "others will be cleared, and it would not be fair to name them now", said this salaried representative of the American people, dedicated to protecting their health!

An enormous number of animals were studied — 26,000 mice. They were given the pesticides in a perfectly controlled experiment, using as controls other mice which were given compounds known to cause cancer. The tumors found in the mice being investigated turned out to be exactly the same kind of thing as those found in the mice getting the known carcinogen. "We are as anxious as anyone to get this information before the public," said Dr. Kenneth Endicott, Director of the National Cancer Institute, "But we don't intend to frighten people needlessly." He emphatically denied that pressure from the giant pesticide industry had anything to do with their decision not to release all the facts!

Comments from experts around the country were about what one would expect. Dr. Malcolm Hargreaves, retired professor of medicine at University of Minnesota and Senior Consultant at the Mayo Clinic, said, "Since the advent of pesticides in 1947, I've seen and taken inquisitive personal histories on 1200 cases of blood dyscrasias and lymphoid diseases (cancerous conditions of blood and glands). Every patient at some time or another had great exposure to a pesticide, a herbicide, a paint thinner, a cleaning agent, or the like. And I wouldn't exempt organophosphates (other pesticides), which the NCI isn't testing at all. I've had several cases demonstrating their involvement in blood marrow depression, sudden prothrombin changes, liver insufficiency, and thrombocytopenia purpura."

Dr. Wayland Hayes, formerly chief pesticide consultant for the National Contagious Disease Control Center, said "It's obvious that the experts in the NCI study can't make heads or tails out of the results themselves." A scientist chiefly concerned with human environment said, "Show me a pathologist with guts enough and I'll show you deaths secondary to chronic or intermittent exposure to these (chemical) agents."

All of these pesticides have already been tested for safety, we are told by government agencies. And now it comes out that most of the tests were performed by the very companies who manufacture the poisons! Says the FDA's Lessel Ramsey, "The majority of all such tests have been industry-sponsored and many of the 900 chemicals and 45,000 formulations on the market were tested years ago. Since organophosphates (pesticides) were considered relatively safe, some were merely tested in two species of animals for 90 days . . ."

Said Dr. Wilhelm C. Hueper, formerly of National Cancer Institute, "Such tests are a waste of taxpayers' money — they weren't long enough or thorough enough. But they found tumors all right — in both dieldrin and DDT studies. Only the pathologists were meek about it in ruling them nonmalignant." Dr. Hueper also tells, in a story on this whole disgraceful matter reported in *Medical World News* for March 14, 1969, of a Miami University investigation which showed that terminal cancer patients, chosen at random, were found to have high concentrations of pesticide residues in liver, brain and fatty tissues.

One can hardly imagine the state of mind of anyone who would be unaffected and cynical about such a frightful revelation as that of the National Cancer Institute. But a Texas physician, a specialist in pesticide poisoning, who also owns a 1000 acre grain ranch was quoted as saying, "Sure, parathion kills the hell out of fish down here. But we've got better crops and more per acre. I'll admit I'm using twice the parathion per acre that I did five years ago. Maybe something will hit 20 years from now. I'll worry about it then."

The February, 1969 issue of *FDA Papers* has a lengthy article on other means of controlling insect pests, aside from toxic chemicals, ways of doing things that present no hazards at all to the consumer. The author tells us that the Department of Agriculture is devoting much more of its time and money to developing ways of eliminating insect pests that do not involve noxious chemicals. They mention, among ways to accomplish this, many of the methods that are already used by organic growers, and they indicate that it may be years until such methods are economically feasible for commercial growers.

Organic farmers, gardeners, poultry and cattlemen are already using these methods, have used them for years, have taken all the financial risks and absorbed all the extra costs which the Department of Agriculture assures us commercial growers will not be able to do for years, after economical methods have been developed by government experts, using, of course, your tax money for this work.

Organic gardeners and farmers perform all the extra work, go to all the lengths that are necessary, in order to produce food that is free from toxic pesticides. They do this because they believe in the principles of organic gardening and they must garden and farm according to their principles. They cannot remove the threat of eventual harm which hangs over us all because of the worldwide pollution of our planet with pesticides. But they can promise you that the foods you buy *from them* will be grown as free from all toxic chemicals as it is possible to grow food.

A threat to health which is not often mentioned in regard to commercially grown food came into the scientific spotlight at the 1968 meeting of the American Association for the Advancement of Science when Dr. Barry Commoner of Washington University, whose field is ecology, spoke on the present pollution of our environment with nitrates.

During the past 25 years, said Dr. Commoner, nitrogen from sewage which, of course, pollutes most of our waterways, has increased no more than 70 percent. But oxides of nitrogen from power plant fumes and automobile exhausts have increased by 300 percent and the use of nitrogen fertilizers has increased by 1400 percent! These last two processes add some 10 million tons of nitrogen compounds to the environment each year, more nitrogen than is cycled annually inside the United States by all the processes of nature combined!

The nitrates run off into the water supply and they remain on food which is grown with heavy applications of this kind of fertilizer. The nitrates which are accumulating in our water supplies pose a serious threat to health. The Public Health Service limits the amount of nitrogen compounds in drinking water to no more than 10 parts per million. Already the water in one-fourth of the shallow wells in Illinois exceeds this limit; so do many wells in Southern California. In one town in Minnesota, the water supply has been abandoned because of the high concentration of nitrogen it contained.

Children are most at risk so far as nitrates in food are concerned. These are changed by intestinal bacteria into nitrites which are toxic. Poisoning of children because of excessive nitrates in food has been reported in Europe. One French doctor believes that no more than 300 parts per million should be allowed in any food, especially those eaten by children. In a recent study of commercial baby foods, 444 parts per million were found in wax beans, 977 in beets and 1373 in spinach.

Supposedly, says Dr. Commoner, we can somehow manage to control the nitrates released from municipal and industrial wastes, but how can we possibly limit the nitrogen that runs off fields fertilized with commercial fertilizer? As population figures soar, the agriculture industry uses more and more fertilizer in order to get bigger yields. "Science can reveal the depths of this crisis," says Dr. Commoner, "but only social action can resolve it."

In *Science and Citizen,* January–February, 1968, Dr. Commoner tells the story of fields kept in continual use at a Missouri Agriculture Station since 1888. With proper crop rotation and the use of manure the annual value of the crops produced by the plots of soil increased over a 50-year period. Nitrogen in the plots remained at essentially the same concentration during this time. In later tests when chemical fertilizers were used, the organic or humus content of the soil decreased and nitrogen not used by the plants leached out of the soil and ran off the fields. And today, says Dr. Commoner, "at the heavy rates of chemical fertilization now widely used in the U. S. . . . plants grown on heavily fertilized soil contain much increased amounts of nitrate."

In children especially the conversion of this nitrate to nitrite can result in destroying the oxygen-carrying capacity of the blood which can lead to respiratory failure and death.

Organic enthusiasts are frequently ridiculed because of their devotion to maintaining "the balance of nature". Says Dr. Commoner, "We have become not less dependent on the balance of nature, but *more* dependent. Modern technology has so stressed the web of processes in the living environment at its most vulnerable points that there is little leeway left in the system. I believe that unless we begin to match our technological power with a deeper understanding of the balance of nature we run the risk of destroying this planet as a suitable place for human habitation." Somber words indeed.

A recent report by Dr. Arnold Schaefer, Chief of the Nutrition Program, Division of Chronic Disease Programs, Public Health Service, revealed that, in a study of 12,000 people, 13 percent of everyone examined had blood levels of vitamin A that were less than acceptable for good health. Several months before that, a Canadian study provided proof that "a shocking incidence" of low or non-existent liver stores of vitamin A had been found in autopsies on 500 supposedly healthy people. Eight of these in Ottawa had no vitamin A at all in their livers; in Montreal 20 percent of those examined had no vitamin A stores whatsoever.

In all these cases the investigators have said they do not know the cause of such conditions. Is it possible that people are just not eating foods that contain enough vitamin A? That's possible, of course, but it's just as possible that the nitrates in the food they are eating are destroying vitamin A wholesale and hence creating deficiencies in this extremely important vitamin.

In additon to pesticides and harmful residues from fertilizers, commercially grown and processed foods may contain one, several or very many of a large number of food additives, chemicals permitted by the Food and Drug Administration for use in and on foods. Fresh vegetables and fruits may be dyed and waxed. They may be packed in containers or wrappings drenched in preservatives. Canned and packaged foods sold in supermarkets may legally contain any or all *of approximately 2500 different chemical additives.*

Addressing industry representatives at the annual Food and Drug Law Institute in December, 1968, C. C. Johnson, head of the newly formed Consumer Protection and Environmental Health Service, singled out chemical food additives as "among several environmental problems so complex as to appear almost beyond remedy. We know too little about the effects of these additives, pesticide and drug residues," he said, "especially in their combination with the rest of the chemical barrage that reaches us from other parts of the environment."

He went on to say that the use of food additives for color, flavor or other reasons has risen 50 percent in the past decade and that each *American now consumes about three pounds a year of such chemicals.*

Dr. Herbert Ley, Food and Drug Administration Commissioner at that time , said, at the same meeting, "The range of such additives is enormous." In 1966 about 700 million pounds of some 2500 different food additives were used. It is estimated that by 1974 the amount will exceed one billion pounds. Among the fastest-growing chemical additives are: preservatives, stabilizers, thickeners and nutritional ingredients. This last additive is to restore some of the vitamins and minerals removed from foods when they are processed.

You do not have to use any of these additives when you cook good, wholesome, nourishing foods at home. Yet somehow the giant food industry finds that it just cannot fill the supermarket shelves with colorful, flavorful, acceptable foods without adding 700 million pounds a year of some 2500 different chemical additives!

The history of food additives is littered with stories of chemicals which were at first thought to be quite safe, later found dangerous in one way or another. With new additives and petitions for their use pouring into the FDA offices in Washington at a rate of more than 300 a year, officials fear that the sheer number of new chemicals in man's diet may create troublesome effects from unpredictable combinations.

What is meant by "unpredictable combinations"? Two scientists of the National Cancer Institute write in a recent issue of *Food and Cosmetic Toxicology,* of experiments with animals involving cancer-causing chemicals. They have found that such experiments are valid only under carefully controlled conditions where every other kind of chemical was carefully restricted. Once other chemicals were present you might find that one of these had caused the substance you were testing to become cancer-causing, even though it would not be so under other conditions! This phenomenon is called "potentiation" among chemists. It means simply that one element mixed with another may produce harmful effects which neither would produce alone. When you think in terms of 2500 chemicals that are deliberately added to foods, plus all those, like pesticides, that get into foods although they are not wanted there, plus all the other chemical pollutants to which we are exposed in the course of one lifetime, it seems a small miracle that any of us survive.

In regard to chemicals that cause cancer, it is well known (and pointed out again in the article above) that exposure to the cancer-causing chemical may not result in cancer for many years, at which time, of course, it will be impossible to do anything about it.

Say the authors, "It is fair to say that trace amounts of carcinogens (cancer-causing substances) surround us and probably enter our bodies with our food, air or water. What zero tolerance in respect of food additives really means is that deliberate addition to the carcinogenic (cancer-causing) burden already upon us should be avoided where this is at all feasible."

By "zero tolerance" they mean the FDA regulation now in effect which says that no substance known to cause cancer is allowed in our food. Obviously, this regulation just cannot be enforced. DDT has been shown to produce cancer in laboratory animals. Yet all of us have DDT in our bodies as a result of past exposure. In 1964 the FDA announced that no pesticides at all would be allowed in milk. Since then and right up to this moment many tests by the FDA have revealed pesticides in milk. There seems to be no way by which this contamination can be prevented. Officials just make their reports, express their discouragement and that ends it. Finally, in 1966, the FDA revised their standards of no pesticides permitted, by saying that this is not "realistic", so they revised the legal limit upward to permit the levels of pesticides then being found!

Dr. Wilhelm Hueper, retired chief of the National Cancer Institute's environmental cancer section, has been outspoken in his concern about chemicals which cause cancer getting into our food supply. He believes that a number of food additives are potential cancer-causers and he has pleaded for many years for more stringent control of these chemicals.

Nutrition Reviews for November, 1966, whose editor at the time was Dr. Fredrick Stare of Harvard, reported "today we find ourselves with a growing body of evidence from a number of sources that the nonessential dietary components of foods and feeds may indeed play a very important role in the world-wide incidence of cancer."

The authors describe an epidemic of liver cancer

among trout which was traced to a food additive in their feed, and cancer in chicks traced to a new ingredient in commercial feed. Such experiences should warn us, they say, "of the folly of accepting new food processing methods or new food additives without adequate testing for possible carcinogenic effects."

They go on to say that cancer is often the result of a long exposure to low concentrations of a cancer-causing substance. And "It is becoming clear that we cannot afford the luxury of debate about 'safe' levels of one carcinogen alone when in actuality it may act synergistically with other environmental agents such as radioactivity in the atmosphere or air pollutants." The studies they have referred to should warn us, they say, of the possibility of "disastrous problems ahead."

So you can stand in front of the supermarket counter and remember everything you now know about what has happened to the food arrayed so attractively before you. This way, you'll find it gets more and more difficult to eat. You'll find that you dread the shopping trips. You'll find yourself developing obsessive care in washing fruits and vegetables. You can't wash off a systemic pesticide, you know. And you can't wash off the myriad waxes, dyes, packaging chemicals and so forth, so don't bother.

In view of the evidence presented above, it may cheer you greatly to know that you can probably do more to save your family from the hazards of modern commercially produced food than you can to prevent harm from water and air pollution, radioactivity and the other technologically created pollutants in today's environment.

If you have even a tiny patch of land, you can plant

a garden and raise your own vegetables without any sprays or chemical fertilizers. There's nothing hard about it. Even if you've never put a trowel into the ground, you can produce a worthwhile crop the first year, with a lot of hard physical work that will be ever so beneficial in terms of good health, weight-watching, and satisfaction. You can pack a good-sized freezer with enough vegetables to last for quite a few winter months.

You can raise berries the same way, if you have enough room. Fruit is a bit harder. You will have fruit that does not look exactly like the splendid, identical fruits the commercial growers produce. You will have some worms and some grubs. An orchard where no sprays are used demands hard work and great devotion, for you must plant the area around the orchard as well, to attract birds which are your chief insect killers. Birds are good neighbors and good friends. The bugs that come to eat your apples are banquets for them all summer long. The grubs that prey not just on orchard trees but all unsprayed trees are feasts for winter birds. You'll have chickadees and juncoes, nuthatches and woodpeckers to cherish all winter.

If you have enough land and equipment, it's possible to raise your own grain, grind it into flour yourself, and make your own bread without using any pesticides or commercial fertilizer. It's hard work. You'll have disappointments and failures. But you'll learn. You'll be an example to your neighbors. Refrigeration provides the best way to store grain or bread so that it is not attacked by all the pests that like grain as much as we do.

For meat and eggs, raise your own if you can manage it. If not, seek out some source of meat, poultry and eggs that have not been produced with the usual modern methods. As like as not there are, living near you, people called organic gardeners and farmers. These are people dedicated to the same high principles as you. They want food untainted with manmade chemicals. They work hard, take appalling financial risks and develop tough skins to ward off ridicule. You'll find their products advertised in health magazines and *Organic Gardening and Farming.* A new guide to sources of organic food is published every year at Rodale Press, where the whole idea of organic gardening started in this country many years ago. If you live in some part of the country where there is absolutely no hope of procuring organically grown food, try to talk some farmer into giving or renting you a patch of land where you can try your luck at gardening. Remember the Victory Gardens during the war? We all somehow found patches of soil and raised our own vegetables. You'll be surprised at how soon the farmer and his neighbors will become interested in your efforts and will come around to see if you succeed. Perhaps you can persuade a farmer to raise cattle, chickens, sheep or hogs for your family and friends to share, but raise it the way stock used to be raised — in the open, maturing as nature designed the process, staying healthy without drugs.

One final word on chemicalized food. Glancing through *Chemicals Used in Food Processing,* published by National Academy of Sciences — National Research Council, one is struck with the number of times the words "beverages, ice cream, ices, candy, baked goods, chewing gum, gelatin desserts, puddings, prepared mixes," and such words appear, in the listings of chemicals and the foods in which they are used.

Fruits, vegetables, meats, poultry, eggs and dairy products are, as I have pointed out above, treated with many chemicals in their agricultural production. Once they are produced, however, and ready for sale, there is little anyone can do to chemicalize them further. (What can anybody do to an egg, safe inside its shell?) But when the food industry begins making things for "convenience" and putting together all manner of fancy concoctions designed not so much for any purpose but making you fat, the quality and variety of chemicals goes up by leaps and bounds. Candy, soft drinks, baked goods, packaged mixes, sauces and toppings, things in aerosol cans, cheese "spreads" and shortenings must be doctored with countless additives like sequestrants, antioxidants, preservatives, stabilizers, thickeners, buffers, synthetic flavors, foaming agents, texturizers, binders, anti-caking agents and dyes.

The safest way to avoid all this mess of potential trouble is just not to buy any of these foods. Make your own. What should you buy? Just these:

Meat, as is on the counter, not prettied up into fancy dishes either in the freezing compartment or in dried or canned form. Plain frozen meat has suffered little damage, nutritionally speaking.

Fish. Ocean fish is probably one of the safest foods, from the point of view of pollutants. We have not yet managed to pollute the ocean to such an extent that tuna, cod, haddock, salmon and so on pose any significant hazard. Inland fish come, mostly, from highly polluted rivers and lakes. When did anyone last check the mercury, the lead or the sewage in any local waterway — do you know?

Poultry. Stick to fresh or frozen poultry, not the stuff made into pies, salads or casseroles. Make your own.

Eggs are the food they've found hardest to derange, technologically speaking. They're trying hard. You will hear of vast research projects which promise us eggs already broken, which we will buy in plastic bags. Who needs broken eggs? Obviously not you or I, who are still presumably not so devoted to sedentary living that cracking an egg is too hard work. But selling eggs in plastic containers will save money for the producers, you see, since they have considerable loss in breakage.

Milk and cheese are still good foods if you stay strictly away from the deranged kinds: chocolate milk and processed cheeses chiefly. Buy good, honest store cheese and skip the fancy spreads and dips.

In the field of *fruit and vegetables,* stick to the fresh ones or the ones frozen without any added sauces, syrups or other goodies which the label and the ads glorify as something you just can't do without. You *can* do without them. Prepare and cook your vegetables yourself. Eat your fruits raw.

Bread, flour and cereals? What happens to flour and cereals in the processing that takes place after they leave the harvest field is unimaginable. If I told you in complete detail, we'd need another long book for the story and, chances are, you wouldn't believe it anyway. If the milling and baking industries had set out, at the beginning of the century, with the avowed purpose of totally destroying grains as a basic, nourishing food for human beings, they would probably not have succeeded as well as they have in the destruction of this basic food. They had no such avowed purpose. They took the easy way, the profitable way.

They found that the germ of the cereal, the part in which most of the nutriments are concentrated, gums up milling machinery and becomes rancid in storage. So they took it out, leaving nothing much but starch. They fed the cereal germ to stock animals which thrive on it.

It's a long, expensive process to "age" flour to make things easier for the baker. They "age" it now with chemicals. In the case of cereals, they found that, by taking out just about all the nutriment and puffing the thing up into some fancy shape, adding sugar, dyes and flavors to make it taste less like cardboard, and preservatives so it will keep on the supermarket shelf practically forever, they could, with expensive advertising programs aimed chiefly at children, convince America that this unhinged, deranged product in the box with the premium will nourish them. It's not so. Quite recently some heroic laymen with no pretensions to degrees in nutritional science, have been telling congressional committees some of the above and have been getting a good press.

So far as I am concerned, there is no bread, no cereal and no flour on the supermarket shelf today that the environmentally concerned person should buy. If he cannot get along entirely without cereals and breads in any form, then he must buy organically grown flours and make his own bread, organically grown cereals to eat at breakfast. There is no other choice.

In the case of food chemicals, as with other pollutants, you can always complain. Write to the people who make the product you wanted to buy but decided against. Tell them why you didn't buy it. Tell them you don't have to use chemicals like this when you cook at home, why should they? Tell them you don't want "convenience" foods, that you have plenty of time to cook and lots of skill. You will get in return some of the fanciest literature you ever saw, both pictorially and content-wise. Never mind. Don't be dissuaded. You will have made your point. At the next directors' meeting, somebody will be saying "Maybe we'd better begin to listen to these complaints. Why not change over and make ours the product with no chemicals in it?"

CHAPTER 13

On Writing Good, Effective Letters

"Any woman who wants to change things must survey, pinpoint, document, threaten, cajole, publish, petition, telephone, write and vote. She must be hard-headed, stubborn and charming in discussing her goals with neighbors, educational institutions, industrial managers, city councils, mayors, governors and Congressmen. From time to time she may be frustrated or angered by resistance to change, but the experience will be exciting and rewarding."

Senator Edmund S. Muskie
Ladies Home Journal
February, 1970

"Today's homemaker spends about the same time for family work as she did 40 years ago. The time has changed for different homemaking duties as reflected in a 30-minute decrease each day in food preparation and meal clean-up with the use of convenience foods and dishwashers. This is counterbalanced by an increase of over 30 minutes for marketing, record keeping and management."

Food and Nutrition News
April, 1970

"If real and steady progress is to be made in improving the quality of the environment, then, perhaps, continuous and steady, albeit moderate, inputs of alarm, panic and hysteria are required of interested citizens. Otherwise progress comes haltingly, if at all. . . . Only when the complaints of the citizenry have become strident, when some measured alarm, panic and hysteria come on the environmental scene, has any real action toward general pollution abatement taken place. The rational, systematic, scientific approach seems to work better with a healthy dollop of emotion added."

Melvin J. Josephs
Chemical and Engineering News
Aug. 17, 1970

"Give me the liberty to know, to utter and to argue above all liberties."

John Milton

I want to take exception to the "Make-a-Scene-at-the-Supermarket" school of environmental activists. I don't believe the local supermarket manager has much to say about what his chain of stores does nationally. He is stuck with the kind of packaging they send him and the rules they lay down about returnable bottles. The manager of our local market is a very cooperative chap, who allows us to put on his bulletin board the newsletter of our environmental action group, petitions against a superhighway, notices of meetings and fund raising events.

I think the supermarket manager is a good man at heart who has no evil wishes to poison the environment or make life difficult for the rest of us. He is caught in the environmental dilemma as we all are. He makes his living selling us things, wrapped, cartoned, canned and bottled in ways to which we object. If he were to investigate the way we make our livings, he could probably find that we cause just as much destruction of the environment as he does, only it's not quite so obvious. Where do you work — a steel company? A power plant? A paper mill?

Furthermore, I think that stamping my foot, throwing packaging material on the floor and demanding my money back will accomplish nothing much except to embarrass the manager, the check-out girl, myself and anybody else standing around. I need the help and cooperation of these folks, in my fight against the superhighway that threatens us all, the nuclear power plant that's on the way, the dam they're planning to build in the next county. Why should I antagonize them?

It seems to me that well thought-out, concise, helpful letters to the heads of companies which make and package products will accomplish much more than scenes at the supermarket. I write letters. I get the addresses of manufacturers from my library where the reference librarian is always helpful.

It is my opinion that the receipt (in a week, say) of fifty such letters as the ones below, by the president of one manufacturing firm would be quite enough to cause a mild panic and a hasty assembling of the planning board to make some quick changes in company policy. Firms with national coverage don't want the public's ill-will. They spend millions of dollars on campaigns to keep your good will. If enough of us insist that we simply will not buy anything from a paper company bent on creating "a disposable environment" (see below) there's a very good chance the paper company will begin to think seriously about discontinuing this line of products.

Here are some letters I have written.

The first is to the president of a national grocery firm which runs the local supermarket.

"Dear Sir: I am sending you herewith a number of polystyrene egg cartons in which I have bought eggs for several past months. These will not disintegrate in my compost pile as the paper ones do. I do not care to send them to our incinerator for reasons that the attached clipping will explain.

"Every day I breathe the smoke from that incinerator. Mr. Reese of *C and EN* may feel that the amount of phosgene gas given off in burning polystyrene is inconsequential. As I recall, we used to think the same thing about the phosphates in detergents, the carbon monoxide in our car exhausts and the mercury dumped so carelessly into our waterways.

"You may have the doubtful pleasure of burning these egg cartons in Chicago. I am — at great personal cost in time, money and convenience — going to buy my eggs in another store from now on — a store where eggs are packed in paper cartons."

The reference in this letter was to an article in a chemical journal which revealed that phosgene gas is given off when polystyrene is burned. Phosgene gas is "nerve gas".

Here is a letter to a detergent company.

"At my neighborhood grocery store the manager handed me a sample of your product and we got into a discussion of the problem of detergent pollution.

"I note that your product contains NTA. I have written several articles on detergents and collected a file of information on the subject. I cannot find any environmental expert anywhere who has any knowledge of what the long-term effects of NTA on waterways may be. Most of the experts who have made statements on this subject have said that the effects may be much worse than those produced by the phosphates in ordinary detergents.

"Since you have presented this product with a great deal of confidence, I assume that you have made some kind of test of what the effects will be. I would greatly appreciate having any information you may have."

The National Sales Manager of this company wrote me that they didn't really know anything about NTA's potential for polluting waterways. "We have researched NTA as much as we can" he said,". . . if you have information that would make you believe NTA is harmful in any way, we would certainly appreciate hearing about it."

I sent him references from several technological journals which seem to show that the nitrate pollution from NTA may be as great a problem as the phosphate in ordinary detergents. Nitrates are the likely cause of as much pollution in Lake Erie as the phosphates from detergents. I also sent him a note saying that NTA has the ability to sequester or chelate heavy metals. We are just beginning to discover with horror the burden of mercury, lead and other toxic metals in our waterways. It sounds as if NTA may be about the worst element ever loosed on the environment if it turns out that this ingredient can indeed bring these heavy metals up from the sediment at the bottom of waterways and make them available to water organisms.

I quoted to him the statement of David Dominick of the Federal Water Pollution Control Administration who said that they are working on a provisional algae assay procedure which will not be completed until 1972. *Until that time no one can say what potential harm may reside in any substitute for phosphate in a detergent.*

One of the big paper companies ran an ad in *Life* calling for a "disposable environment". It outlined all the things a new baby needs, then recommended that all these should be made of paper, because paper is disposable. Disposable paper diapers, sheets, pillow cases, blankets, shirts, sleepers, training pants, furniture, curtains, carpets and finally — a paper house, which presumably the baby (now grown up) will discard every year or so. "The disposable environment," crowed the ad, "the kind of fresh thinking we bring to every problem. Nice to know it's at your disposal, isn't it?"

Here's my letter.

"Disposable environment indeed! You have put your finger right on the most sensitive spot. With every school child in the nation aware that our first priority is to prevent pollution and the flagrant destruction of our failing natural resources, you announce with triumph the coming of disposable paper furniture, curtains, carpets, houses!

"How is it possible for an industry to be so totally irresponsible? Yes, I know, paper products don't present so much of a solid waste problem as aluminum cans and junked cars — but why should you present us with any solid waste problem at all? Why not just quietly withdraw from the manufacture of paper and convert your machinery into something that may, in some small fashion, help out in the environment crisis, rather than making things so much worse? . . .

"You are the second paper company which has announced in full page ads its determination to despoil our natural resources and overwhelm the solid waste facilities of every community in this land, just as fast and as thoroughly as you possibly can. I told the other paper company, and now I tell you I will not buy any product made by you, and I will ask my friends, relatives and neighbors not to buy any product made by you. I consider your irresponsibility and greed to be quite beyond the pale of civilized behavior at this moment in history."

Later I found disposable paper sheets and blankets listed in a mail order catalog. I wrote and objected, sending copies of my letter to both paper companies. The mail order house wrote me they would certainly keep my viewpoint in mind when they made up their next catalog. The paper company wrote me one of the most flagrantly evasive and specious letters I have ever received, concerned mostly with their vast concern for American forests, which they "manage" by cutting down trees, then planting more trees to cut down. I have a feeling a lot more letters from determined boycotters would help.

Here are some other letters on assorted subjects.

"Gentlemen:

"Recently I wanted very much to buy a product of yours. I did not buy it, because it was in a plastic container. I think you are aware that solid waste experts know of no way to dispose of discarded plastic except to burn it (causing dangerous and destructive air pollution) or to bury it, which causes problems at the landfill, since plastic materials do not settle into the soil as paper and metal ones do. They also apparently last forever once they are buried. I am not buying any more plastic products of any kind, until the plastics industry develops some sensible, non-polluting way to dispose of discarded plastic."

"Gentlemen:

"I have been buying your product for many years. My family and I like it. The last time I picked up a jar, the label informed me that you have added a chemical to this fine food.

"Sorry, but we are just not interested in adding any more possibly harmful chemicals to the thousands of such substances to which we are exposed every day. I know all the arguments for adding non-essential chemicals to foods. I also know the histories of many chemicals that have turned out to be dangerous years after they came into general use. I do not use chemicals at home when I prepare food. I see no reason why you should use them in preparing your product."

"Gentlemen:

"I have reluctantly decided to stop using your fine coffee and switch to another brand. I and my family like your coffee. It will be a hardship to switch. But I have discovered a store where I can buy unground coffee in a paper bag and grind it myself at the store.

"Your coffee comes only in a can with an additional plastic lid. I must somehow dispose of both the can and the lid. The sanitary landfill in my small township is already in serious trouble. There is no other place to go with all the trash and packaging material I must discard every time I shop for groceries.

"I am sure you are aware of the immense problem

this country faces in disposing of solid waste. Since industry seems almost totally unconcerned, it appears to be up to us consumers to take whatever steps we can to improve the situation. From now on, we will buy only coffee and, whenever possible, other products packed in paper bags which present no problem of disposal. They disappear almost magically into my compost pile."

Our lieutenant governor ran for governor this past year. He made a campaign speech castigating the nation's young folks for not properly revering "law and order." I wrote him asking what kind of example they got from federal and state authorities who do not enforce the laws on pollution. I cited several cases of complete disregard for our state's fine air pollution law. In one of these cases the pollution from an incinerator burning polyvinyl chloride (plastic) had been going on for a number of years. Doctors had protested to the governor that their patients had to move from the vicinity because of the pollution. Orchardists had protested in vain the loss of crops because of pitting of the fruit. The final event was a bus accident costing many lives and serious injuries. It was thought (though never firmly proven) that pollution from the incinerator may have caused the film on the wet road, on which the bus skidded.

I had a pleasant, meaningless acknowledgement from an assistant to the man I had written, enclosing a copy of a fiery speech he had made on air pollution. I replied that I did not consider this an answer to my letter, but instead a piece of tokenism. I got a letter from the lieutenant governor by return mail. He asked me for documented cases where air pollution laws were not being enforced. I sent them. I had a reply by return mail stating that the proper authorities would immediately investigate. They are.

That was an election year. But, in any year, you can get remarkable amounts of action, and quickly too, from almost any politician, with a firm, polite letter giving well-documented facts on whatever it is you want straightened out. Don't be fobbed off with token responses. Insist on action. Point out that the laws are there. They must be enforced.

CHAPTER 14

Let's Go on a Wartime Basis!

"We have yet to realize that to rescue the environment, we will have to restrict production and consumption at least of some goods. A single-minded concern for increasing production was what got us into this mess. To get out we must ask what things cause more public sorrow than private joy. This involves a radical reversal of form."

John Kenneth Galbraith
Life magazine
March 27, 1970

". . . the realization up and down the company ladder is that better products for better living rings increasingly hollow as a total objective. Industry has more of a social commitment to perform. Company spokesmen want involvement in what is stirring in the hearts and minds of social planners."

Reynold Bennett, Vice President
National Association of Manufacturers,
Science and Technology

SAY NO!

"A recent Gallup poll indicated that three out of four Americans are willing to support higher taxes for conservation work. Since 1963 states have more than doubled the non-federal funds appropriated, nationwide, for soil conservation use."

Soil Conservation
February, 1970

"Society has been and still is, on a great growth kick. If we are interested in a long-term future for man, we will regard rapid growth with suspicion. We will look for, and point out, the unexpected and unpleasant consequences of exuberance long-continued, and seek to moderate it before irreparable damage has been done."

Philip H. Abelson, Editor
Science
October 11, 1968

"Unless the American people are really prepared to pay pollution 'taxes' and meet the costs of environmental restoration, no political authority can control the excesses of affluence or rampant technology — no political authority, that is, that would be tolerable to our society."

Robert Finch, former Secretary
Health, Education and Welfare

A few years ago, you may remember, the paper industry went into an excited flurry about paper dresses. The fashion pages were full of the hideous things, and they sold for a while until all the dupes who bought them discovered how uncomfortable, unattractive, incendiary and totally unappealing they were. But there seems to be no stopping the paper industry from selling us — if we can be sold — any outlandish gadget or useless trinket so long as it's made of paper. The *New York Times* carries pictures of paper furniture. You use it for a while, then throw it away.

The plastics industry is bent on burying us in a welter of trash from their industry. An ad in the British publication, *New Scientist* for July 17, 1969 was headed "The Disposable Furniture Era" which said, "The 1970's might be the decade of planned obsolescence. When nearly everything you buy is designed to last only for as long as you like the look of it . . . ." They went on to talk of disposable furniture, made of plastic, of course, and boasted of the role of plastic in "every sphere — building, transport, engineering, shipbuilding."

An article in the year-end financial pages of the *New York Times,* January 11, 1970, announced that the 16-billion pound production of plastic materials in 1969 outpaced production of all nonferrous metals combined and will outdo steel volume in the eighties. An industry spokesman was quoted as predicting that "very soon now we will have plastic houses, automobiles, electronics appliances, furniture and agricultural equipment."

It is worthy of note that the plastics industry, in the 100 years or so of its existence, has made no effort, until the past few years, to discover ways of disposing of these products without polluting the environment. Plastic just doesn't break down, you know, in a landfill, a dump or a compost pile. It lives eternally, for it is what is now known as "non-biodegradable". That is, soil organisms do not like to feast on it, as they do on things made of paper or wood. Soaking in water leaves it untouched. It doesn't burn — not completely, that is. In an incinerator, it melts down into a lump of something which then has to be disposed of somehow.

A Massachusetts Institute of Technology study recently reported "there seems to be at present no re-use possibilities for the mounting quantities of plastics which are disposed of. We found upon inquiry that even large chemical companies such as DuPont have no method of disposing of their considerable quantities of scrap plastic except by burying it."

There's no need to remind any housewife of what she undergoes every day in the daily battle with plastic bags. It's impossible, in most stores in our area, to buy fruit or vegetables that are not already packaged in plastic. This is undoubtedly so that several rotting or near-rotting pieces can be concealed in the center of the bag. But even in stores where you pick out your own fruit and vegetables, you must confine them to a plastic bag before you can take them to the check-out counter. You have no choice.

The thrifty individual has a natural desire to save plastic bags. They're handy for a thousand things. But you soon find there's no space for anything else. The saved plastic bags occupy every drawer in the kitchen. So you throw them out. If your community buries its trash in a landfill, you can be sure that every scrap of plastic you throw out will still be around, even centuries from now, clogging the landfill, making it impossible for the soil to be compacted around and over it, so that the landfill can eventually serve some useful purpose.

How many plastic bottles of bleach or detergent have you used this year? What happened to them? They're lying, eternal, uncrushed, just as you threw them away, and there they will lie. There are 200 million of us buying laundry products and thousands of other things in plastic bottles. How long will it take until every acre of land around any city, town or village is completely buried under plastic bottles?

The industry is now planning plastic houses, furniture, machinery and automobiles as soon as they can discover a way to stamp out the auto bodies as easily as metal bodies are stamped out. What kind of landscape will we have when, instead of millions of junked cars made of metal which can, eventually, be made into scrap and recycled, millions of abandoned plastic cars will clutter every corner of the land? The idea is intolerable, but the industry goes right ahead with such plans, assuring you in expensive advertising that they are doing all this just for your own pleasure and welfare. By the time the plastic cars, houses and furniture are already swelling profits in every discount store in the country, it will be too late to do anything about them, just as it is too late now to do anything about plastic bags, plastic bleach bottles and all the other plastic trash that threatens to bury us.

In 1969 Senator Muskie held hearings on a proposed law, the Resource Recovery Act of 1969, which would help solve our immense problem of solid waste. In this session he was talking to an expert from M. I. T. about research to develop an incinerator that might be able to burn solid waste without creating massive air pollution.

David Wilson of M. I. T. is speaking, "In the report I saw last year, the President of Gillette said that it took 40 engineers and scientists to work for two years to produce hot, foaming lather."

Senator Muskie: "To produce what?"

David Wilson: "Hot, foaming lather. The cost of that was so stupendous and they followed it with a production program and so forth. About the same time we had the chief engineer of one of the best-known incinerator manufacturers or rather designers to talk to our students at M. I. T. and we said, now incinerators are facing enough problems at the moment. What sort of research do you have, what percentage of your gross profit goes to research? And he said, 'We have never done any research at all.' "

Forty engineers and scientists working for two years to produce something called "hot, foaming lather", which I presume is nothing but a new kind of shaving cream, but not a single penny or expert available to work on designs for equipment to solve what is at present the world's most pressing problem — our poisonous, destructive mountain-high piles of garbage and solid waste!

On December 9, 1970, the *New York Times* printed an outline of what the average American family has been convinced is essential for a happy life, hence owns. Eighty-six percent of all American families have an electric coffee-maker. Forty-seven million home hair-dryers have been sold since 1961! Hair dryers! Twenty-two million electric carving knives have been sold since 1964. The meat you eat is so contaminated with hormones, antibiotics, pesticides and preservatives that no self-respecting member of a primitive society would touch it, but, by golly, you've got an electric carving knife, so you won't have to put in that strenuous, overwhelming amount of exertion it takes to slice a piece of beef!

Eighty-five percent of all families in Detroit have two or more cars. Ninety-five percent of all families have television, which is exactly the same number who have indoor toilets. And 29 percent of us have two or more sets. Forty percent of all families now own color TV. The average family now owns five radios. Almost one-fourth of us own dishwashers. We're too feeble to wash our dishes by hand.

The family interviewed by the *Times* reporter, a married schoolteacher with one child, described how they had been persuaded to pay $25 extra for a refrigerator with an automatic ice-maker. "We really didn't want it," said Mrs. McRea, "We didn't need it. But now, it's just so neat to reach in and not mess around with a tray of ice cubes when you only want a couple of cubes."

"You asked for it," the manufacturers keep telling us, "You demanded it. We are supplying these things only because you demanded them!" They would have us believe, you see, that for the past 25 years we have been on our knees pleading for plastic furniture, paper dresses, electric fruit ripeners and carving knives, hot foaming lather, and all the other idiotic junk they throw at us. And unfortunately many friends of the environment fall into the trap, beat their breasts with guilt at the beginning and end of every speech they make and wail, "We have met the enemy and he is us!" Are you as tired of that slogan as I am?

I think that slogan is being promoted by the people who manufacture all the imbecilic trash in our civilization, then snow us under with million dollar advertising campaigns. Then, when the weak-minded among us have succumbed and bought the junk, used it a while, then discarded it, they complain to us (on their way to the bank!), "See, it's your fault! We made this stuff only because you wanted it! You're stupid and greedy and without any taste, so it's your fault the planet is being buried in pollution and solid waste!"

I propose that we outwit these libelers by calling for an embargo, a boycott, a rationing on all unnecessary goods. If you want to, you can do it the temperate way Jerry Goldstein suggested. Jerry is Executive Editor of *Organic Gardening and Farming* and Editor of *Compost Science,* author of *Garbage as You Like it*— an expert on solid waste and other kinds of pollution. He has developed the concept of "tolerable inconvenience". This can be a guiding standard whereby you will decide for yourself which things you can delete from your personal life without giving yourself a nervous breakdown or a bad name in the community.

Can't you do without most paper and plastic trifles without too much inconvenience? Sure, it means washing more dishes and more laundry. It means keeping refrigerated food and frozen food in metal or glass containers that last for years. It means saving paper bags instead of buying more for lunches. It means saving envelopes that can be re-used instead of throwing them away. It means eliminating most of the Christmas and other holiday mess of tinsel and junk that wears out every year, and every year gets more preposterously ugly, ubiquitous and tiresome.

It means buying one good outfit and wearing it for years. It means never going near a discount store, so you won't be tempted, just because it's all so terribly cheap! It means getting along with one car and using it as little as possible. It means saving the children's clothes and toys and handing them down instead of throwing them away. It means sorting out the garbage from the paper, bottles and cans, putting the garbage into the compost pile, taking the glass and cans to the recycling center. If there is none where you live, start one. It's more work. It's inconvenient. But it's tolerable.

Myself, I think tolerable inconvenience won't solve our environmental problems. I think it's too late for that. I think we should go, nationally and internationally, on a wartime basis. There is no human enemy in this war. The enemy is technology and, no, we aren't going to clean up the mess with more technology. The only way to clean it up is with less technology. By going on a wartime basis, with technology as the enemy, we will manage to get along with less technology and use what technology we have or can develop to clean up the mess our love affair with technology has produced.

Those readers who are under thirty won't know what I mean by a wartime economy. Your children who grew up with a dishwasher, a boat and two cars, a snowmobile, a summer home, a ride-on power mower, air conditioning, electric heat, a new outfit every three weeks or so, a TV in every room, automatic cameras and tape recorders and all the rest don't know what is meant by a wartime economy. Let me tell you how it was in the 1940's.

In April, 1941 the Office of Price Administration was established. On April 28, a government regulation brought 60 percent of all civilian food items under a form of price-fixing.

In January, 1942 ration boards were set up in every county in this country with 30,000 volunteers to handle the paper work. Ninety percent of everything sold in the country was eventually regulated by ration books. Although there were at the time 30 million Americans who owned cars and who needed desperately to get to factories where bombs and airplanes were being made, tires were rationed. If you owned more than five tires you were required to turn the extras in.

As rubber became more and more scarce, because sources were cut off and immense amounts were being used in war industries, everything rubber was rationed and everything rubber that was not being used was turned in to the government for salvage. Some 335,000 tons were collected.

Gas rationing began in May, 1942. President Roosevelt announced a ban on all pleasure driving, a 35-mile speed limit on all roads and the allocation of A, B and C gas stickers for all cars. An A sticker provided only four gallons of gas a week. This was your share if you were not driving a car pool into a war plant every day. If you were, you got a B sticker and a few more gallons. A C sticker with more gas allotted was only for those people in highly critical, essential work, a doctor, for example. Gasoline taxes immediately showed a decline — from $13,500,000 way down to $6,600,000 in New York state in the first three-month period of rationing. Traffic deaths declined dramatically. Anyone found driving for pure pleasure was likely to lose his ration card. At one time, a bit later, gas rations were lowered to two gallons a week.

Says Richard R. Lingeman in *Don't You Know There's a War On?* "In some areas of the country, especially the East Coast, there were times when you couldn't get any gas at all. In the summer of 1942 the pumps literally went dry; most stations closed and motorists and truckers were stranded. Some stations remained 'closed' or 'out of gas' to all save old customers. In New York, drivers would sometimes tail a gasoline tank truck until, like a pied piper, the truck had collected a string of cars following it to its destined delivery point. Cars would line up for blocks — sometimes as many as 350 of them — when word spread that a filling station had received a gasoline shipment."

Couldn't you walk or ride a bike? Most people did. But bicycles were also rationed because of lack of metal, and you were permitted to buy only 3 pairs of shoes per year.

In May, 1942, food rationing began. You got a ration book with stamps which you had to forfeit in the grocery store (there were no supermarkets then — only small grocery stores on almost every corner — nice, friendly, homey places.) Sugar was rationed, butter, cheese, meat and canned goods. Your ration book allowed you one pound of coffee every five weeks.

Cigarettes and liquor were scarce. When you heard that a store had received a carton of cigarettes, you rushed to stand in line, hoping you'd be one of the lucky ones who could buy a pack. Liquor was rationed. If you knew a lot of teetotalers, you could make out fairly well by borrowing or buying their stamps. Nylon and silk stockings were not to be had for most of the duration of the war. You did without. You wore the most awful substitutes made of twine or cotton net or anything the hosiery business could devise. Fuel oil rationing began in the winter of 1942–43. Your coupons were figured on the basis of square feet of home.

Mr. Lingeman tells us one of the most desperate war crises came when bakers stopped slicing bread. Housewives who owned no bread knives and could not find any in the stores were reduced to tearing bread apart or slicing it with the paring knife. Burning more lights than you needed became unpatriotic. Neon signs were forbidden. Store windows were unlighted. A brownout was ordered by the federal government.

At the same time, the drive to recycle everything hit some kind of a record. Every teaspoon of fat (bacon fat, pork drippings) was collected by the patriotic housewife and turned in at the butcher's. Since he got some kind of accolade for accumulating a lot, the housewife who cooperated with him was likely to be favored with a bit of information as to when the next shipment of meat or cigarettes might be expected. Tin cans (actually made of steel) had their tops and bottoms cut off, and placed inside. Then they were flattened to use up as little space as possible and turned in to the scrap drive — to save steel. *Everybody* saved cans. We also saved copper, aluminum and many other kinds of metal. And turned them in.

Described by Lingeman as probably "the most popular of all the civilian war effort tasks", Victory garden projects sprang up everywhere. There were finally, he says, about 20,000,000 Victory gardens which produced about 40 percent of all the vegetables grown in the country. You dug up the back yard, you finagled a little plot of land behind a factory, you talked your neighbors into a joint project on whatever land was available, you persuaded a farmer to give you a patch of ground and you walked to it every evening after work, carrying your garden tools. You took the whole family along. You carried home the harvest and canned it yourself for wintertime eating. It was fun. It was healthful. It was patriotic.

Slogans dreamed up by the finest public relations men in the country urged Americans to cooperate in the government's goals. "The food you save can help win the war", "Joe needs long-distance lines tonight" (don't use the phone). "The Kid in Upper 4" was an ad designed to keep you off the trains, so GI Joe could use them.

The paper shortage was so acute you carried a basket to the store and put most purchases in with no packaging. Whatever had to be purchased in a bag you brought home carefully, smoothed out the paper and put it away to use again. In offices we typed letters on the backs of those we were answering. We used carbon over and over until it fell apart in shreds. There were no such niceties as paper napkins, paper plates and paper cups. You used cloth napkins and handkerchiefs until they fell apart. You washed dishes. And detergents were unknown. Soap was scarce.

Such things as power mowers, TV sets, tape recorders, air conditioning, snowmobiles, golf carts, sports cars were unknown. And you'd be amazed at the fun we had anyway!

Sure, there were people who cheated. There were black marketeers. There were people who somehow could always get enough butter and cigarettes and gasoline. But most of us tried our best not to cheat. We honestly wanted the war effort to succeed and we were convinced that every bit we could do would help. It did. And, do you believe it, you readers who are under 30? We didn't really mind it very much at all! It was astonishing how easily you could get along without most things, so long as everybody was going without and there was something brave and patriotic about the do-without movement.

Meanwhile, businesses "converted". If you were making a product non-essential to the war effort, you just couldn't get raw materials, so you converted. Here is the list from a 1942 *Business Week* of items cut back or forbidden: Bicycles, electrical appliances, flashlights and batteries, metal household furniture, household utensils, plumbing fixtures, radiators, razors and blades, metal signs, toys and games, metal tubes for toothpastes and shaving cream, vacuum cleaners, vending machines, etc. Mr. Lingeman describes in his book the way in which large and small businessmen switched to essential objects or to materials needed for the war.

The Kleenex company made machine-gun mounts. A floor wax manufacturer made gear housings for antitank guns. An organ company made airplane parts.

Boy scouts gathered immense amounts of thistledown for use in life jackets. A spider farm provided threads of spider webs for use in gun sights and bomb sights.

At this moment in 1970 we are listening to warnings of experts that we are running out of minerals and other raw materials. The list is long and depressing. It is obvious that unless we begin very soon to recycle every bit of metal we use, as well as many other commodities, we will be in serious shape in a very short time. So we will *have* to go on a wartime basis, whether we want to or not. We will have to get along with substitutes for things like zinc, copper, nickel, silver, cobalt, cadmium. Ways of substituting will have to be developed. They will be expensive. The federal government announced in September, 1970, that a comprehensive study will be made of the nation's mineral resources — the first since 1950. But experts on all sides have already predicted serious shortages within 20–30 years.

Why wait until there's a crisis? Why not begin now to moderate our demands for the things made from these already scarce materials? Do we really care so little for the welfare of our children and grandchildren that we are willing to bequeath them a world depleted in so many raw materials, in addition to being thoroughly polluted and totally bereft of wilderness and peace?

Let's decide now to limit industries that are, strictly speaking, non-essential. Let's pick an example.

Pick an industry!

Let's decide we can get along without the cosmetic industry. What would we do without? A 4.6 billion dollar industry which makes things like hair sprays, dyes, rinses and tints, dressings, permanents, cream rinses (26 million dollars annually) wave sets, lipsticks (256 million dollars annually) makeup bases, eyebrow pencils, mascara, eye shadow, face lotions, rouge and something called "blusher". Toilet water and cologne account for 225 million dollars annually, bath salts and oils almost 50 million. Face creams cost American women 203 million dollars, nail polish and remover 86 million. These are some of the products we could learn to do without. Almost all of them are products developed in the past 30 years. Before that, somehow, we managed to get along without them. And somehow we managed to be reasonably presentable, reasonably satisfied with the way we looked, felt and smelled. And today it's quite stylish among knowledgeable young people to eschew cosmetics entirely and to rely on clean, shining faces and hair, bright eyes and graceful figures for beauty, instead of artificial props. Why not?

Let's convert the cosmetics industry into an industry which would make only equipment for controlling sewage pollution, or air pollution, or an industry which would work on ways to dispose of solid waste or recycle junk cars. Let's give the cosmetics industry the job of finding a way to refurbish our strip mines into pleasant hillsides once again. Surely a company which can employ 40 engineers and scientists for two years to produce hot foaming lather might be able to come up with a way for getting commuters to their jobs without pollution, noise or stress. And the waste and environmental loss of resources incidental to the manufacture of cosmetics would be eliminated.

They can keep all their personnel, their salesmen, their advertising agencies, their expensive plants. But the facilities and skills of all these would be turned to the solution of environmental problems.

Why couldn't we convert the photography industry into something a lot more helpful in terms of environment? Has anyone ever counted the environmental cost of all those billions of pictures of Johnny playing with the dog or Frank foolishly gazing at the Grand Canyon or Mother cutting the birthday cake? Are we really so immature that we could not give up this luxury, or at least some part of this luxury, for the sake of preserving the planet for another few generations?

Once you start eliminating industries, it is amazing how easy it seems, somehow, to get along without most of these appurtenances of Western life. Almost everybody else in the world gets along without them all the time, of course. And we are told by at least one prophet of doom (Dr. Wayne Davis, School of Biological Sciences, Kentucky University) that this is what will save the "undeveloped" part of the world, while our part of it goes down to ruin.

Says Dr. Davis, in an article in the January 10, 1970 *New Republic,* "The average Indian eats his daily few cups of rice . . . draws his bucket of water from the communal well and sleeps in a mud hut. In his daily rounds to gather cow dung to burn to cook his rice and warm his feet, his footsteps, along with those of millions of his countrymen, help bring about a slow deterioration of the ability of the land to support people. His contribution to the destruction of the land is minimal.

"An American, on the other hand, can be expected to destroy a piece of land on which he builds a home, garage and driveway. He will contribute his share to the 142 million tons of smoke and fumes, 7 million junked cars, 20 million tons of paper, 48 billion cans and 26 billion bottles the overburdened environment must absorb each year. To run his air conditioner, we will strip-mine a Kentucky hillside, push the dirt and slate down into the stream and burn coal in a power generator. . . .

". . . . We are destroying our land at a rate of over a million acres a year. We now have only 2.6 agricultural acres per person. By 1975 this will be cut to 2.2, the critical point for the maintenance of what we consider a decent diet, and by the year 2000 we might expect to have 1.2. . . . If our numbers continue to rise, our standard of living will fall so sharply that by the year 2000 any surviving Americans might consider today's average Asian to be well off. Our children's destructive effects on their environment will decline as they sink ever lower into poverty."

CHAPTER 15

The Silent Minority on This Planet

Little Things

Little things, that run, and quail,
And die, in silence and despair!

Little things, that fight, and fail,
And fall, on sea, and earth, and air!

All trapped and frightened little things,
The mouse, the coney, hear our prayer!

As we forgive those done to us,
— The lamb, the linnet, and the hare —

Forgive us all our trespasses,
Little creatures everywhere!

Collected Poems
James Stephens

"The huge 'think factories' of our time are the equivalent of the Lancashire cotton mills of the industrial revolution. The scientists are many, and they are very busy producing staggering quantities of 'knowledge'. Their product, however, is increasingly taking on the alienated character of assembly line production, with no rhyme or reason or discernible relation to a meaningful whole. To call this mushrooming mass-production of information a flowering of science, makes only a little more sense than to call the booming output of television commercials a flowering of poetry and dramatic art."

Paul R. Zilsel
Bulletin of the Atomic Scientists,
April, 1964

"Raise thy head. Take stars for money."

George Herbert

One of the most frightening, heart-rending and little-appreciated books of our time was written in 1968 by Mel Morse, President of the Humane Society of the United States — *Ordeal of the Animals.* Mr. Morse, who has been in the work of the Humane Society for thirty years, has seen it all. His book recounts sorrowfully the somber facts that, in our enlightened, humane century, in almost every encounter with human beings on any level whatsoever, animals are mistreated in such a horrendous variety of ways that even the most forbearing and forgiving individual is almost forced to conclude that the entire human experiment was a mistake and the sooner it comes to an end the better, for all the rest of the universe.

Mr. Morse describes the horrors of rodeos, "bloodless" bullfights, cock fights, dog fights, horse racing, roadside carnivals and zoos, the massive poisoning of wildlife "predators" pursued by our Department of Interior. He quotes a veterinarian who says, "If we scratched all the sore horses going to the post, there would be no racing at all." He describes state laws forbidding the mutilating of dogs and the way they are flagrantly disregarded. He tells you the story of the Tennessee Walking Horse whose every step is agony, for his hoofs have been "sored" by unbelievable forms of torture so that he will step high.

Livestock auctions and slaughterhouses in our country are scenes of unmitigated cruelties which most of us are totally unaware of, and which most European countries have long since outlawed. The hunter doesn't seem to comprehend that "two out of every three deer he wounds are going to escape and die, and starve while dying — lower jaw shot away, leg broken, innards trailing, gangrene." More than 116,000 deer kills were reported by hunters in our state last year. The total of wounded is, of course, unknown. Twice that? Three times?

"For almost a decade now," says Mr. Morse, "the little town of Harmony, North Carolina, has made the rabbit a rather odd symbol of Christmas. The local post of the American Legion sponsors a charity banquet during the yuletide and rabbit is the chief item on the menu. To procure a sufficient supply of rabbits, hundreds of able-bodied citizens and youngsters fan out through the countryside and drive the frightened wild rabbits into fenced enclosures. When enough rabbits have been assembled in this manner, they are beaten to death by club-wielding and stone-throwing men, women and children . . ."

Mr. Morse's book should be required reading for every American. I could not in one chapter consider even a small part of the wanton, senseless cruelties he describes. But we conservationists must become aware of them. Caring about birds and animals is not just a question of saving the endangered species and paying out tax money for wildlife preserves.

Just the matter of spaying pets is of paramount importance when you consider the figures Mr. Morse gives us on the catastrophic pet explosion which is filling our animal pounds and producing an estimated 15 million wild dogs roaming in packs, to say nothing of uncounted millions of feral cats which starve, freeze, drown or perish under the wheels of cars. A female dog, bred every time she comes in heat — and this will happen if the entire situation is not controlled — can be responsible in a seven-year lifetime for 9,540,912 offspring, if her descendants are also unspayed. One unspayed cat can produce in a 20-year lifetime an astronomical number of offspring, if all her descendants are not spayed, and practically all of them destined for lives of lonely hardship and cruel death. One continues to marvel at otherwise humane people who think having unwanted kittens is somehow amusing and cute.

Early in his book Mr. Morse tackles forthrightly the stickiest of all dilemmas relating to animals: the research laboratories. As Joseph Wood Krutch says in his fine introduction to the book, "Of all the forms of deliberate cruelty prevalent, those which take place under the banner of Science are the most nearly immune to criticism. Once the Inquisition was not only tolerated but justified because it was supposed to operate in defense of a church beyond criticism. Today Science is similarly sacrosanct. Whatever is done in a laboratory by men who call themselves scientists is assumed to be justified. Scientists themselves are assumed to be intelligent and dedicated men. They would not torture an animal unless there were compelling reasons for doing so. Do we not owe to their investigations the blessings of modern medicine? Such comfortable convictions can hardly survive the evidence of this book. And yet, though the United States is far behind England, where many leading scientists criticize our apparent inhumanity in the name of Science, attempts to bring our laws up to minimum standards are being actively resisted by special interests."

Along with almost everyone else in the country, I once believed that animal research was essential and humane. We have insulin, after all, and a polio vaccine. And you wouldn't want doctors experimenting with human beings, now, would you? About 20 years ago my work made it necessary to read every day a number of medical and scientific journals. I began to file abstracts of laboratory experiments. I sent for the original papers. I now have a file case full of records of the most astonishing laboratory experiments, not just of unwarranted cruelty, repeated hundreds of times in one laboratory after another, but of trivia, irrelevance, and scandalous waste of talent, time, resources and money.

The money, almost without exception these days, is yours and mine. We pay for the whole nationwide operation. According to *The New York Times* for November 1, 1970, science and technology grants constituted almost ten percent of the entire federal budget in 1968 — $17,030,000,000. Only a part of this went for laboratory research having to do with health and/or medicine.

But a surprisingly large number of laboratories using animals are working for NASA and the Pentagon which take the biggest bites out of our research money. In 1968, the National Cancer Institute received almost 200 million dollars, National Heart Institute almost 160 million, National Institute of Dental Research 29 million, National Institute of Arthritis and Metabolic Diseases, 137 million, National Institutes of Neurological Diseases and Stroke, 101 million, National Institute of Allergy and Infectious Diseases, 102 million, and so on.

In addition to all this, there are the billions of dollars available from all the tax exempt foundations which, of course, you pick up the tab for, too, since these tax exemptions make your taxes that much higher. The many foundations established by commercial organizations, of course, add the cost of the research money to the price of the product, as well as deducting it from their taxes, so you pay in two ways for this kind of research.

You have nothing at all to say about what goes on in research laboratories, neither do your elected representatives in Congress, nor the bureaucrats in Washington who give out the financial grants. No one is concerned with how many times in how many laboratories the same unspeakable experiment is performed, so that someone can write a paper or get a degree. And meanwhile the incidence of cancer, diabetes, circulatory disorders, nervous and mental diseases, metabolic disorders, stroke, congenital defects increases year after year. The latest figures on infant mortality rate placed the United States 14th on the list internationally, in spite of the fact that pregnant animals and their newborn offspring, as well as pregnant women and their newborn children are the subject of endless experiments in research laboratories and hospitals. Is one not entitled to expect that, over the years, the country spending the most money and doing the most experiments involving pregnancy and infants might begin to show an improvement in the infant mortality rate rather than the opposite?

In a country where $200,000,000 a year is allocated by the government to cancer research, and countless other millions donated by foundations and public drives, should one not expect that the rate of cancer incidence might begin to go down after a while, instead of up?

We are living in an environment where we are almost universally exposed day after day to chemical substances which cause cancer. They are in the air we breathe, the water we drink, the food we eat, the radioactivity in the effluents from our nuclear power plants and bomb tests. We spread them all over the soil and through our waterways in pesticides and pollutants. We feed them to the stock animals which we then eat. We rub in our hair and on our skin, take into our mouths, eyes and every other body opening a thousand and one cosmetics, drugs, tonics, pills, dyes, creams, laxatives, inhalants, and so on whose potential for causing cancer is practically unknown.

Almost never does any scientist who devotes his time to cancer research lift his voice to protest this universal poisoning of the world with cancer-causing substances. Instead, the cancer researchers appear bent on only one thing — finding a "cure" for cancer. To me at least, this seems a bit like submerging the entire population in a tank full of water, then trying to find a "cure" for drowning, rather than turning the faucet off and draining the tank. Preventing diseases by cleaning up the environment never seems to occur to anyone in our health establishment. Of course, there isn't any money in it.

Laboratory researchers seem to share the technologist's point of view that the more elaborate and complex the machinery you use, the more successful the experiment will be. Judging from the descriptions and photographs appearing in scientific journals, much of the time of the laboratory researcher is spent designing machines in which animals can be forced to perform some function which may or may not be related to some function of human beings, like smoking, for instance. And usually the researcher points out that the results of his experiment should not, of course, be applied to human experience since animals are never exactly like human beings and the conditions of any experiment are bound to be totally artificial. If you write and ask him why then he performed the experiment, you will probably not receive an answer.

Here is an example. One would assume that the condition of shock is quite common in the emergency room of any hospital. And one would assume that observing and recording the symptoms of shock would be mandatory in such cases. One would also assume that a given number of such patients die, hence could be fully studied at autopsy. Does it not seem reasonable, therefore, that the doctors probably know or could know more about the condition of shock than any other human condition? Studying shock in animals is such an obsession with medical researchers that entire laboratories are being built just for this one study.

Here is a description from *Ordeal of the Animals* of one mechanism used in laboratories for producing shock.

"The Blalock is best described as resembling a grape press or an old-fashioned printing press. Through a screw arrangement, two facing metal plates, each boasting rows of dull steel teeth, are forced against each other. The press is used to study the cause and effects of shock. Dogs are commonly used in this experiment and the general idea is to exert enough pressure to crush the flesh of the legs without breaking the bones. Pressure in the thousands of pounds per square inch can be applied, and in the final stages anesthesia is not given to the dog. This method of producing shock is so popular that at one time — if one has faith in medical periodicals — a hundred identical studies were being conducted at as many different laboratories with a grand total of over 4,000 dogs as unwilling subjects." A committee of the House of Representatives was told about these experiments in 1962 by the executive director of the Humane Society of the United States, who described experiments at the University of Rochester which crushed more than 400 dogs in this manner, giving no anesthesia or sedative while the dogs lived for from five to 12 hours strapped to tables.

Mr. Morse says "When one laboratory's research on animals establishes something significant, scores of other laboratories repeat the experiment, and more thousands of animals are needlessly tortured and killed. . . . . Every day of the year, hundreds and often thousands of fully conscious animals are scalded, or beaten, or crushed to death, and more subjected to exotic surgery and then allowed to die slowly and in agony. . . . . All this and more has been aired in one congressional hearing after the other, but nothing much happens . . . . the billion-plus dollars are granted without supervision or controls. The money is federal, but the laws of most states provide laboratories with immunity from inspection. . . ."

Here are some clippings from my file which are typical of the kind of reading one finds in scientific journals.

Electric blasting caps were exploded inside the brains of 225 dogs. Of those which survived for 15 minutes, some were immersed in ice water for five minutes, others were heated to see whether heat or cold had any effect on the amount of brain damage. Some of the dogs survived for four weeks. The experimenters discovered that neither heat nor cold appears to lessen brain damage in dogs whose brains have been destroyed by electric blasts.

Journal of the American Medical Association
February 20, 1967

Infant monkeys, 12 hours after birth, are injected with human cancer cells, then kept in complete isolation *for the next five years.*

New Scientist
September 20, 1965

"A scientifically significant experimental model has been developed for reproducing head injury by impact in the monkey. . . . Eighty monkeys received blows on the head with a piston activated by compressed air which," (to the surprise of no one), "produced concussion." Say the experimenters, "Perhaps the greatest remaining difficulty with such a model is evaluation of the state of consciousness of animals subjected to trauma under anesthesia."

Science
July 8, 1966

"In our laboratory, devocalizing dogs (removing the vocal chords) is necessary because of the human patients in neighboring wards. We have used electrocautery (burning) for devocalization of more than 3,000 dogs."

Journal American Veterinary Association
November 1, 1963

Seventy dogs were subjected to "ischemic amputation", that is, circulation in their legs was stopped. After 10 hours, there was 100 percent mortality.

Archives of Surgery
November, 1964

The heads of one hundred and thirty dogs were severed, cooled and kept "alive" for up to 8 hours. "When the heads were later mounted on a holder and perfused with heparinized warm blood, there was lacrimation, salivation, panting and . . . reaction to pain and light . . . a living brain."

Medical World News
September 17, 1965

Dogs were repeatedly hit on the head with a two-pound hammer to see whether padding on the head reduced damage. The experimenters concluded that football players wearing helmets would suffer less damage than those which do not. These researchers received more than $500,000 in grants from the National Institutes of Health for these experiments.

The A–V
October, 1965

"At Wayne State University, Detroit, a dog was operated on and left unattended in a basement. His cries were so terrible they disturbed patients at a hospital a block away. A patrolman, John Mobley, was summoned. He investigated Wayne State's laboratory and found it, in his words, 'a cesspool of cruelty'. 'If this is called for in the advancement of science', he stated in sworn testimony, 'then God help us all.'

"Afterward the assistant dean of Wayne State declared that only two 'irregularities' had occurred: 1. the dog should not have been left in a basement *with the window open,* and 2. the dog should have been 'debarked.'

"Last summer the caretaker at the Naval Medical Research Unit of the Great Lakes Training Center quit his job because, he stated, 'after three and a half years there I couldn't stomach the treatment of the animals any longer.'

"Today, as I write these words, a biologist on the medical faculty of one of our country's leading medical schools has just delivered to me examples of half a hundred experiments. He has classified these as 'Cruel', 'Not cruel', 'Necessary' and 'Unnecessary'. More than a dozen of them are clearly marked 'cruel' and 'unnecessary.' 'I cannot write to the *Times* myself,' he says, 'I would lose my job.'

"The patrolman at Wayne State is not an 'antivivisectionist'. Neither is the caretaker at Great Lakes. Neither is the biologist. Neither am I. All of us, however, are not surprised that Mr. Galton chose to ignore a vast area of commercial experimentation — by the cosmetic companies, for example, that put row upon row of unanesthetized rabbits in stocks, their eyes clamped open, in order to test, on these animals' eyes, hair dyes and permanent wave lotions.

"Why didn't he tell us how at St. Joseph's Hospital, St. Paul, Minnesota, they managed to produce what they called 'the ultimate smoking tool' — the dog which, by the extension of a graft to the bronchial tube through the chest wall, was literally forced with every breath he took to smoke himself to death! And why didn't he mention how, again at our old friend, Wayne State, they managed to spend over a half a million dollars of Government grants, plus large sums from the Kresge Foundation, to crush the heads of hundreds of dogs with pneumatic hammers? All to test what? Cancer? Heart trouble? No, doctor — football helmets. . . . . ."

Cleveland Amory,
President, Fund for Animals
in a letter to the *New York Times* concerning an article by Lawrence Galton, bewailing the activities of antivivisectionists.

"It was with horror that I read in the *New York Times* of April 23 a news report that Navy scientists have trained porpoises carrying explosives in body harnesses to ram enemy submarines. The iniquity, the utter moral degradation of such conduct is beyond words. That anyone could conceive of such a scheme is bad enough, but to propose seriously to carry it out is utterly reprehensible and calls for the strongest possible protest.

"The scientists engaged in this work and their employers in the United States Navy, no doubt view the blowing to bits of porpoises as a regrettable necessity, but efficient. Have those involved in such work abandoned all moral scruples? How can anyone engage in securing the confidence and trust of such especially friendly creatures as porpoises, and then plan to shatter them to bits in the service of the worst of all man's cruelties — war?

"Have we not already worked sufficient harm upon the whole of animated nature that we must now give it both scientific and official sanction? I hope others will join me in protesting against this particularly revolting piece of inhumanity."

Ashley Montagu,
In a letter to the *New York Times*
April 23, 1966

Dogs given lethal doses of abdominal irradiation can be kept alive for 153 days by cutting out the pancreatic duct. Untreated dogs lived only 4 days.

Archives of Surgery
November, 1970

Bleeding dogs to the point of hemorrhagic shock causes death unless treatment is given immediately.

Archives of Surgery
February, 1968

25 to 50 percent of body skin of dogs was surgically peeled off in sheets. 14 dogs had 20 to 40 percent of skin replaced by skin from a donor dog. There was 86 percent mortality and 26 percent of the grafts rotted. The dogs were allowed to live three to 26 days. The experiment was financed by two federal grants, one for $224,208, and one for $236,942.

Ad in *National Observer*
August 17, 1970

Animals were given "crush wounds" in order to see which antibiotic would stop infection.

Archives of Surgery
July, 1969

Dogs were bled of 40 percent of total blood volume in order to study what happened in the gastrointestinal tract.

Archives of Surgery
July, 1969

Mice were struck blows on the head sufficient to produce symptoms of concussion to see whether there was brain damage.

Texas Reports of Biology and Medicine
Spring, 1969

The psychiatrists are looking for an "animal model of depression". No one really knows what depression is. But they feel certain they can so torture, misuse or deprive some animal (preferably a primate) that they can induce depression.

Archives of General Psychiatry
August, 1969

A living brain of a rhesus monkey was kept alive for several hours. "The difficult job of peeling away the monkey's flesh occupies most of this time". . . . "The rhesus body now is lifeless, but the brain, naked in the network of wires and tubes, functions as it had only hours before while contemplating a banana." The application of this research to human health involves "moral and social factors . . . The passage of a considerable period of time may be required to lessen the impact of these factors."

Industrial Research
April, 1968

(Ed. It also might be enlightening to know, of course, whether pain is suffered by the "living brain". What pain? Well, the pain of having all one's flesh peeled away, leaving nothing but a brain!)

I mentioned the trivia for which billions of dollars of your tax money have been spent. Listen!

Infant monkeys were reared from birth in an elaborate apparatus which did not allow them to see any of their body parts. After 35 days, scientists at M. I. T. watched and reported on what the baby monkey did when he was finally allowed to see one hand.

Science
February 10, 1967

SAY NO!

Young mice are grafted to old mice with grafts from tail to shoulder. University of California scientists believe they can thus discover whether the young mouse will keep the old mouse alive for a longer period.

Medical World News
August 4, 1967

Scientists can now make songbirds sing by stimulating electrically one part of the brain. The article gives 28 references to other work in which various animals and birds were caused to vocalize by planting electrodes in their brains. The money was provided by the Public Health Service.

Science
August 27, 1965

Laboratory rats trained to push a lever for food resulting in an electric shock to a rat in another cage refused to push the lever.

New Scientist
July 17, 1969

(Ed. This experiment brought the following letter from a Queen's University, Canada, scientist in the August 21, 1969 *New Scientist:* "Are we to conclude . . . that the rats who were used in the experiment showed more pity than did the men who arranged it?")

5,000 laboratory rats at the University of Pittsburgh are subjected to stress chambers where bright lights, buzzers, clanging bells and jet takeoff noise sound like a big city. This experiment has gone on for 11 years. The rats become hypertensive, irritable and dangerous to handle.

Medical World News
March 6, 1970

Hamsters with their olfactory organs removed could not mate. But those which had been blinded could mate.

Science
January 16, 1970

Thirsty laboratory rats will lick a stream of dry air pumped through their drinking tube. And when they are very thirsty you can get them to lick a piece of cold dry metal. Hamsters which were reared from birth without any access to water (!) licked cold metal. The authors conclude "that tongue cooling is a primary reward for thirsty rodents." This valuable piece of information was partially financed by grants from the National Science Foundation and the National Institutes of Mental Health.

Science
December 25, 1970

After prolonged exposure to their reflected images in mirrors, chimpanzees marked with red dye showed evidence of being able to recognize their own reflections. Monkeys did not appear to have this capacity. This research was supported by a financial grant from the National Institutes of Health.

Science
January 2, 1970

Scientists at the University of Wyoming have spent $75,000 in federal funds over the last 13 years trying to find out if mosquitoes like biting millions of victims, and have not made much progress.

New York Times
November 5, 1968

Two small mongrel dogs were trained to wear masks which separated nose and mouth air flow. Three scientists at Duke University then studied exactly how dogs pant.

Science
September 11, 1970

In rats that would not ordinarily kill mice, injection of a chemical "elicited killing".

Science
February 6, 1970

The biologically active component in catnip was force-fed to cats to find out what becomes of it in the cat.

Science
June 13, 1969

Lamb fetuses have been kept alive in artificial sacs for over two days before they succumb to infection.

Medical World News
May 30, 1969

The University of Mississippi, using a $600,000 grant from the Department of Defense, is experimenting to see if birds can be trained for military duties. "I read it, I re-read it and I read it again," said one scientist, "and I still couldn't believe it. It's insane."

AP Dispatch
October 8, 1969

Irrelevance is another characteristic of much laboratory research. As Professor J. W. S. Pringle of Oxford University said in *New Scientist,* September 22, 1966, "Biologists seem bent on making factual the mythical treadmill of the expert, condemning themselves to learning more and more about less and less until they know everything about nothing. By the time they've discovered everything there is to know about any particular species, they'll probably have dissected it into extinction. . . ." The article dealt with the fact that the common frog is all but extinct in England, because it is the preferred creature for hacking to bits in biology labs.

Your money has paid for the following irrelevant experiments.

Six dogs had their legs broken (the bone sawed in half) to test whether an elaborate heating mechanism strapped to the leg would cause healing in less time. Results were "vague".

Canadian Medical Association Journal
August 5, 1967

Dr. José M. R. Delgrado of Yale School of Medicine plants electrodes in the brains of female monkeys, then commands them by a radio signal to reject their young. "I don't want people to think we are against motherhood," quipped Dr. Delgrado.

New York Times
March 22, 1967

Monkeys were given asthma by injecting them with serum from human asthmatics. "Periodically the sensitized monkeys would drop from the erect position to all fours. This apparently was an effort to find a position in which it was possible to breathe with less discomfort." These experiments have gone on for 3½ years. The experiments consist of giving the monkeys asthma, nothing more.

Journal of the American Medical Association
February 20, 1967

In ninety-two dogs the coronary artery was severed. 77 percent of those left in this condition died. "Controlled ventilation with room air" saved 41% of the rest.

Journal of Thoracic Cardiovascular Surgery
June, 1967

Dogs bled until they were in a condition of shock were studied to see what effect a certain kind of oxygen had on them.

American Journal of Pathology
September, 1967

The implantation of . . . . magnesium aluminum wire in the lumen of the thoracic aorta of nine rabbits resulted in marked hypertension . . . . and lesions of the kidney.

Canadian Medical Association Journal
January 30, 1965

Ninety percent of the small intestine was removed in 31 dogs. Then they were given poison. The poison killed all the dogs which had not been operated on. Of those operated on, 52 percent survived for 48 hours.

Archives of Surgery
September, 1967

Weights are suspended from the legs of rats, which are restrained in holders, then in response to electrical shocks delivered to electrodes imbedded in the legs, the legs can be moved back and forth. This method is advised to exercise the animals since rats, forced to run or to swim to complete exhaustion, have found ways of staying alive.

Journal of the American Medical Association
September 4, 1967

Dogs were raised in cages which blocked nearly all stimulation from the outside for the first 10 months of their lives. "When they came out, the animals froze, then became hyperexcited and went into whirling fits. They learned poorly, and didn't seem to know enough even to avoid a painful electric shock."

Science News
December 2, 1967

Brains are kept alive for tests after removal from monkeys. "Everyone can think of millions of things to use (this information) for", said the experimenters.

New York Times
June 4, 1964

Dogs "exposed to aspiration of water" drowned.

Anesthesiology
January–February, 1966

A Washington surgeon traveled to Africa to shoot leopards, lions, buffalo and elephants with a bow and arrow to produce shock but not immediate death. While the animal lingers in anguish, its body may produce a chemical which could be useful to humans, he thinks.

Associated Press
August 9, 1967

Crush injuries of animals were found to respond better to antibiotics sprayed on them immediately rather than four hours later.

Archives of Surgery
July 1, 1968

Twelve chimpanzees reared for three years in complete isolation in closed boxes did not demonstrate normal sexual behavior when they were released from isolation.

Science News
August 31, 1968

Five donkeys were forced to inhale cigarette smoke equivalent to 36 cigarettes in one to two hours.

Archives of Environmental Health
January, 1969

Direct two-way radio communication between an animal's brain and a computer was established by implanting electrodes in the brain of a chimpanzee. The promise of establishing direct electronic communication from one brain to another suggests promising new ways of treating mental and physical disorders in humans!

New York Times
September 15, 1970

(Ed. I can't wait!)

Monkeys whose eyelids were sewed shut after birth showed "severe visual impairment".

Archives of Ophthalmology
August, 1970

Albino rats can reliably distinguish between the odors of stressed and unstressed rats. The experiment, using electric shock, was performed to suggest the need for controls in studies where odor from a "stressed" animal might affect behavior of nearby animals. The research was financed by a grant from the Public Health Service.

Science
August 9, 1968

Experimental transplants of the uterus have been carried out on dogs "although the uterus is not an organ essential to life and there is no justification for performing such transplants." "We feel we should be able to perform such transplants should we ever be required to do so," said the two researchers.

New York Times
August 6, 1969

"Look today among the countless long faces of a malady as old as life: into the mouth of a screaming, snapping beagle isolated in a laboratory cage at Bar Harbor, Maine." The puppy was confined in total isolation for 13 weeks.

Medicine at Work
February, 1966

(Ed. Scientists must torture animals, it seems, in order to discover that living things, completely isolated from other living things, suffer loneliness.)

". . . neither the monkey nor dog represents an ideal model animal for predicting the metabolic fate of a drug in man . . ." Maurice H. Seevers (University of Michigan) has been studying the problem of drug addiction for more than 40 years using monkeys . . . Monkeys addicted to morphine are withdrawn from the medication for 14 hours. By this time "profound withdrawal symptoms" have appeared. The drug to be tested is then given to the monkey. If the withdrawal symptoms are relieved, the test drug is considered addictive.

Science
June 30, 1967

(Ed. It is obvious how valuable such research is to human beings. You have only to look at newspaper headlines in regard to the prevalence of addiction, to see what great benefits to human beings have come over the past 40 years from the work of this researcher and the hundreds of others who spend their entire lifetimes making addicts out of animals. The man in charge of an FDA program making drug addicts of animals said in 1966, "Our present drug-oriented society is probably more due to sociological conditions than to pharmacological." He then continued with his experiments on animals.)

Creighton University starved groups of dogs for periods of up to 65 days. When the animals were given food they "often appeared ill or in pain." At Cornell University the sight, hearing and sense of smell of a "small army" of cats were destroyed surgically. Over a period of ten years the mutilated cats were subjected to electric shocks, blows and other torments. "Just what was learned in these ten years is not clear."

At Johns Hopkins University one cat survived 139 days of torture during which the tail was subjected to a variety of noxious stimuli: burns, electric shocks, surgical clamps, etc., "leaving us the knowledge that the feline tail has a nervous system."

Ordeal of the Animals

At a time when conservation of living animals, especially those nearing extinction, has become an international crusade, the demand for experimental animals threatens many species with extinction in one locality after another. Small mammals of many kinds are being hunted to extinction in the East and South America to supply American laboratories. The primates are threatened with extinction in many parts of the world because they happen to be the animals most closely related to man.

At Emory University, the Yerkes Primate center has 11 gorillas, 27 orangutans, 73 chimpanzees and 200 monkeys. "The orangutans, which cost about $2500 each, are so scarce in the world that it would be difficult to replace them at much greater prices."

Journal of the American Medical Association
August 16, 1965

Using tranquilizing drugs to capture sea-going mammals has resulted in "the pointless deaths of a number of whales, none of which appears to have been recovered even as a carcass for useful study."

Letter to *Science,* August 11, 1967
From a group of Woods Hole Oceanographic Institution scientists

Huge nylon tents covering entire islands were used by two Harvard zoologists who then gassed all animal life on the islands in order to study recolonization by insects and other life.

New York Times
January 14, 1968

"The last meaningful rhesus (monkey) population census was taken nearly a decade ago when India exported 200,000 to 250,000 annually, of which more than 85 percent were juveniles . . . . in 1965 the export had dropped to 38,870 rhesus of which 24,456 went to the USA. The latest figures indicate that the U. S. is now receiving three-quarters of the exported Indian primates. . . . Roth reckons that only about 50 percent of the collected total number of primates become subjects of meaningful research. The remaining 50 percent are a total loss. An average of 15 percent perish between trap and export compounds, some die in transit . . . if the slaughter of primates continues at present rates, researchers will be obliged to change their policy, as there won't be enough animals to go around."

John Hillaby in *New Scientist*
October 10, 1968

"The mass slaughter of wild primates for biomedical research is causing serious depletion of some stocks. So far, the effects of overkill have scarcely reached research workers, but soon the supply from wild populations must fall behind demand."

The Lancet
November 2, 1968

According to World Wildlife Fund, the University of Detroit alone placed an order for 10,000 monkeys from Thailand for "research in behavioral and related studies." Conservationists in Thailand say there are not enough monkeys left in the whole country to supply this one order.

New Scientist
October 22, 1964

Monkeys are used to study conditions of immobility. They are put into casts or paralyzed, then the minerals of their urine are studied. The fact that millions of immobilized human beings in hospitals are already being studied every day has not lessened the flow of money into animal experiments which provide the same information.

U. S. Government Research Development
Report 41(20), 81, 1966

"If some of the possibilities we're investigating in the viral transmission of cancer get hot, medical research could eliminate the entire chimpanzee population in a year or two . . . and you can state this possibility for other species in other areas of investigation."

Journal of the American Medical Association
November 6, 1967

When Dr. Michael A. Epstein of London announced last summer that he had infected three African green monkeys with lymphomatous (cancerous) material from a child, the research world buzzed with excitement. A key chapter had apparently been unfolded in the mystery of possible cancer transmittal from man to animal. But pathologist Dennis H. Wright of Kampala, Uganda now claims that the monkeys did not develop lymphomas at all. He says they simply had a vitamin deficiency.

Medical World News
December 4, 1964

An increasing number of animals of all kinds are used by high school students in experiments of which one leading biologist says,

"One-fifth of 802 biology projects at 10 recent (high school) science fairs involve pain or death to higher animals. Considering the vast array of biological problems, the great array of plants, protozoa, and insects, and the many studies of animals which can be conducted without harming them, it is profoundly disturbing that one student in five now chooses a topic in which animals are hurt or killed."

F. Barbara Orlans in a letter
to the Editor of *Science*
January 10, 1969

Westinghouse Science Talent Search awarded a $250 prize to a high school teenager who bought ten house sparrows and blinded five of them by removing their eyeballs. Then she tried to train the birds to respond to light by giving them food or electric shocks. She gave some birds no food for six days and concluded that they are "likely to die when starved to 70 percent of their body weight."

Another teenager received an award for "botched up attempts" to implant electrodes in a monkey's brain. "These projects were in full conformity with current Science Service guidelines on the use of animals by high school students."

Letter to the Editor of the *New York Times*
June 7, 1969

"A glance through American pedological literature shows a wide-spread acceptance of the view that students should be allowed to do whatever they like in animal work, and that the production of abnormalities is encouraged and usually gets the prize in science competitions. Small animals are whirled around in centrifuges until they either become partially paralyzed or die. Others are launched, dangling precariously below homemade rockets to simulate space-flight conditions, a project which, although unscientific and monstrously inhumane, was recently cited for its 'excellence' in the Washington, D. C. educational area. At the high school of Our Lady of Good Counsel in Montgomery County, Maryland, mice were starved in vitamin deficiency experiments. Elsewhere goldfish were bathed in detergents and, for some inexplicable reason, rats poisoned with vodka. Splenectomies are being conducted by 15-year-old school children in New York.

"In what seems to be an effort to keep up with contemporary culture, experiments with thalidomide are popular in Huntington, West Virginia, and heart transplants in Columbus, Ohio. In that city, students dressed up in surgical masks and gowns, opened up live bull frogs in front of television cameras. Ice was used in place of a more conventional anesthetic, but as it melted under the hot studio lights, the performers could no longer rely on the tapes fastening down their victims, and were obliged to restrain the squirming animals by hand. . . . What can be made of these horrifying reports?"

John Hillaby
New Scientist, January 9, 1969

A high school boy was given a Federal Bureau of Drug Abuse Control award for his work giving LSD to spiders, in the basement of his home. The LSD was provided by Emory University which got it from the FDA under a grant from the National Institutes of Health.

New York Times
November 5, 1967

A New Jersey high school girl injected mice with a certain acid, then exposed them to lethal doses of radiation. The one which died, she said, "may have been sick to begin with or its resistance to the radiation was abnormally low".

Medical World News
June 17, 1966

The idea that animal experimentation is essential because experiments on human beings are illegal and immoral comes in for some honest open observation once in a while when some especially revolting experiment performed on old people, newborn children, or psychotics makes the headlines. The 1966 scandal when old people in a Brooklyn hospital were injected with cancer cells stirred the medical community into such a furor that medical journals are still resounding with protestations, equivocations and breast-beating on the subject of human experimentation.

Meanwhile the experiments go right on. Schizophrenics are deprived of sleep for 85 hours, psychotic patients are given a hormone "whose potential for harm is unknown", unborn children are exposed to lack of oxygen to see what the effects will be, and once in a while some researcher says frankly,

"I believe that even a casual acquaintance with medical research will reveal that those engaged in it are coming to what would appear to be a logical conclusion: The human patient is the ultimate experimental model."

Robert Legate, M.D., Los Angeles
Medical World News
March 25, 1966

American laboratories spend 50 million dollars a year for stolen pets alone, says Mel Morse in *Ordeal of the Animals.* Trucks roam communities picking up any animal they can find. Sal LaManna, of the National Council for Humane Action, says that an estimated two million dogs a year are stolen for laboratories. It's commonplace for a laboratory to place a purchase order for 300 dogs with a dealer. LaManna knows one dealer who clears $750,000 a year.

It's comforting to pretend that scientists in laboratories don't know that they are using stolen pets. One can't help but wonder where they imagine the two million dogs and the armies of cats come from, when everyone else who works in the humane movement knows their origin. Dog auctions are held in many parts of the country. Panel trucks from many states are there. Dogs and bills of sale are exchanged for a dime or so, and the trucks return to laboratories in their home states. It is impossible to believe that any intelligent person, shown such a bill of sale, could believe that this was not a stolen dog. Yet we are told time and again that these honorable men in laboratories would never do such a thing as burn, scald, crush, starve, drown or otherwise experiment upon "somebody's pet".

If your dog or cat disappears, says LaManna, they have speedily been whisked into another state and become a nameless, homeless phantom worth $40 to the dealer. The Council urges everyone to have dogs permanently marked, with a painless tattoo which will identify him. There is no assurance that this will protect him in a laboratory in another state or that anyone will bother to return him to you. But it is surely the least you can do, the smallest gesture you can make toward trying to protect him. Write for further information to: National Council for Humane Action, Box 37, Clifton, New Jersey, 07011.

The Society for Animal Protective Legislation, P.O.

Box 3719, Georgetown Station, Washington, D. C., 20007, and the Animal Welfare Institute, P.O. Box 3492, Grand Central Station, New York, N. Y., 10017, have excellent literature on every aspect of the care of laboratory animals and much material on endangered species, roadside zoos, the pet trade, circuses and carnivals. Along with other humane organizations they worked hard for the final passage of the Whitehurst Bill, (late 1970) which provides for proper care and handling for experimental animals, as well as those in transport and trade for pet shops, roadside zoos, carnivals, and so on. Any federal law, of course, pertains only to animals which cross state lines. So it's up to you to press for such a law in your own state. The Council of State Governments, meeting in May, 1970, approved a model state law which would empower state agriculture departments to set and enforce standards of animal husbandry for pet shops, pounds, dog wardens, animal shelters and animal dealers within state boundaries. You may obtain a copy of this model law from the U. S. Animal Health Association, Animal Welfare Committee, Dr. Grant Kaley, Dept. of Agriculture and Markets, Division of Animal Industry, Building #8, State Campus, Albany, New York, 12226.

In May, 1967 the *New Yorker* magazine examined the trade in skins of endangered animals. "Fun furs" was the title of the piece. Due solely to examples set by several pampered darlings of the jet set, spotted cat furs became the new rage. The figures given in the *New Yorker* article boggle the mind: one thousand skins of Bolivian ocelot piled in the store room of *one* New York dealer. The price is fifty dollars a skin. Four hundred and sixty-four Somali leopard skins bought by *one* dealer from the Somali government. Says the *New Yorker,* he guessed that, in all, the skins of 7,000 leopards reached New York last year.

In 1966 another dealer was able to get only 16 tiger skins at $325 each. "With the supply of tigers drying up, he is attempting to promote puma from Brazil and Mexico." A customer came in to look at leopard skins and complained about paying $500 for a skin with bullet holes. "Leopards don't die in bed," said the dealer.

You must have eight Somali leopards to make one coat. As many as 25 skins of smaller cats go into one coat. "They must be killing these animals off very, very fast", said one dealer, "I wouldn't be surprised if they disappear entirely. They are so beautiful it's a crime to kill them just for this! . . . I handle the skins of animals that were in the jungle three days before. They are flown in here with the blood still on the fur. To look at these beautiful things makes me want to cry. I would get out of the business if it would change things, but someone would take my place."

"The demand for Somali leopards is unlimited. The finest skin is worth twenty-four hundred dollars . . . a coat could cost $20,000 . . . The demand has risen ever since we sold a coat to Mrs. John F. Kennedy in 1962. We have created our own Frankenstein monster — a demand that destroys the raw material. . . . We assume there are jaguars in unexplored regions of Brazil, but no one really knows. No one really knows much about any of these cats. . . .

". . . Four years ago the Fauna Preservation Society of London estimated that fifty thousand leopards were killed annually in East Africa. . . ."

In September, 1968 and again in December, 1969

Jacques Kaplan, managing director of Georges Kaplan, Furriers, placed ads in the *New York Times* announcing "If you respect life wait 20 years before you buy your next leopard coat from us." The ad went on, "there has come a point in my life when decency and reason must prevail over monetary profits". He has stopped dealing in the skins of threatened animals: leopard, tiger, cheetah, polar bear, Spanish lynx, jaguar, red wolf, sea otter, ocelot and vicuna. He invited other furriers to follow his lead and offered his ad as a public service. So far as I know, no one took him up on it. When a law was passed in Congress which forbad the importation of hides of endangered species, and state laws were beginning to surface in several localities, furriers ran ads, saying in essence, "This might be your last chance to get in on the kill — your last chance for one of these exotic furs!"

A local department store ran such an ad. Through the efforts of people who got on the phone and called everyone they knew, letters poured in to the store. Most were answered with phone calls and assurances that this would never happen again. It was the height of the hawk migration season and some 10,000 nature-lovers visited nearby Hawk Mountain that weekend. The ad was posted prominently at Hawk Mountain with a few well-chosen words by the curator.

In October, 1969, a man's fur coat made from mountain lion (an endangered animal in most parts of our country) was featured in an ad in the *New York Times,* drawing a sharp protest from a Ph. D. and an answer from the furrier that he was only following the international Red Book which lists endangered species all over the world. The Director the New York Zoological Society took up the cudgels in a sizzling letter to the *Times* in which he explained that the Red Book lists only those endangered animals for which scientific information is available. A single species may be pushed to extinction in one country, but not in another, hence is not listed in the Red Book.

He goes on to say, "The United States is, by far, the world's largest importer of wild-animal fragments. For example, in 1967, 22 million pounds of wild animal skins alone went through U. S. Customs. These included 115,458 ocelot skins, 35,748 otter skins and 970,809 deer and antelope skins. . . . The wildlife products trade is demonstrably endangering a number of wild animals ranging from leopards and blue whales to tigers and alligators. . . . How can an informed person look at a mountain-lion coat without seeing fine big cats in their death agony, stripped, fly-blown carcasses lying in a gully, starving cubs in some remote crevice, and maimed animals who got away suffering in a nearby forest?

"Isn't it about time that informed, civilized human beings stop killing diminishing wild creatures for their skins? Isn't it about time for the *Times* to inform its readers about the implications of products made from wild animals?"

The fight to stop the brutal clubbing of seals in Eastern Canada has just begun. Leading the forces for decency is Friends of Animals, whose president, maligned and libeled by those who profit from the slaughter, said in an ad in the *New York Times,* May 8, 1970:

"Don't believe furriers who would persuade you that Friends of Animals has been 'misleading' you, that any slaughter anywhere is done for the benefit of the seals.

"I, Alice Herrington, testify that on March 21, 1970 — the second day of the Canadian season on seals — I saw the same brutal massacre against which Friends of Animals, of which I am president, has been protesting for years. As the bubble-domed helicopter flew low over the first day's kill, I saw mother seals nuzzling the skinless corpses of their babies. Standing ten feet away from the killers on the ice floes, twenty miles out in the Gulf, I saw baby seals clubbed twice, and then sliced open. Other babies were battered as many as fourteen times while the mothers watched in terror and stress."

It appears probable that if most Americans were forced to watch the massacre it would stop, for most of us have at least some humane scruples left which are strong enough to force even the laziest of us to protest such senseless, useless brutality for no purpose other than profit. When you protest in writing, as I have many times, you are fobbed off with the same dreary, evasive excuses. The seals really want to be clubbed is the implication. And besides, it's "good for the herds". And then, what would all those poor Canadians do, who make a few dollars every year clubbing seals? Everyone knows that people in this part of Canada are miserably poor. Obviously, if the Canadian government cared about the welfare of these people, they would give them something to do — and something a lot more profitable, pleasant and satisfying than this. And, obviously, if the seal herds were unable to maintain themselves in good health without the yearly slaughter, they would have become extinct long, long ago.

Brian Davies of the International Fund for Animal Welfare is quoted in the *San Francisco Chronicle* as saying that if the seals were protected and made a tourist attraction and *as few as 1000 people came to see them each year,* the tourist revenue would make up for the revenue lost by stopping the seal hunt!

Lest you think the Canadian government stands alone in sanctioning these murders, get involved sometime in what's going on in the Pribilof Islands where another seal herd is annually "harvested" by the U. S. Department of Interior and/or the Fouke Company, which sells furs. (It's hard to know where the Department begins and the Fouke Company leaves off in these arrangements, but it's quite apparent that the Fouke Company makes all the money and the taxpayers pay for the slaughter).

Says the *New York Times,* August 31, 1968, "Alaska seals, which are made available to American processors by the United States Government (Department of Interior) will be . . . about 53,000. On September 19, the current consignment will be put on auction . . . by the Fouke Company". I got into a long correspondence with both the Department of Interior and the Fouke Company about this slaughter.

The Department of Interior sends you a form letter along with a mass of expensive propaganda, *paid for of course by your money.* The Fouke Company sends you a personal letter on fancy stationery, enclosing the same propaganda from the government, paid for by your money. The gist of the message is always the same. The seals are being murdered only for their own good, by concerned conservationists of our government and the Fouke Company, who have arrived at the extraordinary conclusion that nature simply doesn't know how to maintain living things and, unless some kindly sealers paid by the Department of Interior, club to death a given number of seals every year, why, who knows what might happen! It seems incredible that the department in our government which is entrusted with conservation thinks they can mail out nonsense like this to concerned conservationists in the year of Earth Week! But they continue to do so.*

And now it's time for the American people to stand up and be heard. And I mean you, the reader of this book. I mean you are being made a fool of by a Federal bureaucracy which uses your money to destroy in the most inhumane and senseless manner, one of the most beautiful and appealing of all our animal resources to enrich a company which profits from the slaughter. This is the same Federal bureaucracy which, using your money, spreads deadly poison over vast areas in the West to kill "predators" — chiefly the coyotes, which control rodent populations and other pests, as the balance of nature necessitates. Any other animal which finds the poison, including pets, dies an agonizing death.

Take No for an answer. Tell your congressman you will simply no longer permit this cruel exploitation. If he or the Department of Interior send you some blatant, expensive piece of equivocation, write again and demand that they cease these operations at once.

Friends of Animals has other suggestions for action. Borrow or rent a fur or leather coat. Wear it with a placard telling the story of death, the welter of suffering.

* Recently the seal slaughter was transferred to the Department of Commerce, National Marine Fisheries Service, by this peculiar operation transferring mammals into the classification of fish. In March, 1971 Senator Fred R. Harris introduced S 1315, the Ocean Mammal Protection Act of 1971, to protect seals, whales, otters, porpoises, walruses, sea lions and polar bears. It's a fine bill. Let's get it made into law fast! Write your senators!

An average full-length coat is made of: "Seven Helpless Seals Hang Here." "Lots and lots of Ocelots — 25 Are In This Coat", "Seven Beautiful Leopards Were Stripped of Their Coats To Make This Coat", "Forty Raccoons Trapped in Jaws of Steel Are In This Emblem of Barbarism", "This Coat Shrieks With Pain".

Signs to carry on demonstrations might be placards with enlarged paste-ups of seal slaughter, animals in traps, slogans like "Save the Seals", "Stop the Murder of Wildlife", "When You Wear Fur You Wear Death", and so on. Friends of Animals organizes nationwide protests. You need only get in touch with them to help. The address is: 11 West 60th Street, New York City, 10023. And they have many, many fine projects in addition to their work in the anti-sealing campaign.

Friends of the Earth ask environmentalists to sign a pledge that they will not wear skins of the endangered animals. You can get copies of the pledge by writing them at the address given in the appendix of this book. The Sierra Club, the Audubon Society, the World Wildlife Fund, the Fund for Animals, Friends of Animals, Canadian Wolf Defenders, the Humane Society, Defenders of Wildlife are some of the many other organizations involved in the fight to save endangered animals. Some of these organizations, as well as many others concerned with birds and animals, go much farther in their convictions about killing *any* animals for *any* purpose that is not absolutely essential.

The best way to find out which organization best represents your views is to write to a number of them and ask for literature on furs, on vivisection, on conservation, on dog fights or the maimed Tennessee Walking Horses, or whatever is your chief field of protest. You will get plenty of literature. Unless your stomach is strong, you'd better approach the photographs cautiously. Many humane individuals who identify with animals or who simply believe in the Golden Rule find they cannot eat or sleep after seeing photographs of crippled horses, beheaded laboratory dogs, poisoned coyotes, raccoons mangled by steel traps, baby seals beaten and skinned alive.

And many humane people use their aversion to such sights as an excuse for doing absolutely nothing about what is happening to birds and animals all over this planet in the midst of our supposedly enlightened and civilized age.

"I'm just too squeamish," they say, "I just can't stand to think of all those horrible things." You don't have to think of all the horrible things to mail a check to some of the steadfast, courageous people who are not too squeamish to face the facts. You can sign your name to a petition. You can write a letter to an editor. You can cancel your charge account at a store. You can write or wire your senator or congressman about legislation which may bring some small, late benefit to those living things on this planet which are not human beings.

You can put up no hunting signs on your property. You can discourage the use of snowmobiles — one of the most recent threats to all wildlife everywhere. (It's almost time for a book on the various ways an animal can be killed with a snowmobile — for pure pleasure, of course.) You can teach your children and those in your neighborhood to be humane, and to shun, no matter what the cost, any activities which hurt or kill birds or animals senselessly.

You can check on the laws of your state which concern animals. Do you have a humane slaughter law? Do you have a law which protects endangered birds and animals in your state? Is some state legislator looking into the model State law for protection of animals in transportation, in pounds, in trade? (We mentioned this earlier). Does your children's school encourage vivisection? Have your dogs and cats been spayed? If you have a pet, is it well cared for, or do you just turn it loose to roam, trusting that it won't be run over, poisoned, stolen, scalded, or crippled in a fight?

Do you drive carefully in country areas, on a constant lookout for wildlife crossing the road? Do you protest the destruction of wildlife habitat in your community, encourage the establishment of sanctuaries and parks? If you live in a new housing development have you made any gestures toward caring for the myriad animals and birds whose homes were destroyed so that your home could be built? Food and water for songbirds, shelter and protection for squirrels, rabbits and chipmunks cost almost nothing and pay back part of the huge debt you owe these homeless ones.

Do you have an animal shelter for strays in your community? If not, why not start one, with a sound program for spaying pets and strays and finding homes for unwanted and lost animals? The Lehigh County Humane Society and the Allentown (Pennsylvania) *Morning Call* co-operate in an excellent, long-standing program to place stray dogs and cats. Every Sunday the "Dog and Cat of the Week" are featured in appealing photographs. Almost all of them find homes with loving families by the next morning.

In case you are kidding yourself that there's plenty of time, that the people crying "sadism", "senseless destruction", "extinction" are just alarmists or old ladies in tennis shoes, it's time for you to wake up and face the cold facts that, as things are going now, with pollution, over-population, possible worldwide famines, over-exploitation of all our resources for such trivialities as furs, sports and eradication of the fire ants, we are facing the total extinction of any meaningful amount of life on our planet other than human.

If you collect clippings pertaining to animal welfare, as I do, you might find in your file the following. All these are headlines from the past few years:

Alaskans React to Criticism of Their Bounty on Wolves

Curbs on Hunting Polar Bear Eased

Extinction Threatening Ceylon's Elephants

Poisoning of Wolves is Causing Concern

Vicunas Struggle Against Extinction

Efforts Reported to Get Whales Off List of Endangered Species

22 Species Added to List of Animals Facing Extinction

Scientists Call for Stiffer International Controls on Whale Hunting

Alaska Assailed Over Wolf Policy

U. S. Asked to End Woodcock Season

Bluebird is Added to Imperiled List

In Time of Urbanization, Bear is Still Fair Game

The Vanishing Jungle: Two Wildlife Expeditions to Pakistan

Many Species of Asian Wildlife Periled by Population Rise

Vast Projects Affecting Wildlife in West Stir Controversy

A Rare Breed (Sea Otters) Imperiled by a Nuclear Test

Beaver Trapping (Penna.) Brings in 2,874 Skins
Tiger Hunting Banned (Jaipur, India has only 10 tigers left)
Philippines Battling to Preserve Rare Wildlife
Survival of All Seven Species of Marine Turtles in Critical Stage
Montana Weighing Wild Horses' Fate
The Brown Pelican Declining Rapidly
Many Unique Australian Species Disappearing at an Alarming Rate
Hunter Shoots Two Cougars Same Day (a famous local hunter who uses only bow and arrow, and boasts of his many kills of animals nearing extinction).
Craze for Pet Parrots Threatens Jungle Ecology
Bobcat Hunt Using Snowmobiles
Licensed Depredation — 600,000 Tortoises Imported as Pets
Canadian Boy Scout Troop Enters Trapping Business
78 Types of Wildlife Species Face Extinction
Canada's Caribou Face Extinction
U. S. Urged to Help Wild Horse Herd
Rhodesian National Parks Face Ecological Ruin
U. S. Bans Importing of Gray Jungle Bird
Yellowstone Park Applauds Sighting of Six Wild Wolves
Studies Imperil Marine Life Off California
Canada Faces Immense Task Preserving Rare Natural Habitat of Arctic
U. S. Alligator Skin Sales Ban Unlikely to Curb Fashions Here
Extinction Fear for Mexican Grizzly Bear

Pollution Problems Facing Sea Otters
Killing of Rare Tule Elk Arouses Dispute (there are only 400 of these animals left of the former immense herds. California officially sponsors a cold-blooded hunt in which 50 are killed each year).
Death Comes to the Peregrine Falcon
Pollution Threatens Extinction of 2 British Sea Birds
Bill to Protect Striped Bass, Endangered Species in Hudson River
War in Cambodia Perils Oxen of Fossil Species
Alaskan Bears Decimated by Oilmen and Killing from Air
Only 40 Condors Counted in U. S. (This is the magnificent thunderbird, worshipped as a god by Indians).
Naturalists Book Predicts That Wildlife Will be Wiped Out in New Jersey By Century's End
Protection is Ordered for Eagles
Netting of Birds is Fought in Europe
Are Kangaroos Doomed by Current Slaughter for Meat and Hides?
"Sportsmen" New Peril to Offshore Mammals
Genocide at Sea — Whales Grossly Over-Exploited
Naturalists Fear Wolves About to Disappear
Smuggling of Birds Big in New Zealand
Man Threatening Peru's Wildlife
Baboon Kills Big in Rhodesia
Elk Hunt in Yellowstone Opposed by Sportsmen
Ten Rare Asian Lions Poisoned in Indian Forest
Seattle to Offer Sea Otter Pelts
Wildlife in Soviet in Peril
Canada to Permit Hunting of Muskox
Siberia Offering $1500 Bear Hunt

Orangutans Victims of Malaysia-Indonesia Fighting
Atlantic Salmon Doomed
Galapagos in Trouble Again
Butterfly Called a Victim of Cities (Imagine, after all butterflies are extinct, trying to describe to a child — your grandchild, perhaps — what a butterfly looked like!)
Kenya Killing Elephants to Save Park
798 Animals Seen in Danger of Extinction Around World

Naturalists who understand most deeply our relation to other living things know that we cannot survive without our bird, fish, insect and animal life. It's not just a matter of insects taking over completely once we have destroyed all the birds, and millions of people starving once we have so polluted the oceans that they cannot support food fish. It's a matter of loneliness.

Dr. Alfred G. Etter, Western representative of Defenders of Wildlife, whose dog was poisoned by strychnine set out by a few state fish and game agents "to kill a few magpies to save a few pears," put it this way, "It is strange how unimportant each of us may seem in the great fairy ring of life, yet how good it feels to touch a dog, to hug her big head, to feel the beating tail against your leg. In the great range of time and earth, it is good to know the feel of other life, to wipe away the loneliness of being man."

The Silent Minority on this planet have no voice of their own, no legislators, no political influence. They can erect no barricade to fend off their despoilers. They have no weapons. They must depend on you for their protection, for their survival. Part of their welfare depends on how well you protect the environment they must have for survival. Another and equally important part depends on how well you protect their moral rights to live and thrive on this planet which is theirs, as surely and as eternally as it is ours.

Bibliography

Here's Some Good Reading on Ecology and Environment:

Carr, Donald E., *Death of the Sweet Waters.* What we have done to destroy our streams, rivers, beaches, lakes, and how we may be able to save ourselves from water starvation. Norton, $5.95.

Carson, Rachel, *Silent Spring.* The book that started it all, by the eminent biologist who was also one of the great prose artists of her time. A Fawcett Crest book, paperback, 75 cents.

Coleman-Cooke, John, *The Harvest That Kills.* The story of agricultural chemicals and what they are doing to soil, animals and man. Odhams, London.

Commoner, Barry, *Science and Survival.* The man who was featured by Time magazine during Earth Week, one of the most quoted biologists of our time, Commoner charges that the present state of science and technology endangers the existence of all life. Viking Press, $4.50.

Compost Science, a bi-monthly journal on waste recycling, presenting the views of official experts and daring innovators in this important field. Rodale Press, Emmaus, Pa. 18049, $6 a year.

Conservation Directory, 1970. Directory of all organizations, agencies and officials concerned with natural resources and management. Natl. Wildlife Federation, 1412–16th St., Washington, D.C., 20036, $1.50.

Crisis of Survival. An issue of Progressive magazine devoted to this subject with important articles by leading authorities.

One to 10 copies $1 each, from Progressive, Madison, Wisc. 53703.

Curtis, Richard and Elizabeth Hogan, *The Perils of the Peaceful Atom.* What our peacetime nuclear program means in terms of future catastrophe and present health hazards, Ballantine Books, paperback, $1.25.

DeBell, Garrett, Editor, *The Environmental Handbook.* Prepared for the first national teach-in on Earth Day, 1970. Background material on ecology and ecotactics. Ballantine Books, paperback, 95 cents.

Ehrlich, Paul R., *The Population Bomb.* The book on overpopulation which made the world realize this is the most serious problem humanity has ever faced. Ballantine Books, paperback, 95 cents.

Ehrlich, Paul R. and Anne H., *Population, Resources, Environment.* A full account of what world overpopulation is doing to our world and our future, with some helpful suggestions for change. Freeman, $8.95.

Ellul, Jacques, *The Technological Society.* A learned analysis of what technology is doing to human beings and their world by a famous French sociologist who doesn't hold out much hope for the future. Alfred A. Knopf, $10.95.

Environment. A monthly journal published by the Committee for Environmental Information, 438 N. Skinker Blvd., St. Louis, Missouri, 63130. $8.50 a year.

Environment Action Bulletin. A weekly newsletter on health and human ecology, published by Rodale Press, Emmaus, Pa., 18049, $10 a year.

Fisher, James, et al., *Wildlife in Danger.* A handsome book on our vanishing wildlife, the official publication of the International Union for Conservation of Nature and Natural Resources. Viking Press, New York, $12.95.

Gofman, John W. and Tamplin, Arthur R., *Population Control Through Nuclear Pollution.* Man's eventual destruction of man by the poison of pollution. Nelson Hall, $6.95.

Gofman, John W. and Tamplin, Arthur R., *Poisoned Power.* A description of the dangers we face from atomic energy plants and alternatives we can take. Rodale Press, Inc., Emmaus, Pa. $6.95.

Goldstein, Jerome, *Garbage as You Like It.* A plan to stop pollution by using garbage to create soil conditioner, and other solid waste to replenish our dwindling resources. Rodale Press Inc., $4.95.

Graham, Frank, Jr., *Disaster by Default.* The politics of water pollution. Private and public apathy, cynicism and ineffective laws are responsible, says this author. Evans, $4.95.

Graham, Frank, Jr., *Since Silent Spring.* What has happened in the field of pesticides and the harm they do, within the past 10 years. Houghton Mifflin, $6.95.

Harrison, Ruth, *Animal Machines, The New Factory Farming Industry.* Horror stories of how stock animals and poultry are raised in modern farming. Vincent Stuart, Ltd., London. 21 shillings.

Herber, Lewis, *Crisis in Our Cities.* Pollution of all kinds, physical and emotional stress, crowding, lack of privacy are only a few of the urban problems taken up in this book. Prentice-Hall, $5.95.

Herber, Lewis, *Our Synthetic Environment.* The artificiality of our technological world: drugs, pollution, chemical additives, urban problems. Alfred A. Knopf, $4.95.

Hunter, Beatrice Trum, *Gardening Without Poisons.* How to do without the toxic pesticides that have proven themselves a daily risk to health and environment. Houghton Mifflin, $5.00.

Hunter, Beatrice Trum, *Consumer, Beware! Your Food and What's Been Done To It.* A slashing, well-documented attack on modern chemicalized food. Simon and Schuster, $8.95.

Johnson, Huey D., *No Deposit, No Return.* Speeches delivered at a symposium of the U.S. National Commission for UNESCO. Many fine statements by people well worth consulting and quoting. Addison-Wesley Publishing Company, Reading, Mass. $2.95.

Leavitt, Emily Stewart, et al., *Animals and Their Legal Rights.* The laws of the fifty states in regard to protection of animals.

Essential if you want to go into humane work. Animal Welfare Institute, p.o. Box 3492, Grand Central Station, New York City 10017.

Leavitt, Helen, *Superhighway, Superhoax*. The story of Interstate highways all over the nation and the Federal Highway Trust Fund that makes them possible. We are strangling in a concrete straitjacket that pollutes the environment. This book tells why. Doubleday, $6.95.

Lewis, Howard R., *With Every Breath You Take*. How the poisons of air pollution are injuring our health, and some suggested remedies the layman can pursue. Crown Publishers, $5.00.

Lingeman, Richard R., *Don't You Know There's a War On?* The story of the many things we did without because we had to. G. P. Putnam's Sons, New York, $7.95.

Linton, Ron M., *Terracide*. The author was an important figure in the Federal Department of Health, Education and Welfare. He takes up chemicals, food, crowding, urban problems, and so on. Little, Brown and Co., $7.95.

Loebsack, Theo., *Our Atmosphere*. An ecology book dealing with the earth's atmosphere and its effects on our lives. New American Library, paperback, 50 cents.

Longgood, William, *The Poisons in Your Food*. There are at present, as a conservative estimate, 10,000 chemicals in the American food supply whose potential for harm has not been investigated. Simon and Schuster, $3.95.

Marine, Gene, *America the Raped*. A stinging, slashing attack on what the author calls "the engineering mentality" which has nearly destroyed whole sections of our nation, largely through the efforts of the Army Corps of Engineers. Simon and Schuster, $5.95.

Marx, Wesley, *The Frail Ocean*. Oil spills, sewage, land reclamation, destruction of estuaries—are we ruining our oceans? Ballantine Books, paperback, 95 cents.

Milne, Lorus and Margery, *The Balance of Nature*. An attractive, interesting book on ecology for beginners, by two well-known naturalists. Alfred A. Knopf, $5.00.

Mitchell, John G. and Constance L. Stallings, Ed., *Ecotactics.* The Sierra Club handbook for activities the layman can take to help preserve our environment and prevent pollution. Pocket Books, paperback, 95 cents.

Morse, Mel, *Ordeal of the Animals.* Man's encounters with other living things almost always bring disaster to the other living things. Prentice-Hall, Englewood Cliffs, N.J., $5.95.

Mowbray, A. Q., *Road to Ruin.* A critical view of the Federal highway program and its scandalous highway trust fund which is destroying our landscape and polluting our air. Lippincott, $5.95.

Nicholson, Max, *The Environmental Revolution.* A history of international conservation movements up to the present, with notes on their effectiveness in dealing with environmental problems. Hodder and Stoughton, London.

Novick, Sheldon, *The Careless Atom.* The editor of *Environment* magazine tells the full story of what our peacetime nuclear program is doing to our environment, our health, our future. Houghton Mifflin, $5.95.

Ogden, Samuel R., Editor, *America the Vanishing.* Nostalgic word pictures of our past landscapes, rustic pleasures and abundant wildlife, by famous American writers. The Stephen Greene Press, Brattleboro, Vt. 05301, $6.95.

Organic Gardening and Farming. Monthly publication dealing with ways to farm and garden without the use of chemical pesticides and commercial fertilizers. Many articles on readers' experiences in this eminently satisfying way of living. Rodale Press, Emmaus, Pa. 18049, one year subscription $5.85.

Paddock, William and Paul, *Famine 1975!* Two experts on population figures and food production say the world cannot possibly avoid extensive famines by 1975 due to uncontrolled overpopulation and unwise use of resources. Little, Brown, $6.50.

Perry, John, *Our Polluted World, Can Man Survive?* Timely facts on pollution by a famous naturalist. Franklin Watts, $4.95.

Policies for Solid Waste Management. Official publication of the U.S. Public Health Service covering past policies and future recommendations in the field of disposing of garbage and trash. There are valuable statistics here. Superintendent of Documents, Washington, D.C. 20402. 50 cents.

Pringle, Laurence, *The Only Earth We Have.* A book on ecology for young people by a staff member of the American Museum of Natural History. Macmillan Co., $4.50.

Restoring the Quality of Our Environment. Report to the President's Science Advisory Committee, Environmental Panel. Superintendent of Documents, Washington, D.C. 20402.

Ridgeway, James, *The Politics of Ecology.* How it works out when environmental dilemmas get into the hands of politicians and big business. Discouraging. E. P. Dutton and Co. $5.95.

Rienow, Robert and Leona Train, *Moment in the Sun.* A summary of our environmental troubles and the deteriorating quality of the life around us. Ballantine Books, paperback, 95 cents.

Rockefeller, Nelson A., *Our Environment Can Be Saved.* Cheerful, positively ebullient. There's no problem we cannot solve! Doubleday and Co., Inc. Garden City, N.Y. $2.50.

Rodale, J. I and staff, *The Organic Way to Plant Protection.* How to raise garden and ornamental plants without using pesticides. Rodale Press, Emmaus, Pa. 18049, $5.95.

Rodale, J. I. and staff, *Our Poisoned Earth and Sky.* Health, pollution, chemicals in food, pesticides and so on. Well documented facts. Rodale Press, Emmaus, Pa. 18049, $9.95.

Rudd, Robert L., *Pesticides and the Living Landscape.* A survey of where we stand in regard to pesticide harm, commissioned by the Conservation Foundation and written by a specialist in the field. U. of Wisconsin Press, paperback, $1.95.

Scientists' Institute for Public Information Workbooks. Paperback books planned for teachers on *Air Pollution; The Effects of Weapons Technology; Environmental Education,*

1970; Nuclear Explosives in Peacetime; Environmental Cost of Electric Power; Hunger; Water Pollution; Pesticides. Order from SIPI, 30 East 68th Street, New York City 10021, $5.00 for the set.

Shurcliff, William A., *SST and Sonic Boom Handbook.* The horrors of the future if we allow the government to proceed with production of the supersonic transport. Ballantine Books, paperback, 95 cents.

Stewart, George R., *Not So Rich as You Think.* Pollution and the hideous waste of our natural resources which cancel out what we think of as "progress." Houghton Mifflin, $5.00.

Storer, John H., *The Web of Life.* A basic book on ecology for everyone, young or old. New American Library, paperback, 50 cents.

Swatek, Paul, *The User's Guide to the Protection of the Environment.* What to buy and not buy and what to do with it after you're through with it. Ballantine Books, New York, $1.25.

Udall, Stewart L., *The Quiet Crisis.* The urgency of our environmental crisis. By a former Secretary of the Department of Interior. Avon Books, paperback, 95 cents.

Vosburgh, John, *Living With Your Land.* A guide to conservation on the city's fringe. Cranbrook Institute of Science, paperback, $1.

Whiteside, Thomas, *Defoliation, What Are Our Herbicides Doing to Us?* The story of 2,4,5-T and other herbicides and what they have destroyed. Ballantine Books, paperback, 95 cents.

Whyte, William H., *The Last Landscape.* The way our landscapes look and the way they can and should look, with proper planning and legislation, is the gist of this book by a Pennsylvania expert. Doubleday Anchor Book, paperback, $1.95.

Wilson, Billy Ray, *Environmental Problems.* Pesticides, thermal pollution and the interactions of one kind of pollution on another by a Rutgers biochemist. J. P. Lippincott, $5.25.

Appendix

Here are the names of organizations which can give you help in environmental education and projects. There are hundreds of other organizations listed in *Conservation Directory,* $1.50, published by National Wildlife Federation, whose address is listed below. This directory, containing also lists of state and federal officials concerned with all aspects of the environment, is an absolute necessity for your conservation library.

Canadian Wolf Defenders
Box 3480, Station D
Edmonton, 41 Alberta, Canada

Conservation Foundation
1250 Connecticut Avenue N.W.
Washington, D.C. 20036

Defenders of Wildlife
2000 N. Street N.W.
Washington, D.C. 20036

Environmental Action
1346 Connecticut Avenue
Washington, D.C. 20036

Environmental Defense Fund
P. O. Box 740
Stony Brook, New York 11790

Friends of Animals
11 West 60th Street
New York City 10023

Friends of the Earth
451 Pacific Avenue
San Francisco, Cal. 94133

Fund for Animals
1 Wall Street
New York City

Humane Society of the U.S.
1145 19th Street, N.W.
Washington, D.C. 20036

National Audubon Society
1130 Fifth Avenue
New York City 10028

National Wildlife Federation
1412 16th Street N.W.
Washington, D.C. 20036

Nature Conservancy
1522 K Street N.W.
Washington, D.C. 20005

Planned Parenthood
515 Madison Avenue
New York City 10022

Scientists Institute for Public Information
30 East 68th Street
New York City 10021

Sierra Club
1050 Mills Tower
San Francisco, California 94104

Trout Unlimited
5850 E. Jewell Avenue
Denver, Colorado 80222

Wilderness Society
729 15th Street N.W.
Washington, D.C. 20005

World Wildlife Fund
Suite 728, 910 17th Street N.W.
Washington, D.C. 20009

If you are looking for an environment group near your home, here is a list compiled by Environment Action Bulletin, state by state. We can not guarantee every address, for these things change with time, but we are sure you can find any neighborhood group in your locality from this list.

ALABAMA

GASP, Inc.
800 South 20th St.
Birmingham, Alabama 35205

Greg Fuller
705 Spraggin St. S.W.
Decatur, Alabama 35601

Arthur N. Beck, Technical Secretary
Alabama Water Improvement Commission
State Office Building, Room 328
Montgomery, Alabama 36104

ARIZONA

Eco Contact
% Betsy McDonald
1028 E. 6th St.
Tucson, Arizona 85716

Arizona State Department of Health
Environmental Health Services
Division of Air Pollution Control
4019 North 33rd Avenue
Phoenix, Arizona 85017

Cochise County Air Pollution Control District
Cochise County Board of Supervisors
Willcox, Arizona 85643
W. R. Moore, Chairman

Bureau of Air Sanitation
Maricopa County Health Department
1825 East Roosevelt Street
Phoenix, Arizona 85006
Robert Taylor, Director

Mohave County Health Department
305 West Beale Street
Kingman, Arizona 86401
John G. Lingenfelter, M.D., Director

Coconino County Air Pollution Control District
Coconino County Health Department
2500 North Fort Valley Road
Flagstaff, Arizona 86001
William Thomas, M.D., Director

Greenlee County Air Pollution Control District
P. O. Box 1372
Clifton, Arizona 85533
Lawrence A. Dahners, Officer

Air Pollution Control District
Pima County Health Department
151 West Congress Street
Tucson, Arizona 85701
W. F. R. Griffith, P.E., Chief

Yuma County Health Department
145 Third Avenue
Yuma, Arizona 85064
E. V. Putnam, M.D.

Phoenix Civitan Club-Operation Smog Stop
2641 East McDowell Rd.
Phoenix, Arizona 85008

GASP
% Teri Fornara
9 Brookside Blvd.
Prescott, Arizona 86301

ALASKA

Department of Health and Welfare
Division of Environmental Health
Juneau, Alaska 99801

CALIFORNIA

Environmental Action Group
%Paul Leech
1570 Notre Dame Ave.
Belmont, California 94002

Ecology Information Group
% Larry Luce
20 Crystal Way
Berkeley, California 94708

H.O.P.E.
Humboldt State College
1550 B Street
Arcata, California 95521

HOPE
% Ross Hunter
Route 1, Box 4
Bayside, California 95524

Ecology Action of Berkeley
Box 9334
3029 Benvenue
Berkeley, California 94709

Ecology Action-Chula Vista
% Kaeti Pittman
3419 Evergreen Rd.
Bonita, California

APPENDIX

Students for Ecological Action
% Casey Murphy
Box 583
St. Mary's College
Moraga, California 94574

Experimental College Ecology Class
Napa College
Napa, California 94558

Ecology Action-Merrit College
% John Kaltenbach
Merrit College
5701 Grove
Oakland, California 94609

Montera Ecology Act. Comm.
6701 Pinehaven Rd.
Oakland, California

Cal State Hayward Conservation & Ecology Club
% Bob Ulrich
22302 Center St.
Castro Valley, California 94546

Ecology Center
116 W. 12th St.
Chico, California 95926

Mount Shasta Ecology Action
% Jeff Dennis
General Delivery
Mt. Shasta, California 96067

Coachella Valley Ecology Action
% Garlan Salzgeber
General Delivery
North Shore, California 92254

Laney Ecology Club
% Laney College
1001 Third Avenue
Oakland, California 94606

Oakland Tech. H. S. Ecology Action
% Ted Donaldson
115 Alpine Terrace
Oakland, California 94618

Jared Mays
26200 Mesa Drive
Carmel, California 93921

Ecology Action of Chico
% Etidorpha Natural Foods
114 W. 12th St.
Chico, California 95926

Environmental Studies Center & CASE
Orange Coast College
2701 Fairview Rd.
Costa Mesa, California 92626

Monte Vista HS Conserv. Club
% Linda Mitchell
Sec., 866 Rose Blossom Dr.
Cupertino, California 95014

Mrs. Raymond E. Jacksman
Route 2
Box 235 A
Fort Bragg, California 95437

Ecology Action
Calif. State College
800 North State College Blvd.
Fullerton, California 92631
Attn.: Leonard Hitchcock, Philosophy Dept.

Ecology Action-UC at Santa Barbara
% Scott Daulton
Box 624
Goleta, California 93017

Sonoma St. Environmental Action Comm.
% Rick Bergman
Outdoorsmen's Club
Sonoma State College Activities Office
Cotati, California 94928

Ecology Action
% Ray Dragseth
4984 Hillhurst Dr.
Fair Oaks, California 95628

Ecology Action-Fullerton
% Robert Fufer
101 S. Lillie
Fullerton, California 92631

STAMP OUT SMOG
P.O. Box 5128
Garden Grove, California 92641

Glendale HS Conservation Club
% Dianne Beilly
2220 Risa Drive
Glendale, California 91208

Politics Ecology Act. Coalition
% Greg Knell
708 Bolton
Wlk No. 104
Goleta, California 93017

Ecology Workshop
Grossmont College
El Cajon, Calif.

Lompoc Ecology Center
308 N. "H" St.
Lompoc, Calif. 93436

John E. Miller (Organic Gardener)
Wormy Acres
San Diego, Calif. 92104

Sacramento County Air Pollution Control District
2221 Stockton Boulevard
Sacramento, California 95817
(916)454-5458 Activated December 7, 1959
Nemat O. Borhani, M.D.
Acting Director of Public Health
Mr. Philip S. Tow
Chief, Division of Air Sanitation

San Bernardno County Air Pollution Control District
172 West Third Street
San Bernardino, California 92401
(714)889-0111, Ext. 376, 456, 548, 549
Activated June 19, 1956
Mr. John H. Fairweather, Control Officer

APPENDIX

Sutter County Air Pollution Control District
Sutter County Office Building
463 Second Street
Yuba City, California 95991
(916)673-7005 Activated July 28, 1969

Air Resources Board
1108-14th Street
Sacramento, California 95814

Bay Area Pollution Control District
939 Ellis Street
San Francisco, California 94109
(415)771-6000 Activated September 1955
Mr. J. D. Callaghan
Chief Administrative Officer

Calaveras County Air Pollution Control District
Government Center
El Dorado Road
San Andreas, California 95249
(209)754-4251 Activated March 6, 1970
D. L. Albasio, M.D., Health Officer
Mr. Carl Overmier, Senior Sanitarian

SMART Organization
Allan Hancock College
800 S. College Drive
Santa Maria, Calif. 93454

LIFEHOUSE
P. O. Box 187
La Mesa, Calif. 92041

San Diego County Air Pollution Control District
Civic Center
1600 Pacific Highway
San Diego, California 92101
(714)239-7711 Activated May 1955
J. B. Askew, M.D., Health Officer
Mr. Clark L. Gaulding
Chief, Air Pollution Control Services

Tulare County Air Pollution Control District
County Civic Center
Visalia, California 93277
(209)732-5511 Activated June 25, 1968
Lowell F. Chemberlen, M.D., Health Officer
Mr. Pete Manson, Director of Sanitation

Ventura County Air Pollution Control District
3147 Loma Vista Road
Ventura, California 93001
(805)648-6181 Activated March 12, 1968
Stephen A. Coray, M.D., Health Officer
Mr. Richard B. Atherton
Air Pollution Control Engineer

Colusa County Air Pollution Control District
County Court House
Colusa, California 95932
(916)458-4516 Activated June 3, 1969
Mr. Andrew R. Clark
Executive Secretary to Board of Supervisors

Los Angeles County Air Pollution Control District
434 South San Pedro Street
Los Angeles, California 90013
(213)629-4711 Activated June 1947
Mr. Louis J. Fuller
Control Officer

Kern County Air Pollution Control District
P. O. Box 997
Bakersfield, California 93302
(1700 Flower Street)
(805)325-5051 Activated March 12, 1968
Owen A. Kerns, M.D., Health Officer
Mr. Citron Toy, Senior Sanitarian

Madera County Air Pollution Control District
216 West Sixth Street
Madera, California 93637
(209)674-4641 Activated June 11, 1968
Douglas F. Pratt
Director of Sanitation
(Acting APCO)

Merced County Air Pollution Control District
P. O. Box 1350
Merced, California 95341
(240 East 15th Street, next to General Hospital)
(209)723-2861 Activated January 14, 1969
A. Frank Brewer, M.D., Health Officer
Mr. Bill Norman, Director of Sanitation

Humboldt County Air Pollution Control District
5630 South Broadway
Eureka, California 95501
(707)443-3091 Activated February 4, 1964
Mr. Charles P. Sassenrath
Air Pollution Control Director

Kings County Air Pollution Control District
1221 West Lacey Boulevard
Hanford, California 93230
(209)582-3211 Activated March 19, 1968
Douglas B. Wilson, M.D., Health Officer
Mr. Tony Maniscalco, Director of Sanitation

Placer County Air Pollution Control District
155 Fulweiler Avenue
Auburn, California 95603
(916)885-4517 Activated March 3, 1970
Gordon Seck, M.D., Health Officer
Mr. Albert A. Marino
Chief, Division of Environmental Health

APPENDIX

San Joaquin County Air Pollution Control District
P. O. Box 2009
Stockton, California 95201
(1601 East Hazelton Avenue)
(209)466-6781 Activated May 9, 1967
Mr. J. Don Layson
Director of Environmental Health

Orange County Air Pollution Control District
1010 South Harbor Boulevard
Anaheim, California 92805
(714)774-0284 Activated September 1950
Mr. William Fitchen, Control Officer

Riverside County Air Pollution Control District
Room 234, Health-Finance Building
3575 Eleventh Street
Riverside, California 92501
(714)787-2416 Activated June 13, 1955
Mr. Galen Kinley, Acting APCO

Fresno County Air Pollution Control District
515 South Cedar Avenue
Fresno, California 93702
(209)485-8000 Activated August 8, 1968
William A. DeFries, M.D., Health Officer
Mr. R. E. Bergstrom
Director of Environmental Sanitation

Nevada County Air Pollution Control District
Willow Valley Road
East Basement Wing
Nevada City, California 95959
(916)265-2461 Ext. 264
Activated April 28, 1970
Peter J. Keenan, M.D., Health Officer
Mr. Hal Cox, Senior Sanitarian

Mariposa County Air Pollution Control District
P. O. Box 5
Mariposa, California 95338
(on Hy. 140, next door to Frosty Shop)
(209)966-3689 Activated April 9, 1968
Robert John Evans, M.D.
Acting Health Officer
Mr. Herb Davis
Chairman, Board of Supervisors
County Court House
(209)966-2396
Home (209)966-2109

Monterey-Santa Cruz County Unified Air Pollution Control District
P. O. Box 487
Salinas, California 93901
(Courthouse)
(408)758-3583 or 424-8611 Ext. 383
Activated July 1, 1968
Mr. Edward W. Munson, Control Officer

San Luis Obispo County Air Pollution Control District
P. O. Box 1489
San Luis Obispo, California 93402
(2191 Johnson Avenue)
(805)543-1200 Activated April 6, 1970
Mr. Jim Gates
Director of Sanitation

Sonoma County Air Pollution Control District
3313 Chante Road
Santa Rosa, California 95404
(707)527-1111 Activated March 30, 1970
Walter C. Clowers, M.D., Health Officer

Stanislaus County Air Pollution Control District
902 Scenic Drive
Modesto, California 95350
(209)524-1251 Activated August 20, 1968
Robert S. Westphal, M.D., Health Officer
Mr. James Mankin, Director of Sanitation

Open Space Action Coalition
384 Post St., Rm. 203
San Francisco, California 94108

Palomar Pro-Ecology Comm.
℅ Alex Hinds
Route 1, Box 2150
San Marcos, California 92069

Burbank Ecology Council
Box 751E
Burbank, Calif. 91503
(213)843-0800

Hiking Group
Allan Hancock College
800 S. College Drive
Santa Maria, Calif. 93454

"Grassroots, Again"
Box 572
Whittier, Calif. 90608

San Diego Environmental Information Center
7566 Lemon Ave. 26
Lemon Grove, Calif. 92045
(714)461-8311

People of the Valley
Ecology Motivation Group
P. O. Box 1802
Porterville, Calif. 93257

United New Conservationists
487 Park Avenue
San Jose, Calif. 95110

Ecology Action Group
Allan Hancock College
800 S. College Drive
Santa Maria, Calif. 93454

APPENDIX

Ecology Action
715 Lafayette St.
Martinez, California 94553
% Pete Benedict

Merced Ecology Action
% Marsh Pitman
2832 E. Arden Lane
Merced, California 95340

Ecology Action Educational Inst.
Box 3895
Modesto, California 95352

PROBE-% Community Action Coordination
U.S.C., University Park
YMCA, Room 202
Los Angeles, California 90007

World Wide Society of Advanced Engineers & Scientists
P.O. Box 57146
Los Angeles, California 90057

Malibu Park J. H. Conservation Club
% Lee Cooper
29706 Baden Place
Malibu, California 90265

Ecology Action-Contra Costa
% Ted & Kathy Radke
834 Carquinez Way
Martinez, California 94553

Miss Michell Mordell
30562 Troon Place
Haywood, California 94544

L.I.F.E.
P.O. Box 56
La Honda, California 94020

Dan Clancy
Center for Ecological Living
246 Center Ave.
Pacheco, California 94553

Ecology Action
% C. Garnian
Box 1013
Imperial Beach, California 92032

Ecology Action
% Art Jokela
4043 E. Miramar
La Jolla, California 92037

Conservation-Ecology Club
Calif. State College
25800 Hillary St
Haywood, California 94542

Palo Alto Ecology Action
% Jennifer & Ronald Angel
678 Tennyson
Palo Alto, California 94301

Kristi L. Denton
3133 Monterey St.
San Mateo, California 94403

Ecology Action–Terra Linda HS
% Carol Roth
2526 Las Gallinas
San Rafael, California 94903

Fred Alley
% SCAAP Office
University of Santa Clara
Santa Clara, California 95050

Ecology Action
11317 Santa Monica Blvd.
Los Angeles, California 90025

Monterey Peninsula Ecology Action
% Mr. P. A. McCray
640 Palm Ave.
Seaside, California 93955

Ecology Action Council
U.C.L.A.
Box 24390
Los Angeles, California 90024

Ecology Action
% David Wight
Box F312
Raymond College
Stockton, California 95204

Contra Costa J. C. Ecology Action
% Burt Mason
2883 Del Camino Dr.–14A
San Pablo, California 94806

P.E.A.C.
% Assoc. Students
University of Cal.
Santa Barbara, California 93106

Ecology Action
U.C. at Santa Cruz
Merrill College
Box 513
Santa Cruz, California 95060

Mrs. Phyllis Boskovich
1125 Cornell Dr.
Santa Rosa, California 95405

Delta Ecology Club
San Joaquin Delta College
Stockton, California 95204

Nan Woolrych
628 N. Baker St.
Stockton, California 95203

Greg Thompkins
2000
Vacaville, California 95688

Ecology Action–AHC
% Lee Jones
605 Cherry Ave.
Vandenberg AFB, California 93437

Mrs. Petie Baldwin
Citizen's League Against the Sonic Boom
1000 E. Kaweah
Visalia, California 93277

Palo Alto Ecology Action
% Plowshare Bookstore
162 University Ave.
Palo Alto, California 94301

APPENDIX

Ecology Club–Lakewood HS
% Selene Smith
6619 Eberle St.
Lakewood, California 90713

Donna Baty
253 Oakdale Drive
Los Gato, California 95030

PCC Ecology Action
3556 Milton
Pasadena, California 91107
Attn.: Michael Tanchek

Christopher G. Dean
434 So. Topanga Canyon Rd.
Topanga, California 90290

Ecology Action of Solano College
% Talmadge Wright
201 Main St. D-8
Vallejo, California 94590

Conservation Center
1237 E. Main St.
Ventura, California 93001

Walnut Creek Ecology Action
% Ann Hornbacher
2124 Walnut Blvd.
Walnut Creek, California 94596

Ecology Club–St. Genevieves H.S.
% Edward Rhodes
8359 Colbath Ave.
Panorama City, California 91402

Marin Ecology Center
937 Sir Francis Drake Blvd.
Mill Valley, California 94941

Earth's Ecology Action Resource Through Students
% Bob Johnson
Campolindo High School
Morage, California 94556

Ecology Group
% Ron Lal
762 Eagel Ave.
Alamdea, California 94501

April Comm. for Environmental Awareness
P.O. Box 701
Arcata, California 95521

Ecology Action
% Biology Department
Cal Poly-Tech
San Luis Obispo, California 93401

ECOLOGY ACTION Educational Institute
Box 3895
Modesto, California 95352

Paul Heidenreich
% Mr. Aaland
Pleasant Hill H.S.
3100 Oakpark Blvd.
Pleasant Hill, California 94523

Ecology Action–San Fernando Valley
% Russ Salzgeber
6303 Reseda Blvd.
Reseda, California 91355

Ecology Action of Riverside
% Gene Anderson
26386 Ironwood Ave.
Sunnymead, California 92388

Environmental Action Comm.
% Bob Mosher
Sonoma State College
1801 E. Cotati Ave.
Rohnert Park, California 94928

East San Diego Ecology Action Comm.
5307 Lea St.
San Diego, California 92105

Ocean Beach Ecology Action
5005 Niagara Ave.
San Diego, California 92107

San Francisco Ecology Action
1370 Masonic
San Francisco, California 94117

Committee of Environmental Concern
% Stone Church
1108 Clark Way
San Jose, California 95125

People of the Valley
1401 Tea Pot Dome Ave.
Porterville, California 93257

Ecology Action at Cal-State
% Robert J. Larsen
8201 Lindley
Reseda, California 91335

CON-PARC
3701 Canyon Crest Drive
Riverside, California 92507

Students For Ecological Awareness
St. Mary's College
St. Mary's College, California 94575

Ecology Action
Skyline College
3300 College Dr.
San Bruno, California 94066

San Diego State College Ecology Action
San Diego State College
Aztec Center Activities Office
San Diego, California 92115

COLORADO

Ecology Action
1452 Penn Ave., Rm. 22
Denver, Colorado 80203

John K. Green
Box 1038
Boulder, Colorado 80302

APPENDIX

Environmental Action
Univ. of Colorado
Denver Center
1100 14th St.
Denver, Colorado 80202

CONNECTICUT

Environmental Offensive and
Environmental Action Group
550 Osborne Memorial Laboratory
Prospect Street
New Haven, Connecticut 06520

DISTRICT OF COLUMBIA

The Population Institute
100 Maryland Ave., N.E.
Washington, D.C. 20002
(202)544-3310

Environmental Action
Rm. 200
2000 P St. N.W.
Washington, D.C. 20036

Mr. & Mrs. Thomas E. Patton
110-A 'G' St., S.W.
Washington, D.C. 20024

FLORIDA

Environmental Action Group
Box U-6794
Florida State Univ.
Tallahassee, Florida 32306

Air and Water Pollution Control
Department
Vince Patton, Executive Director
400 Tallahassee Bank & Trust Building
Tallahassee, Florida

Environment
P. O. Box 631
Coconut Grove, Florida 33133

HAWAII

State of Hawaii
Department of Health
P. O. Box 3378
Honolulu, Hawaii 96801

IDAHO

Air Pollution Control Section
Idaho Department of Health
Statehouse
Boise, Idaho 83707

Solid Waste
Idaho Department of Health
Boise, Idaho 83707

Water Pollution Control Section
Idaho Department of Health
Statehouse
Boise, Idaho 83707

ILLINOIS

C. R. A. P.
4636 N. Central Park
Chicago, Illinois 60625

C.A.P.
65 East Huron Street
Chicago, Illinois 60611

Students Together Opposing Pollution
% Mark Maley
3703 Bluebird
Rolling Meadows, Illinois 60008

Students for Environmental Controls
University YMCA
1001 South Wright
Champaign, Illinois 61820

Students Against Pollution
6201 Cumnor
Downers Grove, Illinois 60515

R. S. Nelle, B.S.
Water Resource Engineer
535 W. Jefferson
Springfield, Illinois 62706
(217)525-2824

Hoyt Frederick, Acting Chief
General Sanitation Bureau
535 W. Jefferson
Springfield, Illinois 62706
(217)525-6782

Leroy Stratton, Chief
Radiological Health Bureau
535 W. Jefferson
Springfield, Illinois 62706
(217)525-6555

Benn J. Leland, M.S.
Engineer-in-Charge
Sanitary Water Board
1919 West Taylor Street
Chicago, Illinois 60612
(312)341-7290

Kenneth L. Baumann, B.S.C.E.
(Acting)
East Central Region (II)
2125 South First Street
Champaign, Illinois 61820
(217)333-6914 or 333-6996

E. L. Sederlin, M.D.
Southern Region (V)
306 West Main Street
Carbondale, Illinois 62901
(618)457-8102

Robert R. French, Ch. E., Chief
Air Pollution Control Bureau
535 W. Jefferson
Springfield, Illinois 62706
(217)525-7327

APPENDIX

O. S. Hallden, B.S., Chief
Public Water Supplies Bureau
535 W. Jefferson
Springfield, Illinois 62706
(217)525-2027

Arthur E. Sulek, M.D., M.I.H.
Northwestern Region (III)
121 Fourth Avenue
Rock Island, Illinois 61201
(309)786-6471

E. E. Diddams, M.S.P.H. (Acting)
Region VI
9500 Collinsville Road, Unit E
Collinsville, Illinois 62234
(618)345-5141

John W. Lewis, Director
Illinois Department of Agriculture
Illinois Building, State Fairgrounds
Springfield, Illinois 62702
(217)525-2274

A. L. Sargent, Director Emeritus
Illinois Municipal League
1220 South Seventh Street
Springfield, Illinois 62703
(217)525-1220

Dan Malkovich, Director
Illinois Department of Conservation
102 State Office Building
Springfield, Illinois 62706

Richard C. Reinke, Vice Chairman
Illinois Air Pollution Control Board
Secy., Argo Local 7-507
Oil, Chemical & Atomic Wrkrs.
International Union, AFL-CIO
6305 Archer Avenue
Argo, Illinois 60503
(312)458-4900

Raymond D. Maxson
Illinois Air Pollution Control Board
330 Cottage Hill
Elmhurst, Illinois 60126
(312)834-3591

Arthur E. MacQuilkin
Illinois Air Pollution Control Board
Industrial Filter & Pump Manufacturing Co.
5900 Ogden Avenue
Cicero, Illinois 60650
(312)652-8700

William L. Rutherford
Coordinator of Environmental Control
Capitol Airport, Main Terminal Bldg.
North Walnut Street Road
Springfield, Illinois 62702
(217)525-4954

D. B. Morton, B. S., Chief
Stream Pollution Bureau
535 W. Jefferson
Springfield, Illinois 62706
(217)525-6171

Evelyn M. Cunningham, R.N. (Acting)
West Central Region (IV)
Room 173, State Regional Office Building
601 Toronto Road
Springfield, Illinois 62706
(217)525-6482

Franklin D. Yoder, M.D., Director
Illinois Department of Public Health
503 State Office Building
Springfield, Illinois 62706
(217)525-4977

William F. Cellini, Director
Illinois Department of Public Works & Buildings
300 Administration Building
2300 South 31st Street
Springfield, Illinois 62703
(217)525-2276

C. S. Boruff, Ph.D.
6016 N. Mt. Hawley Road–Apt. 101
Peoria, Illinois 61614
(132)682-8572

Samuel T. Lawton, Jr., Chairman
Illinois Air Pollution Control Board
Altheimer, Gray, Naiburg, Strasburger & Lawton
1 North LaSalle, Room 1825
Chicago, Illinois 60602
(312)372-0345

David P. Currie
Illinois Air Pollution Control Board
University of Chicago Law School
1111 East 60th
Chicago, Illinois 60637
(312)643-0800, Ext. 2445

Edgar Peske
Illinois Air Pollution Control Board
Ill. Bell Telephone Company
225 W. Randolph Street
Chicago, Illinois 60606
(312)727-2074

John Post, M.D.
Illinois Air Pollution Control Board
Zenith Radio Corporation
1900 N. Austin Avenue
Chicago, Illinois 60639
(312)745-2000

Franklin D. Yoder, M.D.
Director of Public Health
Ill. Dept. of Public Health
535 West Jefferson Street
Springfield, Illinois 62706
(217)525-4977

George W. Mosley, D.D.S. (Acting)
Northeastern Region (I)
48 West Galena Boulevard
Aurora, Illinois 60504
(312)892-4272

APPENDIX

INDIANA

Joseph Ante
Indiana Central College
4001 Otterbein Ave.
Indianapolis, Indiana 46227

Mr. Terry Whalin
553 E. Main Street
Peru, Indiana 46970

Dennis T. Karas, Director
Dept. of Air Quality Control
4525 Indianapolis Blvd.
East Chicago, Ind. 46312
Ph: (219)398-4200 Ext. 276

John E. Clausheide, Engr.-Smoke Commr.
Dept. of Air Pollution Control
Rm. 207 Safety & Admn. Bldg.
Civic Center Complex
Evansville, Ind. 47708
Ph: (812)426-5595

Joel A. Johnson, Chief Engineer
Division of Air Pollution Control
3600 W. Third Avenue
Gary, Ind. 46406
Ph: (219)949-8486

Air Pollution Control Div.
Indiana State Board of Health
1330 W. Michigan St.
Indianapolis, Ind. 46206

Lake County Health Department
209 W. Joliet Street
Crown Point, Ind. 46307
Attn: Ervin Kmiecik. Ch. San.

Lewis F. Scott, Director
Bureau of Air Pollution Control
City-County Bldg.–Rm. 1642
Indianapolis, Ind. 46204
Ph: (317)633-3800

Vigo County Dept. of Health
Air Pollution Control Division
120 S. 7th Street
Terre Haute, Ind. 47801
Attn: Dr. Noel E. Moore, Director
Ph: (812)232-2148

Division of Air Pollution Control
Department of Public Health
100 W. Michigan Blvd.
Michigan City, Ind. 46360
Attn: Karl Hilberg, Chief

C O P E
423 S. Boeke Road
Evansville, Ind. 47714

ENACT (Environmental Action)
Cindy Airhart (Sec.)
Beeman Hall
Ball State University
Muncie, Ind.

ZPG 206
Stefan P. Shoup
7243 Olcot Avenue
Hammond, Ind. 47374

ZPG 3176
Robert Goebel
1515 N. La Lountaine St.
Huntington, Ind. 46750

Thomas C. Griffing 77
Dept. of Biology
University of Notre Dame
Notre Dame, Ind. 46556

Lafayette C. Eaton 19
Life Sciences
Indiana State University
Terre Haute, Ind. 47809

S.A.F.E. (Students Against a Fatal Environment)
P. O. Box 2103
West Lafayette, Ind. 47906
(317)463-2415

St. Joseph County Health Dept.
1419 S. Michigan Street
South Bend, Ind. 46613
Attn: Calvin L. Frappier, Director
Air Pollution Control Division
Ph: (219)287-2816

Water Pollution Control Div.
Indiana State Board of Health
Indianapolis, Ind. 46206

Air Pollution Control Dept.
5925 Calumet Avenue
Hammond, Ind. 46320
Attn: William J. Harrigan, Chief

Porter County Health Department
552 W. Lincolnway
Valparaiso, Ind. 46383
Attn: Robert Mefford

Committee To Publicize Crisis Biology
205 Morrison Hall
Indiana University
Bloomington, Ind. 47401

Izaak Walton League
Jean Blake (Sec.)
12 Hickory Rd.
Muncie, Ind.

Zero Population 96
C. B. Williamson
Dept. of Zoology
Indiana University
Bloomington, Ind. 47401

ZPG 94
Joseph Ante
4001 Otterbein Ave.
Indianapolis, Ind. 46227

ZPG 20
Jerome H. Woolpy
Earlham College
Richmond, Ind.

L.E.A.F.
Lafayette Environmental Action Federation
P. O. Box 2103
West Lafayette, Ind. 47906
(317)463-2415

APPENDIX

IOWA

Environment & Pollution Control Council, Inc.
1901 Orchard St.
Burlington, Iowa 52601
Thomas R. Martin, Secretary

KANSAS

Ecology Action
% Leland McCleary
1328 Vermont
Lawrence, Kansas 66044

Environmental Action Comm.
% Mrs. Peter Macdonald
111 Countryside Dr.
Hutchinson, Kansas 67501

The Assoc. for Environmental Improvement
Box 26
Wichita State University
Wichita, Kansas 67208

KENTUCKY

Pollution Endangers World
P. O. Box 14008
Iroquois Station
Louisville, Kentucky 40214

Mountain Legal Rights Program
10 College Lane
Prestonburg, Kentucky 41653

Environmental Action
% Paul Hankins
3111 Redbud Lane
Louisville, Kentucky 40220

Louisville & Jefferson County Metropolitan Sewer District
400 South 6th Street
Louisville, Kentucky 40203

Kentucky Water Pollution Control Commission
275 East Main Street
Frankfort, Kentucky 40601

Sanitation District No. 1
Campbell & Kenton Counties
212 Greenup Street
Covington, Kentucky 41011

LOUISIANA

Ecology Center
Box 15149
New Orleans, Louisiana

MARYLAND

Ecology Action of Baltimore
% W. M. Robinson
3012 Abell Ave.
Baltimore, Maryland 21218

Ecology Action Center-American Friends Service Comm.
319 East 25th Street
Baltimore, Maryland 21218

H. Lawrence Lock
% Green Revolution
Heathcote Revolution
Freeland, Maryland 21053

MASSACHUSETTS

Ecology Action of Cambridge
925 Mass. Ave.
Cambridge, Massachusetts 92139

New Politics Coalition
% Janet Clark
25 Main Street
Northampton, Massachusetts 01060

Mr. James L. Dallas, Director
Bureau of Air Use Management
Department of Public Health
600 Washington Street, Room 320
Boston, Massachusetts 02111

Mr. Thomas McMahon, Director
Division of Water Pollution Control
Leverett Saltonstall Building
100 Cambridge Street
Boston, Massachusetts

Mr. John C. Collins, Director
Division of Environmental Health
600 Washington Street, Room 320
Boston, Massachusetts 02111

Boston University Ecology Action
Biological Science Center
2 Cummington St.
Boston, Mass. 02215

Andover Ecology Action
% Phillips Academy
Andover, Mass. 01810

MICHIGAN

Ecology Action of Ann Arbor
% Lynn North
501 Linde
Ann Arbor, Michigan 48104

Mrs. Christine Byrn
2538 Union N.E.
Grand Rapids, Michigan 49505

ENACT-School of Natural Resources
Univ. of Michigan
Ann Arbor, Michigan 48104

Comm. for Environmental Preservation
148 Mackenzie Hall
Wayne State Univ.
Detroit, Michigan 48202

Charles J. Burda
P. O. Box 1665
Midland, Michigan 48640

APPENDIX

PLEA
℅ Students Activities Center
Oakland Univ.
Rochester, Michigan 48063

Ecology Action
℅ Wallace Elton
Dept. of Geography
Michigan State Univ.
East Lansing, Michigan 48823

MINNESOTA

METRO
Clean Air Committee
Mrs. Janet Garrison, Director
1829 Portland Ave.
Minneapolis, Minn. 55404

Environment & Resources Info. Center
℅ SE Branch Library
1222 SE 4th St.
Minneapolis, Minnesota 55414

Students for Environmental Defense
℅ Robert Hertz
1175 S. Cleveland
St. Paul, Minnesota 55116

Carleton Environmental Studies Group
Carleton College
Northfield, Minnesota 55057

Students for Environmental Defense
℅ Fay Brezinka
515 6th Ave. South
St. Cloud, Minnesota 56301

State of Minnesota
Pollution Control Agency
717 Delaware Street S.E.
Oak and Delaware Streets S.E.
Minneapolis, Minnesota 55440

MISSISSIPPI

CLEAN
P. O. Box 643
Starkville, Mississippi 39759

Glen Wood, Jr., Acting Executive Secretary
Air & Water Pollution Control Commission
P. O. Box 827
416 North State Street
Jackson, Mississippi 39205

MISSOURI

Black Survival
4957 Delmar Blvd.
Union-Sarah Gateway Center
St. Louis, Missouri 63108

Coalition for the Environment
Room 706
Security Bldg.
319 North 4th St.
St. Louis, Missouri 63102

Susan Wright
4740 Charlotte
Kansas City, Missouri 64111

Carl Boggs
Dept. of Political Science
Washington State Univ.
St. Louis, Missouri 63130

Missouri Water Pollution Board
P. O. Box 154
Jefferson City, Missouri 65101

Missouri Air Conservation Commission
P. O. Box 1062
Jefferson City, Missouri 65101
ATTENTION: H. D. Shell, P. E.
Acting Executive Secretary

Division of Air Pollution Control
St. Louis County Health Department
801 S. Brentwood Blvd.
Clayton, Missouri 63105
ATTENTION: Donald A. Pecsok, Director

Air Pollution Control
City of Independence Health Department
210 S. Main
Independence, Missouri 64050
ATTENTION: W. W. Stepp, Director

Metropolitan St. Louis Sewer District
2000 Hampton Avenue
St. Louis, Missouri 63139

Kansas City Pollution Control Department
5th Floor, City Hall
Kansas City, Missouri 64106

Division of Air Pollution Control
City of St. Louis
419 City Hall
St. Louis, Missouri 63103
ATTENTION: Charles M. Copley, Commissioner

Division of Air Pollution Control
Kansas City Health Department
City Hall, 21st Floor
Kansas City, Missouri
ATTENTION: Carl C. Potter, Director

Air Pollution Control Authority
Springfield-Greene County Health Dept.
Court House
Springfield, Missouri
ATTENTION: Joe Allen, Director

MONTANA

C. W. Brinck, Secretary
Water Pollution Council
State Department of Health
Helena, Montana

Division of Air Pollution and Industrial Hygiene
State Department of Health
Helena, Montana

APPENDIX

The Concerned Few for the Population Problem
℅ Mrs. Carolline Wright
East Shore Rt.
Polson, Montana 59860

NEBRASKA

Panhandle Environment Council
Box 188
Scottsbluff, Nebr. 69361

Citizens for Environmental Improvement
333 North 14th St.
Lincoln, Nebraska 68508

Don Olson
Douglas County Health Dept.
1201 So. 42nd
Omaha, Nebraska 68105

Nebr. Air Pollution Control Council
℅ Room 1007
State Capitol Bldg.
P. O. Box 4757
Lincoln, Nebraska 68509

Les Sanger
Lincoln-Lancaster Co. Health Dept.
2200 St. Marys Ave.
Lincoln, Nebraska 68502

Nebr. Water Pollution Control Council
P. O. Box 4757
State Capitol Building
Lincoln, Nebraska 68509

NEVADA

Nevada State Health Division
Bureau of Environmental Health
Nye Building, 201 So. Fall St.
Carson City, Nevada 89701

Nevada Department of Fish & Game
P. O. Box 10678
Reno, Nevada 89502

Air Pollution Control
Washoe County District Health Department
10 Kirman Avenue
Reno, Nevada 89502

Air Pollution Control
Clark County District Health Department
P. O. Box 4426
Las Vegas, Nevada 89106

NEW HAMPSHIRE

Brookwood Ecology Center
Route 1, Box 51
Greenville, N.H. 03048

New Hampshire Air Pollution Control Agency
61 South Spring Street
Concord, New Hampshire 03301

NEW JERSEY

Citizens for Environmental Protection
P. O. Box 243
Hazlet, N.J. 07730

Department of Environmental Protection
John Fitch Plaza
P. O. Box 1390
Trenton, New Jersey 08625

Water Pollution Control Program
New Jersey State Department of Environmental Protection
P. O. Box 1390
Trenton, New Jersey

Hudson and Delaware Basins Office
Federal Water Quality Administration
Department of the Interior
Edison Township, New Jersey

Interstate Sanitation Commission
10 Columbus Circle
New York, New York

Delaware River Basin Commission
25 Scotch Road
Trenton, New Jersey 08603

NEW MEXICO

Albuquerque Department of Environmental Health
P. O. Box 1293
Albuquerque, New Mexico 87103

Environmental Services Division
State of New Mexico
P. O. Box 2348
Santa Fe, New Mexico 87501

NEW YORK

Environmental Action Coalition
235 East 49th St.
New York, New York 10017

CEASE
8 Old Pascack Rd.
Pearl River, New York 10965

Frances Cott
Stony Point, New York 10980

Donna Shipsky
Hartigan Rd.
Old Chatam, New York 12136

Preserve Your Environment Organ.
℅ Steven Moore
912 Mohegan Rd.
Schenectady, New York 12309

Ecology Action Earth Groups
3800 E. Genesee St.
Syracuse, N.Y. 13214

SACEQ
(Syracuse Area Committee for Environmental Quality)
Room 411
402 E. Jefferson St.
Syracuse, N.Y. 13202

Ecology Group
Marion Kamp
17 Bellmore Dr.
Poughkeepsie, N.Y. 12603

NORTH CAROLINA

Organ. for Environmental Quality
P. O. Box 5536 C.S.
Raleigh, North Carolina 27607

Ecology Action
% Carol Saffrati
318 Gragan Hall
Univ. of N.C.
Greensboro, North Carolina 27412

E. C. Hubbard, Assistant Director
Department of Water and Air Resources
P. O. Box 27048
Raleigh, North Carolina 27611

Jim Rice
113-A Stephen St.
Chapel Hill, North Carolina 27514

ECOS
% Charlotte Phelps
6598 C.S.
Durham, North Carolina 27708

ECOS
P. O. Box 1055
Chapel Hill, North Carolina 27514

Sheridan Ross
2006 Dartmouth Pl.
Charlotte, North Carolina 28207

NORTH DAKOTA

Mary Bjorneby
614 No. 4th St.
Grand Forks, North Dakota 58201

Campus Conservatives
Minot State College
Box 195
Minot, North Dakota 58701

North Dakota Water Conservation Commission
State Department of Health
Bismarck, North Dakota 58501

State Industrial Commission
State Department of Health
Bismarck, North Dakota 58501

Environmental Health & Engineering Services
State Department of Health
Bismarck, North Dakota 58501

North Dakota Game and Fish Department
State Department of Health
Bismarck, North Dakota 58501

OHIO

Nancy Hedman
524 So. College
Oxford, Ohio 45056

Citizens for Survival
P. O. Box 446
Ashtabula, Ohio 44004

Marty Wolf
1126 N. Fountain
Springfield, Ohio 45504

Dick Roop
Hiram College
P. O. Box 914
Hiram, Ohio 44234

Ecology Action
% Bill Anderson
% Burning River News
13037 Euclid Ave.
Cleveland, Ohio 44112

Environmental Studies Info Center
% Bill Knowland
Antioch College
Yellow Springs, Ohio 45387

Barrett J. Day
30997 Nantucket
Bay Village, Ohio 44140

Like Improvement for Environment
10706 Bernard Ave.
Cleveland, Ohio 44111

P.U.R.E.
(People United for a Respectable Environment)
Heidelberg College
Tiffin, Ohio 44883

The Air Conservation Committee
Mrs. Richard Felber, Chairman
4614 Prospect Ave.
Cleveland, Ohio 44103

OKLAHOMA

State Water Resources Board
2241 N.W. 40th St.
Oklahoma City, Oklahoma 73112

State Corporation Commission
Jim Thorpe Bldg.
Oklahoma City, Oklahoma 73105

APPENDIX

State Department of Agriculture
State Capitol
Oklahoma City, Oklahoma 73105

Department of Pollution Control
P. O. Box 53431, State Capitol
Oklahoma City, Oklahoma 73105

State Department of Health
3400 No. Eastern
Oklahoma City, Oklahoma 73105

State Department of Wildlife Conservation
1801 Lincoln
Oklahoma City, Oklahoma 73105

Putman City West
Ad Hoc Comm. to Save our Planet
℅ Paula Large
7121 N.W. 44th
Bethany, Okla. 73008

Robert F. Rood
4051 E. 43rd St.
Tulsa, Okla. 74135

OREGON

Students for Oregon's Environment
421 S.W. 11th Ave.
Portland, Ore. 97205

Bob Estelle-Ecology Action
1142 Mill
Eugene, Ore. 97401

Ecology Action-Lake Oswego H.S.
℅ John Adams
1250 Sunningdale Rd.
Lake Oswego, Oregon 97034

Nature's Conspiracy
℅ Steve Wilson
Rm. 23, EMU
Univ. of Oregon
Eugene, Ore. 97403

John Dolan or Bob Timm
℅ Linfield College
McMinnville, Ore. 97128

World Ecological Betterment
℅ Nick Bielemeier
1254 James Ave.
Woodburn, Ore. 97071

PENNSYLVANIA

U.A.W. Conservation
Committee Chairman
Robert G. Mowrer
434 Walnut St.
Lansdale, Pa. 19446

Phila. Ecology Action Group
P. O. Box 1600
Philadelphia, Pa. 19105

Mrs. Carol DiGirolamo
16 Valley View Drive
Langhorne, Pa. 19047

Eric N. Jones
B-744 Bucknell Univ.
Lewisburg, Pa. 17837

Dr. Rolf von Eckhartsberg
Assoc. Prof. of Psychology
Duquesne Univ.
Pittsburgh, Pa. 15219

Environmental Crisis Center
℅ Cynthia Mengel
Box 159
Given Hall
Clarion, Pa. 16214

Paul Osher
The Bucknellian
Lewisburg, Pa. 17837

Environment: Pittsburgh
P. O. Box 7380
Pittsburgh, Pa. 15213

Soucon Assn. for a Viable Environment
P. O. Box 26, Coopersburg, Pa. 18036

Eastern Pa. Chapter A.I.A.
James L. Harter, 3131 Diamond Avenue
Allentown, Pa. 18103

Anti-Pol
Eugene R. Modjeski
Box 44, Laurys Station, Pa. 18059

Moravian Environmental Society
Dr. Robert Windalph
2311 Catasauqua Rd.
Bethlehem, Pa.

ECOS- Kutztown State College
Kutztown, Pa. 19530

Penn Northeast Conference
Rev. Paul Peters
Box 177, 470 Delaware Ave.
Palmerton, Pa. 18071

Zero Population
Bradford Owen
RD 4, Bethlehem, Pa. 18015

H.E.L.P.
Cedar Crest College
Allentown, Pa. 18104

Muhlenberg College Ecology Action Group
Carl Oplinger
6 Juniper St.
Wescoesville, Pa. 18090

East Penn Environmental Concern
Jeff Cox
RD 1, Emmaus, Pa. 18049

Mary Aull
272 E. High St.
Philadelphia, Pa. 19144

RHODE ISLAND

Ecology Action for Rhode Island, Inc.
50 Olive St.
Providence, R.I. 02906

Cranston Ecology Action Movement
% Mrs. Marie Hopper
Cranston High School East
899 Park Avenue
Cranston, Rhode Island 02910

TENNESSEE

Birth Environment Movement
P. O. Box 8470
Univ. Station
Knoxville, Tenn. 37916

TEXAS

Ecology Action
% Hillel Foundation
2105 San Antonio St.
Austin, Texas 78705

San Jacinto T.B. & Respiratory Disease Assoc.
Coalition for Air Conservation
2901 West Dallas St.
Houston, Texas 77019

Ecology Action
Jeffrey H. Giles
3506 Gramercy St.
Houston, Texas 77025

Ann Beale
5435 48th St.
Lubbock, Texas 79414

Beautification Committee
% Mr. R. B. Berrie
715 S. Bluebonnet St.
Pharr, Texas 78577

Mr. Don Thurman
Director, Air Pollution Control Program
Dallas County Health Department
1936 Amelia Street
Dallas, Texas 75235

Lea Hutchinson, M.D.
Director, Air Pollution Control Program
El Paso City-County Health Department
222 South Campbell Street
El Paso, Texas 79901

Mr. Harry Markel, P. E., Public Health Engineer
Director, Air Pollution Control Program
Dallas City Public Health Department
2666 Brenner
Dallas, Texas 75220

Mr. William Badgett
Director, Air Pollution Control Program
Denison-Sherman-Grayson County Health Department
P. O. Box 1295, Courthouse
Sherman, Texas 75090

Mr. Guy Wilkinson
Director, Air Pollution Control Program
Galveston County-Mainland Cities Health Department
P. O. Box 95, 1207 Oak Street
LaMarque, Texas 77568

W. A. Quebedeaux, Jr., M.D.
Director, Air & Water Pollution Control Section
Harris County Health Department
P. O. Box 6031
Pasadena, Texas 77502

Mr. Walter Breedlove
Director, Air Pollution Control Program
Lubbock City-County Health Program
P. O. Box 2548, 1100 North Avenue Q
Lubbock, Texas 79408

Mr. Walter Harrison
Director, Air Pollution Control Program
San Antonio Metropolitan Health District
131 West Nueva Street
San Antonio, Texas 78204

Mr. Robert Curry, Director
South Jefferson County Air Pollution Control Program
246 North Dallas Avenue
Port Arthur, Texas

Mr. Bill Westbrook
Director, Air Pollution Control Program
Texarkana-Bowie County Health Department
P. O. Box 749, 10th & Spruce
Texarkana, Texas 75502

Mr. Roy Adams, Public Health Engineer
Director, Air Pollution Control Program
Fort Worth Department of Public Health
1800 University Drive
Fort Worth, Texas 76107

Mr. Bill Berry
Director, Air Pollution Control Program
Greenville-Hunt County Health Department
2500 Lee Street, Room 412
Greenville, Texas 75401

James H. Sterner, M.D., Acting Director
Houston City Health Department
1115 North MacGregor
Houston, Texas 77025
ATTENTION: Mr. Gerald Hord, Public Health Engineer

Mr. John Wheeler
Director, Air Pollution Control Program
Orange County Health Department
701 Second, Box 309
Orange, Texas 77630

Mr. Victor Bateman, Director
North Jefferson Air Pollution Control Program
601 Courthouse Building
Beaumont, Texas

Mr. Albert Cock, Public Health Engineer
Director, Air Pollution Control Program
Corpus Christi-Nueces County Health Department
P. O. Box 49
Health Center Bldg., 1811 Shoreline Blvd.
Corpus Christi, Texas 78403

UTAH

Earth People News
USU
Box 1343
Logan, Utah 84321

Bruce Plank
℅ SDS
U. of Utah Union Bldg.
Salt Lake City, Utah 84112

VIRGINIA

Air Pollution Control Board
902 Ninth Street Office Building
Richmond, Virginia

WASHINGTON

State Department of Health
Office of Air Quality Control
Smith Tower Building
Seattle, Washington 98104

State Department of Health
Olympia Airport
Olympia, Washington 98501

Department of Water Resources
General Administration Building
Olympia, Washington 98501

Mrs. Nancy Arnold
Washington Environmental Council
3744 77th Ave. S.E.
Mercer Island, Wash. 98040

CARHT
(Citizens Agt. the R H. Thomson [freeway])
P. O. Box 147
Seattle, Wash. 98111

WISCONSIN

State of Wisconsin
Department of Natural Resources
Box 450
Madison, Wisconsin 53701

Planned Parenthood
536 West Wisconsin Ave., Rm. 604
Milwaukee, Wisc. 53203
271-8181

Responsible Parenthood–Planned Parenthood
Mrs. Joan Gander
5453 North 39th St.
Milwaukee, Wisc. 53209
463-7611

Root River Restoration Council
Mrs. Richard Densen
2023 Golf Avenue
Racine, Wisc.

Southeast Wisconsin Coalition for Clean Air
Mrs. Robert Jaskulski, Chairman
12004 North Ridge Trail Road
Hales Corners, Wisc.

State of Wisconsin
Department of Natural Resources
Division of Environmental Protection
Mr. Thomas Kroehn, Director
9203 W. Blue Mound Road
Milwaukee, Wisc. 53226
476-8120

Milwaukee River Restoration Council
Joseph Zingsheim, President
1098 17th Ave.
Grafton, Wisc. 53024
377-1417

Racine Coalition For Clean Air
Hank Cole
2010 Charles Street
Racine Wisc.
634-2976

River Edge Nature Center
4311 W. Hawthorne Drive
P. O. Box 92
Newberg, Wisc. 53060

S.O.S. Save Our City Committee
Mr. Jay Franklin
911 E. Ogden Ave.
Milwaukee, Wisc. 53202
276-5304 or 273-4949 or 271-1881

State Committee to Stop Sanguine
P. O. Box 7
Ashland, Wisc.

UMW Cedarburg Bog Field Station
Mrs. Millicent Ficken, Director
Route 1, Box 216
Saukville, Wisc. 53080
(414)675-6844

Political Interest Group–UWM
Women's
Mrs. Lois Zahorik
4515 North Woodburn St.
Milwaukee, Wisc. 53211
964-8665

Zero Population Growth
% Zoology Department of UWM
Milwaukee, Wisc.
228-4214

Wisconsin T.B. & R.D. Association
Mrs. Harvey Cohen, R.N.
Box 424
Milwaukee, Wisc. 53201
933-1161

Pollution Fighters
710 Woodward Drive
Madison, Wisc. 53704

Cedar Creek Restoration Council
Delbert Cook
114 North Washington Ave.
Cedarburg, Wisc. 53012
377-4392

Aldo Leopold Conservation Club–UWM
Jeffrey Macht, Chairman
4454 North Woodburn
Whitefish Bay, Wisc. 53211
964-7916

Center for Consumer Affairs
Dr. Milton Huber, Director
University Extension
600 West Kilbourn Ave.
Milwaukee, Wisc. 53203
228-4421

Committee on Survival of Man in
Changing Environments
Mr. Lawrence Giese
3018 North Stowell
Milwaukee, Wisc. 53211
962-8674

League of Women Voters—
Environment Quality Committee
Mrs. Ann deMille
3817 North Bartlett
Shorewood, Wisc. 53211
332-0141

M.U.S.T.B.E.
(Marquette University Students to
Better the Environment)
Mr. Nick Studzinski, President
547 North 31 Street
Milwaukee, Wisc. 53208
342-1516

Port of Milwaukee Harbor Commission
Mr. Clayton Swinford, Harbor Master
1225 South Carferry Drive
Milwaukee, Wisc. 53207
276-9355

Citizens for the Nine Mile Farm Nature
Center
Mrs. Edward Zieve, Chairman
9481 North Sequoia Drive
Milwaukee, Wisc. 53217
352-5145

Izaak Walton League of America
John Street
Markeson, Wisc.
Mrs. Eugene Dahl
5832 North Lake Drive
Milwaukee, Wisc. 53217
332-3669

League Involved for Environment
(LIFE)
Mrs. Mary Jo Baertschy
128 East Chateau
Whitefish Bay, Wisc. 53217
964-2194

City of Milwaukee Health Department
Bureau of Consumer Protection
and Environmental Health
Mr. George Kupfer, Superintendent
841 North Broadway, Room 105
Milwaukee, Wisc. 53202
276-3711

Milwaukee County Department of
Air Pollution Control
Mr. Fred Rehm, Director
9722 West Watertown Plank Road
Milwaukee, Wisc. 53226
771-3612

WYOMING

Wyoming Department of Health and
Social Services
Division of Health and Medical
Services
State Office Building
Cheyenne, Wyoming 82001

State Engineer's Office
State Office Building
Cheyenne, Wyoming 82001

Wyoming Game and Fish Commission
P. O. Box 1589
Cheyenne, Wyoming 82001

Index

INDEX

INDEX

INDEX

INDEX